What people are say

The Medicine W

Barry has created a meditation on meaning, a most interesting discourse on the Medicine Wheel tempered with Jung and other interesting philosophers, matching and mixing and extracting clarity and knowledge. I hear Barry as I read, his voice is clear and direct, there is no bull here but challenging discussions on teachings and the real meanings behind them. I have just read his lovely piece on aging, a subject I am deeply involved in through necessity, and I feel encouraged, emboldened and enlivened. It is like that through this book, Barry weaves teachings together from Jung to Winnie the Pooh in a most encompassing and enlightening way, always grounded and useable. A really good read! I heartily recommend this book as a good addition to texts on the Medicine Wheel and the mysteries of life.
Leo Rutherford, author of *The View Through the Medicine Wheel* and *Principles of Shamanism*

The Medicine Wheel affirms Plotinus' dictum that 'the native motion of the soul is circular': as we move around the Medicine Wheel's four (or eight) directions, each of which provides a different perspective on ourselves, we approach the four-fold wholeness of the Self so beloved by C.G. Jung. A sensitive and sensible guide to our circumambulation, Barry Goddard offers us telling suggestions and practical advice on how to understand ourselves and to manage life's waywardness. We trust him because he doesn't lay down the law so much as let us in on his own tribulations with endearing honesty and refreshing humility. The lessons we feel he has learnt the hard way are passed on unassumingly – even chattily – until they add up almost imperceptibly to more than the sum of their

parts: a kind of wise Middle Way which may owe as much to his Buddhist background as to Aristotle's Golden Mean.
Patrick Harpur, author of *The Philosopher's Secret Fire* and *Daimonic Reality*

Barry Goddard has written a book about the Medicine Wheel based on in-depth study, clear insights, and personal experience. The Medicine Wheel teachings guide humans on how to live in a way of wholeness, as a part of the web of life. The teachings are highly relevant today in a world that is changing rapidly. They provide a map that can help people understand themselves and the world in general.
Chris Luttichau, author of *Calling Us Home*

The Medicine Wheel

Maps of Transformation, Wholeness and Balance

The Medicine Wheel

Maps of Transformation, Wholeness and Balance

Barry Goddard

MOON BOOKS

Winchester, UK
Washington, USA

JOHN HUNT PUBLISHING

First published by Moon Books, 2022
Moon Books is an imprint of John Hunt Publishing Ltd., No. 3 East Street, Alresford
Hampshire SO24 9EE, UK
office@jhpbooks.net
www.johnhuntpublishing.com
www.moon-books.net

For distributor details and how to order please visit the 'Ordering' section on our website.

ISBN: 978 1 78535 967 5
978 1 78535 968 2 (ebook)
Library of Congress Control Number: 2021941983

A CIP catalogue record for this book is available from the British Library.

Design: Stuart Davies

UK: Printed and bound by CPI Group (UK) Ltd, Croydon, CR0 4YY
Printed in North America by CPI GPS partners

Contents

Preface

I began writing this book nearly a year into the Covid lockdowns. In the seasons of human activity, the lockdowns were winter, when life withdraws, contemplates itself and eventually emerges again, renewed. The lockdown period constituted compulsory introversion for an extraverted world. A time to reconsider who we are, what we are doing, what gives meaning and value to life.

Windows like this don't come very often, and when they do, they change collective humanity – at least, for a while. Things shift on quite a deep level, and it can take some years before we can look back and see the significance. At the time of writing, that re-emergence has not even begun.

As soon as the lockdowns began, I had an inspiration to run a long, experiential course on the Medicine Wheel. On Zoom. Not the most obvious place to be experiential. But I thought why cannot people build their own Wheels, stay with each direction for a month at a time, and share with others their life from the viewpoint of that direction? I hadn't taught the Medicine Wheel much before, though I had been around it and inspired by it for many years, and had held back for lack of a practical venue. Suddenly the lockdown solved my problem. The only way was Zoom!

It worked surprisingly well, and a sense of community built up in the two long courses I ran that year. And I surprised myself by how much I had to say, providing I gave myself the freedom to ad-lib. I view ad-libbing as thoroughly traditional: in the old days you didn't have courses, you had teachers responding to their pupils in that moment. And that leaves room for the Spirit to say what needs to be said rather than what we, with our limited minds, might have planned.

Then in early 2021 I thought, well, there is probably enough for a book here. I had wanted to write a book for many years.

I had been writing shamanic and astrology blogs since 2006, and all that added up to quite a few books. But I wasn't ready. There needed to be something central in me that was substantial enough to create a much longer piece of writing. It was not enough just to put together all the shorter pieces. One morning I thought dammit, what are you waiting for, just start writing now, this minute, and see where it goes. And that was how I started, and I find it is a way that works for many things. It was how I began blogging. Stop thinking about it, just start, now! And ignore those impostors, success and failure. What matters is that you bring forth that which is in you to bring forth, as Jesus put it in the Gnostic Gospel of St Thomas. If you do that, he said, it will save you. If you don't do that, he added, it will destroy you. Spirit is not nice and fluffy. Spirit means business, life means business.

When I write or talk, my intention is always to stay close to experience. And to do this, you need to know what you are talking about. That is why it has taken me so many years to get to the point of writing a book. I was always aware of the degree to which I actually knew what I was talking about, and the degree to which I was just passing on information from others. There is a place for passing on information, and of course, that is part of what this book is about. But my real intention is to draw you into a deeper contemplation of yourself. By talking about my own experience – which I frequently do – I hope that will move you towards your own experience. I hope this book will give you a fresh perspective on many things, including yourself.

This book is a product of topics that I have been pondering for many years. I learnt to think originally and practically from a Buddhist teacher I had in my 20s and 30s. My school and university education had not taught me that, which raises questions as to their value. What I try to do is to ascertain the facts and their status, put aside assumptions and any desires for a particular outcome, and apply reason and experience. One of the hardest things can be to put aside what everyone else thinks, because that often presents itself as 'reality'. But then I find something of my own always appears, that is fresh. I also hope that by watching the way I think (as I watched my teacher in my 20s), you will feel emboldened to find more of your own fresh perspectives.

People sometimes say to me, in a context of appreciation for what I write, that they do not always agree with me. Well, there is only one thing worse than that, and that is people always agreeing with you. I hope you find points in this book where you do not agree with me. Cherish them, for they are often pathways into our own originality. I am sure there is at least something in this book for everyone to disagree with. But that is what comes with thinking freshly: people will disagree with you, and you know that is going to happen, and it means you have to live your life unconstrained by the need for others' good opinion. Now that is a true warrior training!

This book is not an exposition of the Medicine Wheel as a traditional Native American teaching. I am not qualified to do that, and that is maybe just as well, for it has meant I have had to find my own way in. The Medicine Wheel comes from particular peoples, and has different forms, but the principles behind it are universal. It can be adapted locally to, for example, the animals that you know. But we live in a time when more than ever we can see that humanity is one people, with different cultures that we can all share in, and it is in that spirit of universality that I am offering my understanding of the Medicine Wheel.

'Medicine' means that which will heal. 'Heal' comes from 'whole'. A Wheel too is a symbol of wholeness. The more traditional understanding of the Wheel is that it can help bring us into balance with ourselves and with the world around us. They amount to the same thing. I hope reading this book will help you lead yourself to the centre of the Wheel, the centre of yourself, the point of balance and wholeness.

Acknowledgements

I would like to express my gratitude to indigenous peoples everywhere for hanging on to their ancient ways and teachings, despite our modern attempts to eradicate them. And to all those 'worthy opponents' in my life, who have made me what I am, I say thank you through gritted teeth. Thanks to Leo Rutherford, for introducing me to the teachings of the Medicine Wheel. Thanks also to Moon Books for publishing this book, and to Ali Broughton for painting such an amazing cover.

Chapter 1

Introducing The Wheel

First Encounters with Shamanism

I first encountered the idea of the Medicine Wheel in 1997, when I was on a course learning about Shamanic Journeying. One of the guys running the course, Leo Rutherford, also ran a year-long course on the Wheel. I knew nothing about it, but it nevertheless fascinated me, I felt pulled towards it.

This was at a time when my whole life was changing. I had spent my 20s and 30s involved with Buddhist practice, and had reached a point where it was no longer working. I loved many of the ideas in Buddhism, and along with its various practices, they had shown me that my metaphysical quest, my desire for meaning and personal transformation, was a full-time thing, it was at the centre of who I was.

Something deep had taken root in me during those years, and it was that same thing that had brought me to this impasse. The Buddhist teacher I had was an original thinker, and it was his ideas, rather than who he was, that attracted me. And as time went on, and I made my own relationship with his ideas, it became increasingly clear to me that he wasn't very keen on his students thinking outside of his particular box.

The Natural World is Alive

Here, in what we call shamanism, was a very different way of looking at the world compared to the particular form of Buddhism that I had been around. I say 'particular form' of Buddhism, because at the origin of all spiritual or religious teachings is the same search for what is real, what is of value in this short dream we call life. We simple humans like things to be tangible and certain, it is hard for many of us to live with the elusiveness and subtlety and uncertainty of what is real. As TS Eliot said,

> *"Humankind cannot bear very much reality."*

We identify that metaphysical search with the particular forms it takes in our culture, and even start to think that our forms are 'better' than other forms. And those forms get twisted to suit the needs for group control. And then you have religion.

The Buddhism I was around had the idea of 'transcendence' at its core: as with traditional Christianity, this Earth was not a place you really wanted to be. Nirvana, or Heaven, was really where it was at. Shamanism, which can be defined as our modern attempt to replicate the ways of being in the world that one finds amongst early peoples, had the idea that the Earth and the natural world are alive and inspirited. And that we are part of it.

For me, this idea was intoxicating. It is also a very natural idea, but it is one that we have been increasingly forgetting in the West for the last 2500 years. (See *The Dream of the Cosmos* by Anne Baring, p99, where the author points the finger firmly at Plato and his over-emphasis on rationality, which was foundational for Western civilisation.) I call it the Great Forgetting.

I had reached an impasse with Buddhism not just because of the dogmatism of the teacher; it was also because the model of transcendence had made me feel deeply disconnected and out of sorts. This was not just personal to myself, or even particular to the Buddhist group I was with: I also felt out of balance and ill because the culture was out of balance and ill, and had been so for 2500 years.

Shamanism, with its foundation in the sense of being part of a world that is alive and to be cherished, provided a remedy for myself and, I believe, can do so for the same imbalance in the culture at large.

A Note on the Word Shamanism

Shamanism is used to mean different things, and some people eschew the word altogether. It is a term created by Western anthropologists, from the original Siberian term Saman, initially to describe the religious practices of those areas, and then given a wider application by some. In popular usage in the modern world, it has come broadly to mean our attempts to be inspired by indigenous attitudes to living, and to create our own ways. Some people use the term to refer specifically to practices involving altered states of consciousness and the help from guides in those states. There are sometimes endless arguments on Facebook as to the 'correct' meaning of 'shamanism'. And it is usually people with the more specific definition who argue that theirs is the 'correct' usage. Personally, I am happy to move between both ways of using the word. Insisting on a particular definition of a word, particularly in the face of popular usage to the contrary, seems to me to be a kind of fundamentalism.

There are courses available in what is called 'core shamanism', which teaches the work involving altered states. While I have no quibble with the teachings themselves, I think the word 'core' is misleading in our common usage of the word shamanism. It suggests that shamanism begins with altered states. It doesn't. It begins, in my view, with a remembering of our connection to the natural world, the sense that we belong to her and that she takes care of us. Everything flows from that. Anything beyond that – journeying, ceremonies, Medicine Wheels – has that remembering as its basis.

The Nature of the Medicine Wheel

The Medicine Wheel, which has its origins in the Americas (no-one knows quite where) encompasses a philosophy, a way of understanding ourselves, whose aim is finding balance both within ourselves, and in relation to the natural world around us. It is simple and practical and elemental, yet has room for the abstract thought that is also part of our relating to life.

The Medicine Wheel addresses us in our wholeness. It does not divide us into good and bad, spiritual and unspiritual, mind and body, in the way that institutional Christianity and then science have tended to. Furthermore, it is not just about the individual human and their path to wholeness: we are inseparable from the people and the world around us. The human being is primarily relational rather than existing autonomously. This amounts to a fundamental difference in outlook between the modern Westernised world and indigenous societies which are, at bottom, very similar the world over.

The language of wholeness emphasises the human being as an autonomous individual; the language of finding balance emphasises our relatedness. I think both have their place in our exploration of the Medicine Wheel.

The Spirit Perspective

For myself, the two-year period in which I learnt firstly shamanic journeying and the healing methods that come with that, followed by an exploration of who I was through the lens of the Medicine Wheel, changed my life completely. I didn't know that this was what was going to happen. And that was because there was something bigger than my everyday self working through me – Spirit, the Unconscious, the Dreamtime – that, I think, knew very well where I was headed. I was, in a sense, being taken care of.

So much of it was intoxicating for me, it was deeply delicious: the idea that Buddhism didn't have all the answers, that there were other ways of seeing the world; the idea that the world was alive and that I was part of that; and the idea that our problematic sides, that maybe torment us at 4am while everyone else is asleep, are not to be 'transcended' but lived and nurtured and brought into balance: they are 'the cracks where the light gets in', the gateways to our soul.

Vision Quest

There was a particular point towards the end of the Medicine Wheel course where we did a short 'Vision Quest', a night out on a hillside in mid-Wales, completely remote from everyday life, a place where, given time and intention on our part, the Spirit can speak. This is the East of the Wheel, the element of Fire, that speaks of inspiration and initiation. For me, it was the culmination of three years exploration and practice of shamanism; and within half an hour of being on that hillside, an absolute certainty flooded through me that it was time to formally leave the Buddhist organisation that I had been associated with for 19 years. I had never been so sure of anything in my life, it was like a clear light flooding through me from top to bottom. A visionary moment. I wasted no time putting my decision into action when I got home. And when I thought about this series of events, for some years afterwards, a feeling of ecstasy would go through me.

Going Round the Wheel

The Medicine Wheel is a way of exploring who we are through the elements of Fire, Water, Earth and Air respectively (these elements are common to all Wheels, though their order may vary.) These elements are each associated with one of the four directions: East, South, West and North.

Over the previous year I had been round the Wheel, beginning with my initial inspiration to attend the course, which is, of course, Fire; then attending to some of the more troubled sides of myself in the element of Water; finding a way of incarnating those sides in the element of Earth; developing a new perspective on my life in the element of Air; and then arriving back at Fire, with an inspiration to change my whole life. And a major new chapter did indeed begin. The Medicine Wheel came in again 15 years later, and helped change my life radically once more, but that is another story (see below My

Personal Medicine Wheel.)

Making Your Own Medicine Wheel

A Medicine Wheel is essentially very simple, and that is part of its beauty. All you need are four stones, one for each direction. I suggest you make one as a companion to reading this book. one way is to find somewhere unspoilt and go for a walk, and approach any stones that catch your eye. Spend a few moments with that stone, see if it feels happy to come home with you. If not, see if it wants to be moved – maybe the fairies are wanting bit of help with that, which is why it caught your eye. This may seem fanciful, but we are beginning at the beginning, by relating to rocks as we would to plants and animals – as alive. And nature herself as replete with presences that we humans often do not notice in our busyness.

Find a place where you can set out these four stones, one for each direction. We are starting with nature and with ceremony, with direct experience, rather than with intellect, which is always the right way. This Wheel will gradually become a place that carries your dreams and your intentions and your self-knowledge and your sense of the sacred, so treat it accordingly. Put it away in a special container if you do not have a permanent place for it, and make sure you go and talk to it from time to time and give thanks to it for supporting your life.

The Simple and Radical Foundation of the Wheel

This Wheel, this mandala, is so simple, and yet it contains the whole universe, with you at its centre. And it does not describe the universe in the abstract concepts that we are used to in the West – think atoms and dark matter, for example, neither of which anyone has directly seen, but which are fundamental to the modern understanding of the universe. No, think Sun and rain and soil and wind: Fire, Water, Earth and Air. The Wheel brings us back to an understanding of the universe that is immediate to our experience.

This is radical, because for the last 1000 years knowledge of things-as-they-are has been in the hands of specialists, first the priests and then the scientists. And we have become used to there being just one story, that becomes 'the truth'. This makes our minds disempowered and rigid, and it is one way that these vast collectives that we are all part of nowadays keep the illusion that everything is under control. It produces a certain kind of psychological stability for many people. But in reality, no-one is in control, and we need to re-learn to hold in our minds contradictory stories about how the universe is

"without any irritable reaching after fact and reason"

as the poet Keats put it, using the term 'negative capability' to describe this state of mind. We will explore this further when we come to the Air element.

Origins of the Wheel and Making it Your Own

For the same reason, there is not just one Medicine Wheel. There are many, that associate different elements with different directions, each with their own set of meanings. I urge you to make your own connections and meanings as we explore the Wheel. Once you have made it your own in terms of your own experience, then you will have understood it. Before that, you will just have someone else's understanding which, valuable as that can be, does not have the same creative power, the same quality of authenticity that comes when someone speaks from what they know within themselves, and which can then move other people.

The Wheel we will be exploring came to me from Leo Rutherford, who in turn learnt it from Hyemeyohsts Storm and his pupil Harley SwiftDeer. I have no idea who they learnt it from, but I do know that the Ojibwe people, for example, use the same Wheel. As does Lewis Mehl-Madrona, who is part Cherokee and Lakota, in his book *Coyote Healing*. They may well, however, have a different understanding of the Wheel than Storm and SwiftDeer, who were not always accepted as traditional.

The form of the Wheel is traditional, but the understanding of it has morphed as various modern people have made their own contributions. I will (I hope) be making my own contribution. Traditions need to be dynamic, ever-evolving, ever-responding to the needs of the time, or they gradually die, they become mere religion. Jim Tree, a Cherokee who wrote *The Way of the Sacred Pipe*, has a saying (p15):

> *"If it's real, it works; if it works, it's real."*

I think that is a sound principle. Black Elk, a Lakota Medicine man, said that the power of a ceremony lies in the understanding of it. This is not referring to a purely intellectual understanding (which for us is often enough), rather it also needs to make sense in terms of your own experience for there to be true understanding. A Medicine Wheel, or a Sweatlodge, or a Pipe Ceremony will have built up particular forms within particular traditions over the centuries. Every detail of a ceremony carries meaning. When you enter a Sweatlodge, or place yourself around a Medicine Wheel, you are in ceremonial time, sacred time. Everything becomes significant. Those significances are laid out for us in a general way by the tradition, but our personal interaction with the ceremony will also have its own meanings.

Humans, being what they are, become attached to forms, to the 'correct' way of doing or understanding something: that is what 'authentic' can come to mean. Are those teachings 'authentic', is that ceremony 'authentic'? There is a surface meaning, in the sense that if you are claiming that a ceremony comes from a particular tradition, then it needs to do so, otherwise it is not authentic, and you are probably just using the name of that tradition to lend credibility to yourself. But in a deeper sense, authentic is related to 'authoritative' and 'author': it is something that is generated, 'authored', from deep within ourselves, because we have understood it and lived it.

This relates to my Vision Quest experience in Wales. I spent the rest of the night out on that hillside, with a plastic bag over my head to keep the midges at bay, in order to complete the quest. What I hadn't quite clocked was that I had in fact completed the Vision Quest within that first 30 mins, and I could have walked back to base camp with my head held high. But no, somewhere I had it in my head that the Vision Quest was about spending the night on the hillside, rather than about having a vision. Not unlike someone thinking that being a good Christian is about going to church once a week. No harm done, but I was slightly missing the point that this ceremony was essentially about the Spirit speaking to me, not about spending a night outside.

The forms can be very important, don't get me wrong, particularly if they are part of a tradition that has been developed over the generations. But even more important is the reason for those forms, their meanings. "The power of a ceremony lies in the understanding of it." Spirituality, one could say, is always focussed on the inner meanings, religion on the outward forms as ends in themselves.

Cultural Appropriation?

It has taken me many years to feel confident I had the right to talk about the Medicine Wheel. Not just because I needed to live it, but because it comes from the Americas, it is not from my own culture, and we live in a time of sensitivity to what is called 'cultural appropriation'. The idea behind this is that not only has our culture dispossessed and destroyed the societies that came before in the Americas and elsewhere, but now we are also trying to steal what little they have left, namely their traditions.

This is a complex area. Sensitivity is needed, and I certainly think it is inappropriate to claim to be representing any of those traditions without the requisite trainings and permissions from them. But we can be inspired by elements in those cultures, and incorporate from that point of view, without claiming to represent. I am not claiming that the Medicine Wheel teachings in this book are Native American. What I am aiming at is a Wheel that is universal, that largely transcends specific cultures. But it is certainly inspired by Native American cultures, and I am grateful to them on that account.

Humans have always borrowed from other cultures. Shakespeare borrowed many of his plots. It is not something that can be stopped, and it might not be such a good thing if it could be stopped. You are not going to be able to prevent young party-goers in New York wearing Indian feather head-dresses, even though from one point of view it is the height of disrespect and 'cultural appropriation'.

For some years, a Canadian Indian teacher used to come and stay with me. They call themselves 'Indians', and leave the term 'Native Canadian (or American)' to the white people*. I learnt many things from him, often informally around the breakfast table, which for me is often the best way, and probably more like how people learnt traditionally, rather than through the more structured courses we have nowadays. But this teacher didn't have much time for the shamanism we are trying to create in the West; he was quite dismissive of it, but nor did he create openings for us to practise his ways. Native peoples can be closed and fundamentalist just as much as we can (and a certain defensiveness on their part is entirely understandable.) By contrast, I was in a Sweatlodge with a Lakota woman a few years ago, and she was very informal in the way she led it, and very encouraging for all of us to go forth and lead Sweatlodges ourselves. My point here is that claims of 'cultural appropriation' need to be weighed up to see what is behind them, and not just bowed down to because a particular native person is saying it.

*Another Indian told me that the term 'Native American', while appearing to be respectful, has a less obvious political agenda: if Indians are 'Native Americans', then they are one more American minority along with Irish Americans, Hispanic Americans, African Americans and so on, so why should they have any special rights that the other minorities do not have?

If it Works, it's Real

I spent quite some years in a kind of limbo, unsure to what extent it was legitimate for me to run, in a public kind of way, with the ceremonies and teachings I had imbibed. Then a few years ago I had a dream in which I was about to lead a Sweatlodge in a very 'new age' type of context. Sweatlodges are a kind of ceremonial sauna, wooden structures covered in blankets into which red hot rocks are brought, and onto which water is poured to create steam and heat. Prayers are then made. The lodge in the dream, however, was inflatable and made of plastic, with 'new age' type people sitting around inside it in an informal sort of way. And in this dream, it came to me that I knew exactly how to lead this lodge in a way that would help people. At that point, the Canadian teacher turned up and started purifying people in a traditional way with burning herbs. And this completely killed the spirit in which I was about to lead the lodge, and my confidence to do so evaporated, because of this guy, and the attitude he brought, being present.

This dream told me everything that I needed to know. 'If it works, it's real'. I knew how to lead this rather bizarre Sweatlodge in a way that would help people, where bringing in a more traditional approach would not work. An irony of the dream was that this same teacher once said to me that back on the reservation, they get the Sweatlodge fire started by pouring paraffin on it, whereas over here in Europe he could not do that because people would think it was not authentic.

Balancing Tradition and Creativity

There is a dance, a weave to be done between the integrity of tradition, and the need to be adaptable, to bring a creative attitude to our leading, or holding, of ceremonies and teachings. In the modern world, the honest position is that we do not have tradition. Our old tradition, Christianity, is for many of us dead and, I think in many ways that is a good thing. The downside is that it has left us in a world with no sense of the sacred.

But at the same time, it frees us. We do not have tradition and the depth that can come with that. But nor do we need to find our way out of forms that have become rigid, and ends in themselves. We can be inspired by traditions from all over the world, and re-create them for ourselves. This is the spirit in which I am approaching the Medicine Wheel in this book. As a symbol and a ceremony and a philosophy that has its roots in Native American cultures, but which has a universal application, and which we are at liberty to re-create in ways that speak to us: if it works, it's real.

Egregore

A final nod to the past: there is a mysterious way in which symbols and ceremonies acquire power over time. The word 'egregore' describes this phenomenon. You may sometimes feel this with stone circles, that tend to be located at spots that have a certain power anyway, but the combination of ancient and modern ceremony at those places adds another layer of power that one can feel.

For myself, this also works with astrology and tarot. They are both symbolic systems that are used for divination, to help unpack who we are. Their ability to do that lies not just in the divinatory ability of the reader, but in the fact that these symbols have been used for centuries or more in the same way. Reality is not just the visible, tangible material world. It is not even fundamentally that. Consciousness is primary, matter secondary, as quantum physics also reveals. As Max Planck, the originator of quantum theory, said,

> *"I regard consciousness as fundamental. I regard matter as derivative from consciousness. We cannot get behind consciousness. Everything that we talk about, everything that we regard as existing, postulates consciousness."*

It is as if when we sit with, say, the planet Mars, we are also sitting with all those thousands of astrologers from the past and present who have also directed attention to that planet and allowed it to speak through them: it has grown as a gateway to meaning over time. And you find yourself being able to say something to the person having the reading that is true about them, without the prior knowledge one would normally require. This is magical, it is like the universe already knows you. It enlarges and enchants the spirit of the other person.

It is the same with the Medicine Wheel. It is also a tool of self-knowledge that has a divinatory aspect. When we use the Wheel to understand ourselves better, we are plugging in to the power it has developed over time, through all the people who have used it in this way. The Wheel has its own power, it needs to be approached with that kind of respect, and any contributions we might make to that tradition need to be done advisedly.

The Wheel as a Way of Balance

Without further ado, let us plunge into the Wheel itself. As I said, it is essentially simple, yet contains the whole universe. It is founded on the four directions and the four elements, and gives us a way of orienting and understanding who we are.

These directions and elements can be directly experienced. The East is the point on the horizon where the Sun rises, and the West is where it sets. As we face the East, the North, the place of cold and winter, is to our left. And the South, the place of warmth and summer, is to our right. We have Sunrise and Sunset, left and right, all very immediate. The anticlockwise order of the directions is also experiential, describing the journey of the Sun across the sky in the Northern hemisphere every day, from East to South to West and then (after dusk) to North. And then we have Fire, Water, Earth and Air – Sun, Rain, Soil and Wind – again very immediate. A whole symbolic system of correspondences is built around these two sets of four, that differs according to tradition.

Each element is aligned with a direction, and they are arranged in a circle, just as the horizon is a circle. Circles symbolise wholeness and balance. Seen in this way, life is not a progress along a line towards higher and higher levels, but a circling around an ever-deepening centre of wholeness and balance. In this sense, time itself is also circular, repeating itself through the markers of the four seasons (which also have their place on the Wheel) on a yearly basis.

We are immediately into a very different way of thinking about life compared to the Western rational, linear, evolutionary model: which is just that, a model, a story, that has its uses and its limitations.

> *"Evolution is a spirit notion which soul does not recognise. Traditional societies do not evolve. They live within a mythology which contains all imaginative possibilities, Earth Goddesses no less than Heraclean egos... Because we are changing, we think of ourselves as evolving. We are not. We are literalising the old myths... If the rational ego is to disappear it is more likely to be destroyed by the ricochets of ideologies made in its own image."*
> Patrick Harpur *The Philosopher's Secret Fire* (pp 263-6)

I once asked the Canadian teacher I mentioned what was the underlying purpose of his people's ways, and he said it was about becoming a balanced human being. And this is indeed the aim of all the ceremonies and teachings: aligning ourselves with Spirit within and without, and arranging our lives around that. One of my hopes is that in reading this account of the Wheel, you will also find yourself moving towards that point of balance within yourself that the Wheel speaks of.

The central part of this book will be a detailed exploration of each element and its associated direction, as individual aspects of who we are, that interweave with all the other aspects; and that also build as we journey around the Wheel from East to North.

Jung and the Medicine Wheel

Broadly speaking, the four elements of Fire, Water, Earth and Air can be understood respectively as intuition, feeling, sensation and thinking, using the typology that the psychologist CG Jung created. In the 1920s, Jung visited indigenous people in Africa and the Americas and was quickly able to form a rapport with them and their way of seeing the world, which was extraordinary for his time. His own vision of the human being involved wholeness rather than the linear model of progress, and his typology, as noted, is close to that of the elements of the Medicine Wheel.

But in creating this typology Jung was, suggests the astrologer and Jungian analyst, Liz Greene, drawing on his understanding of the four elements as found within astrology. There is a remarkably similar use of the four elements to describe the human being in both the European esoteric tradition and the Medicine Wheel. This lends a universality to the Wheel.

If we expand the Wheel a bit further, we find that there are seven directions rather than just four: the Above, the Below and the Centre as well as North, South, East and West. I mention this now because the Centre can be seen as that point of wholeness and individuation that is central to Jung's psychology; and the above and the below are the attitudes of extraversion and introversion respectively which complete Jung's typology of the human being. We will look at this further in Chapter 8.

Keeping it Simple

I want to move back to just the four directions to keep it simple (there are also intermediate directions that can be used, see Chapter 7). The reason I want to keep it simple is not just for ease of comprehension, but because then it is easier to stay close to the symbolism and the explanatory and divinatory power that comes with that.

I use the same principle in astrology. You can make it as complex as you like, you can even pull in dozens of asteroids if you want, and they will indeed tell you things. But it is also a move towards the intellect on its own, and away from the raw power of the symbolism of the Sun and the Moon, both of which are in our immediate, daily experience. When I do astrology readings, I try to concentrate on the Sun and soon and what they are saying, and gradually draw the other planets in around that.

It is the same with the Medicine Wheel. You can make it almost as complex as you want, and that does have its own relevance and beauty. But then you are having to juggle all that in your head – unless you know the Wheel really well and it has become second nature – and one can't help but to start to move away from the simple power of Sun, Rain, Soil and Wind.

As we explore the Wheel, in which there is no end of ideas and perspectives and correlations to be usefully brought in, I want to keep coming back to that basic set of four, which is foundational. And the simple experience, beyond all concepts, of the four stones of your circle.

Before we go there, I want to do justice the Wheel in its full complexity as a ceremony. There is what is known as the 20-count, where you have 20 stones. Because the Wheel is a map of the universe, there is in a sense no limit to the amount you can put in it, and this works very well in ceremony. Once you know the Wheel, you can create your own ceremonies around it.

For now, here is a diagram of the Wheel along with some of the correlations that we find in each direction.

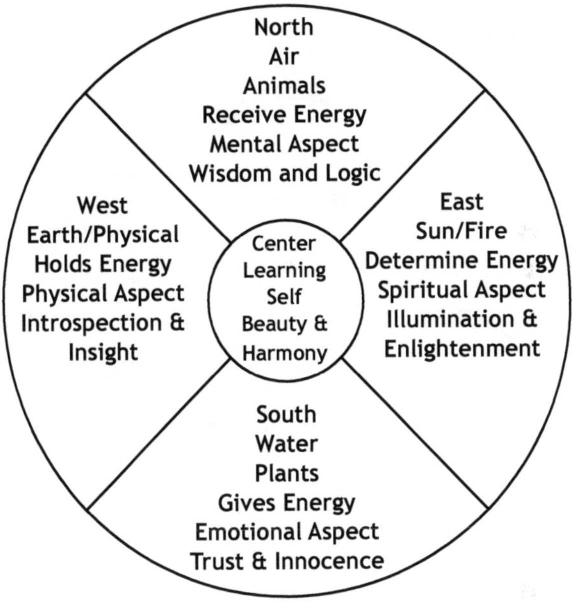

Engaging the Unconscious Mind

Because this is a book, we will be approaching the Wheel largely through ideas rather than through, say, ceremony, or just going outdoors and experiencing the elements.

However, the power of the Wheel, like any symbol, lies in ability to speak to the unconscious mind as much as to the conscious mind. The language of the unconscious is symbol and image and myth and ceremony. And, in a way, the simpler the better.

The Wheel is an example of a mandala, or circle, which is found universally. This was one of Jung's discoveries as he explored symbols and dreams across the world. They are symbols of wholeness. Think Stonehenge. Or Buddhist mandala paintings.

I recommend painting your stones, as the unconscious/ imagination responds strongly to colour. Or else have a painting divided into four quarters with the appropriate colour for each direction: East is Yellow, South is Red, West is Black and the North is White. If you wish, you can put a Green circle in the middle for the Centre.

And then this painting (I know someone who embroidered it, a great exercise) or this circle of stones becomes an object of meditation, it will gradually sink into your unconscious, the dream-world can speak to you through it. And when you come to explore your life through the directions, they can speak to you, insights will come unbidden. Or insights for others, using the Wheel as a counselling format.

My Personal Medicine Wheel

I created my own Wheel in about 2015. I was in a difficult situation, in a long-term relationship that was no longer working, and Spirit came knocking – or rather, hammering, in a way that I had never known, pushing me to move on. It began when my son knocked my Prayer Pipe off a bookshelf and broke it. I managed to fix it, and took it as a message to use it: it had been given to me, but remained unused. When you use a Pipe, you are having a conversation with the natural world about your life and all the things you are thankful for and all the things that need fixing. Then you light it, and the smoke carries your prayers out to the universe. I began using the Pipe, and out of that came the notion that I needed a caravan up the road to create my own space. So I did that, a place where I could talk to the universe in peace.

And then the notion came to me that I needed a Medicine Wheel outside of the caravan. It was a beautiful spot: a paddock with a stream running through it, and with two giant beech trees protecting the space, raining their masts onto the roof of the caravan in the autumn.

I had a strong feeling about doing this, which is how Spirit often speaks to me. Some people experience guides turning up with advice, for me it more like a nudge that has flow and synchronicities around it if I follow through.

There is a particular quarry in Cornwall that I used to get my Sweatlodge stones from, and I knew these would be ideal for my Wheel. So I drove down, and when I got there, I was told they no longer allowed cars in for health and safety reasons, and that stones could only be ordered by the lorry-load. This puzzled me: how could I have had such a strong feeling about coming here to get these stones, and yet it wasn't working out? I realised that all I could do was trust in the situation and start driving back home, keeping my eyes peeled for stones. And sure enough, about a quarter mile up the road was a discarded pile of stones, of exactly the type I needed. It is strange how Spirit works in this tricksy way sometimes, giving us lessons in trust and in not making assumptions about how events 'should' unfold!

I got back to my caravan and created a Wheel outside it, as big as the space would allow. I used the 'intermediate' directions as well, to create a more obvious circle. We will come to the intermediate directions later. They are useful, but do not have the same immediate relationship to the elements and directions as do the cardinal points.

And then I realised I needed to paint them. So this is what I did, and I invented a simple scheme for the intermediate directions, as I was not aware of particular colours associated with them: I painted them each in two colours, comprising the two adjacent cardinal stones. So I had my Wheel

I did not use it in a conceptual way. I was a bit hazy about the meaning of the intermediate directions, for example, and I still sometimes have to think twice about them. But none of that mattered, because what I had created was a living symbol, an ongoing ceremony on the land outside my caravan. And I had a sense of being protected by it, of it carrying the dream and direction of my life, even though I was a bit hazy about that too!

It is important to run intuitively with these things, and not get too tied down by the formal or 'correct' meanings. At one point a friend visited, and she suggested that the Wheel was too large and that a smaller one could contain more effectively the dream I was trying to manifest, which was to move on from the situation I was in, vague as I was about it. I could immediately feel she was right, there was something more 'manageable' about a smaller Wheel. So I reduced it in size, creating a tighter personal relationship with it. A while later I had another visionary moment of absolute clarity (just before entering a Sweatlodge) that it was time to move on. That was the certainty I had been waiting for, and within a couple of months I had left. The Wheel, sitting outside my caravan, overseen by two giant beech trees, had carried my life forward. It felt like the most drawn-out and difficult thing I had ever done, and the Medicine Wheel helped me do that.

Fast forward six months, and I was now living on my own in a local town. And it took me that time to realise that, having a spare bedroom, I could bring my stones over and have that space just for the Wheel. They needed re-painting after being exposed to the weather and to the hooves of sheep. But it meant I had my dream-carrier with me again.

But also, having been around me in this ceremonial way for some years now, they have acquired a power of their own. An egregore that is personal, but which also draws on the power of the Medicine Wheel as a collective thought-form. People coming into the room can feel the power those stones are now holding.

The Wheel as a Counselling Tool

And I have 'invented' a way of using them for counselling.

You get the person to sit in a direction, and to speak about whatever issue it is they are bringing. And I sit in the opposite, complementary, direction, and reflect back to them as necessary. When it feels complete, we move to another direction and repeat the process. And the person will usually find themselves speaking from the quality of that direction, even if they don't know in advance the meaning of that direction. If they are in the South, for example, they may find themselves talking from the 'child' in themselves. That is part of the power, part of the magic of the Wheel. I will keep going round the Wheel with the person until a sense of completion, for now, is reached. It is not about looking for answers so much as it is about chewing over an issue, 'cooking' it, until a sense comes that the energy around it has moved on in some way. This is quite deep work, and like a dream or a shamanic journey, the implications and the changes will often unfold in the months ahead.

There is no set way of doing this. It can be done systematically, starting in the East, the place of inspirations and new beginnings, and working round from there. Or it can be done spontaneously. Moving from direction to direction, from stone to stone, as you or the other person feels, sometimes maybe revisiting a place.

Calling in the Powers of the Directions

When I teach the Medicine Wheel, much of it is often me expounding, in an experiential way, on the meanings of each direction, and indeed that will constitute the centrepiece of this book. But I tend to begin by calling in the powers of the directions, followed by a short, guided meditation. This sets a ceremonial context for the learning. The Medicine Wheel is 'sacred' knowledge: it connects us to, and helps us gain insight into, that which holds most value in our lives; it aligns us, rebalances us, with our Spirit. It is very far from the passing on of information on subjects that do not have a bearing on who we are. That has its place, and is ordinarily what is meant by teaching. It is, of course, important to absorb the information element of the Wheel; but more important is to be moved by it, to let it connect you to yourself and to your relationship with all-that-is.

Each direction is seen as a power in its own right, that is 'out there' and which can be invoked. We do this with humility rather than from a position of 'commanding' the power. We give thanks to that direction for helping us with our lives, and we ask for the particular qualities of that direction to be present as we explore the Wheel.

As modern people, we tend to view the self as autonomous, an entity in its own right, and a corollary of that would be that the qualities of each direction – the inspiration of the East, the emotion of the South, the dream and the incarnation of the West, the wisdom and knowing of the North – as qualities within ourselves to be lived and unfolded.

That view has its place, it works. But only up to a point. The self from a traditional point of view is relational: we cannot separate who we are from our parents and grandparents and all the ancestors before that, as well as from all our living relatives and the natural world around us.

And one reason that the self is, for indigenous people, relational, is that they take into account what we call the 'unconscious' – which Jung once paraphrased simply as 'life'. It is the conscious ego that separates, that sees a barrier between self and other, the inner world and the outer world. If we pay attention to our experience, it quickly becomes clear that the sense of separation is illusory. We sense atmospheres, we quickly feel comfortable around certain people and not around others, when we barely know them. And subsequent experience often verifies our initial instinct (and we learn to pay attention to those instincts by getting burnt when we ignore them!) We have hunches to maybe contact certain people, and there turns out to be a good reason to do so. We get a sense of the people we are close to even when they are not present. How often have you had a message from someone just as you were thinking of them? It is traditional that if you see something unusual in nature, there is probably a message for you in that. The natural world speaks to us, helps us, she is our mother. I could go on and cite what we call 'psychic' experience, but I think I have made my point. We are connected to each other in ways that are not obvious.

The ego is necessary, it helps us function within this dream of time and space, and enables us to make necessary distinctions for that functioning. But it is the servant, not the master. Its way of perceiving the world is provisional. We will explore this more when we come to the North.

In the same way, the directions and their powers live 'out there' in the world, everything we perceive is a blend of those powers (who needs M-theory, the arcane 'theory of everything' in physics, when you have the four directions, which you can actually experience?) When we invoke those directions, we are invoking something awesome, something so powerful that maybe we should merely peep at it lest it burn us up!

This sense of the sublime, of something infinitely bigger and deeply unknowable is the Great Mystery, and it provides the context for everything, for all understanding. Without it, you might begin to suffer from the illusion that you actually know something. And that you have an all-powerful separate self that does the knowing.

The purpose of all 'sacred' activity, whether it is contemplating the Medicine Wheel teachings or whispering with the natural world or entering a Sweatlodge or listening to Mozart is to align ourselves with that Great Mystery. For then we are in balance, then we are a true human being.

The Wheel as a Meditation

After calling in the powers of the directions, I conduct a short meditation. This has the purpose first of all of bringing us to the centre point of the Wheel, which is that still centre within each one of us, that is also the Great Mystery. We are each of us unknowable, and it is this realisation that lies at the heart of that ancient injunction at Delphi to 'know thyself'.

The other purpose of the meditation is to let the Medicine Wheel speak to us at a non-rational level, to become a power within our unconscious, or to connect us more deeply to the great Medicine Wheel that underlies the universe. I ask people to visualise themselves at the centre of the Wheel, with the different directions opening up around them. And I will choose just one set of correlations to connect to.

There are numerous correlations for each direction, and they often link to each other. But for the purposes of a meditation, you need just one set of images that do not demand much of the rational mind and can therefore can sink in deep.

The most basic one is probably the colours. Colours are powerful, they have a deep effect on how we feel, and associations can build up around them. The lack of colour in modern men's clothes shows how disconnected in some ways we have become from Spirit, which loves colour. If you are a man and you go to the bank manager for a mortgage, you would not wear colourful clothes! I'll take this up later when we look at the warrior aspect of the North.

So we let the directions open up around us – having started at that still centre that is beyond time and space and beyond this dream we call life – the Sunyata of Buddhist tradition – and we see a colour in each direction. Moving anti-clockwise, we gaze at each in turn, we let it sink in, and we also become aware of our emotional response to that colour. And at the end we dissolve the visualisation, and in-so-doing maintain its proper context: it is a dream, just as life is a dream.

Or we can visualise the elements in the same way: we see the Sun in the East, an Ocean or Rain in the South, the Earth herself in the West, and we feel the Wind blowing past and even through us in the North.

You can invent these meditations yourself. I meditated for many years in the Buddhist tradition, and undertook years of deity visualisations in that context, in which the dissolution into 'emptiness' (which is really a fullness) at the end is crucial.

Similarly, you can see the stages of your life – birth, childhood, adult and elder – as you go round the directions. All those stages exist outside of time (time being a convenient illusion). Or the seasons. Or a spirit helper that is personal to you. Or an animal that is traditionally associated with that direction. There are many possibilities. But in each case, we are taking just one set of associations, and allowing them to sink deeply into our Spirit.

Re-Enchanting the World

For an indigenous person, their stories about the world are central to who they are, and they have a metaphysical and magical dimension. We have been stripped of that since science 'proved' the Christian mythology, indeed any sacred mythology, to be 'untrue'. Taking a story like the Medicine Wheel, which tells us what we and what the world are made of, and allowing it in in this way – assuming you find it convincing – can help restore that lost enchantment. The world itself is sacred, and if we relate to it in this manner then we shall find ourselves aligned with our spirit in its deepest sense, because we are the world, we are nature, it is a returning to who we are. And the unfoldment of that natural wholeness into four elements and four directions is like gazing at a rainbow and glimpsing the white light that is at its source.

Listening to Ourselves

I am going to be describing each direction in turn, beginning in the East, in such a way that I hope it can act as an aid to reflection on your own life, and who you are, and the bigger patterns that become discernible over time. That is how I teach: I talk about an aspect of the Wheel in an experiential way, and then give participants a chance to talk in turn about that aspect of their lives. In this way we learn about ourselves, not just from our own reflections, but by listening to the reflections of others too.

Another way of describing the Wheel is as a tool for listening to ourselves. What else are we here to do other than to listen to ourselves, and act on what we find there? Society wants us to listen to its version of who it wants/needs us to be. Whereas the Medicine Wheel shows us how to listen to our own version of ourself. Looking back, this is what was so intoxicating about the Wheel for me when I encountered it. I had grown up being told who I should be, and even when I rebelled against that at as a young man and set out on the Buddhist path, to a large extent I applied that path to myself in a way that was familiar: trying to make myself 'fit' the teachings, to be a regular meditator, to know all the lists of teachings etc. I was listening too much to the teachings and to the teacher and not enough to myself, and the teacher had an agenda. Really, one needs to do both. It wasn't that I didn't listen to myself entirely at that time, but it was still well out of balance. I am sure I would have tried to do the same thing with the Medicine Wheel had I encountered it when I was younger.

Chapter 2

The East – Initiation

It is somewhat artificial to talk about each direction on its own, because they are inter-related, and no direction can be grasped without the light shed on it by the other directions. At the same time, the Wheel does have a movement that gathers momentum and wisdom as it rotates on its path from East through the South and West to the North, and back to the East again. This turning describes the whole arc of our life, as well as many turnings on different levels within the course of our lives. We will begin with the East, and take it from there. A structure will emerge…

Colour: Yellow
Element: Fire
Season: Spring
Time: Timeless
Stage of Life: Birth
Animal: Eagle
Some key words for the East: Inspiration, Initiation, Spirit, Imagination, Intuition, Meaning, Beginnings.

Birth and the New

The East is the beginning of things, just as the Sun begins the day in the East. It is the spark that begins life, and it is outside of time. In terms of a human life, being born is not something we have conscious choice over, though perhaps the fact of being born involves choice on a deeper, Spirit level. And sometimes we maybe find we have bitten off more than we can chew! It is the same with Death, in the opposite direction, the West, where the Sun sets. Death generally happens to us at a time of its own choosing, as does birth. For this reason, the East-West Road is the Spirit Road or the Blue Road. The 'Good Red Road' of North-South, Thinking and Feeling, is where we do have choice, and where we can cultivate the ground to provide fertile soil for Spirit when it chooses to enter.

The East is the place where all that is new enters our life, those impetuses that enable life to unfold to the next level. We are like the branches of a tree moving upwards towards the Sun. Our job is to water and to protect the tree.

But the larger pattern that those branches are forming is beyond our knowing, we are mysteries to ourselves. We do not make the bigger inner changes happen; we do not even know what they are until they occur. All we can do is to provide good conditions for them, and to trust and welcome them, uncomfortable as their birth can be.

Initiation

There are certain major changes that correspond to the biological stages of life, but which also reflect inner changes. And there are other major changes which are less biologically determined. In a traditional society, these more regular changes are marked by ceremony and by initiation. Any new phase, where something new enters our consciousness, is an initiation. Birth and death are initiations, in which you cannot know what is coming next. Puberty is a time of initiation, in which we begin to make the transition from child to adult.

> *"A traditional puberty rite usually contains an element of ordeal, and spirit vision/induction into the tribal myths, and acceptance as an adult by the community. For the Sioux in North America, for example, the boy is firstly put through a Sweatlodge (which is characterised by intense heat) and then immediately brought to a hilltop where he is placed in a cramped vision pit for days without food and water. At the end of this time he will, hopefully, have been*

> *granted a vision and been turned from a boy to a man."*
> Patrick Harpur, *The Philosopher's Secret Fire* (pp91-7)

We do not, uniquely, have such rites of passage in our culture, nor do we (again, uniquely) have a prevailing mythology that provides meaning. (See the North for further discussion on this.) It may well mean that many boys and girls take a lot longer reaching adulthood, if at all.

However, it is not my purpose to bemoan this situation. We have what we have and let us not compare ourselves unfavourably, it doesn't usually help. Young people *do* attempt to initiate themselves, albeit without necessarily realising it. It is a natural thing. Life has a way of initiating us anyway. As Patrick Harpur continues:

> *"During a special sacred time of about two weeks in summer, young European initiates fly to the Otherworld where they inhabit a liminal zone between land and sea. By day they are 'cooked' by a process of frying under a scorching Sun, and periodically plunged into cold water; by night they undergo an elaborate Dionysian ritual involving an orgy of wine, dancing and sex. They call this a 'Mediterranean holiday'."*

I would add the drug 'Ecstasy' to Harpur's account, the illegality of which adds an initiatory edge, taking one outside permitted norms. Criminal behaviour, dangerous driving, risk-taking (I still shudder at the blind corner on which I impatiently overtook someone when I was 20) are often also driven by this craving for initiation.

It is worth looking back and seeing where your own need for initiation took you as a teenager and young adult, and the new elements that may have entered your consciousness, and their implications for your future.

For myself, the biggest single initiatory experience of my

youth (in a life that had been heading that way for some years) was a three-month period when I was 20, when I was regularly ingesting magic mushrooms, as they are popularly known. I don't seek out psychedelic experience, but I am open to them if they come my way. There seemed to be a way in which the universe 'gifted' this experience to me, as though I needed it. A group of us had found several thousand of these mushrooms in a field, and we picked them and dried them, and that was my supply. In the 40 years since, if I have ever looked for magic mushrooms, I have not been able to find them, even in places that others recommend. And I have taken that as a message from Spirit that they were useful to me then, but not now. And I am happy with that.

Over a period of a few months the psilocybin (the active ingredient, at least from a scientific point of view) opened me up permanently. I had been brought up to have a 'proper' career in which I would become rich. That idea had been tottering for some time, and the mushrooms finished it off. I now knew for certain that my life would need to be centred around something more deeply meaningful to me than that, though I knew not what. But it was a vision for my life, connected to something bigger than the facts of ordinary existence, and in that sense, it was an initiation.

It was an initiation into heavenly experience, and also into my shadow side. I was seeing my father (who had put a lot of pressure on me) in demonic form, and I experienced crashing waves of depression. This was tough, but ultimately useful, the 'cracks where the light gets in.' However, I was on my own in all this, there were no elders to guide me, and no-one around me seemed to get what I was talking about!

I think this probably reflects our wider situation with those crucial initiatory experiences of our youth (if we have them, and by no means everybody does): they can take a long time to process, they can leave us vulnerable to the predations of gurus and others, and it can be a lonely place in which we can doubt the value of our experiences. However, there are nowadays plenty of 'spiritual' groups around, and yes, they can often be quite limited, and with some strange things going on: but we can still find an initial home for that metaphysical enquiry that has been opened up. And sometimes the limitations and betrayals of 'spiritual' groups and teachers can be exactly where we learn most.

I've opened this exploration of the East around that time in our life where, in an indigenous situation, probably the most significant initiation happens, that can map out, in principle, our whole future. And central to that is a sense of what gets called the 'Otherworld', a visionary dimension that transforms us.

The Magical Child

It is useful also to look back at other East experiences in your life. As a child, what really 'did it' for you, what gave you a sense of wonder, and absorbed you? It is natural for children to be open to the East in this way, before the responsibilities and demands of adult life come in and, quite often, squeeze out that sort of playful magic. The East is the place of the 'magical child' (and the South of the historical child.)

When I was about five, I had a picture story-book with a wizard in it, and the wizard exerted a fascination over me that is still there. Pets also interested and absorbed me, I had many of them at different times. As I got a bit older, cacti came to interest me: I had a small greenhouse full of them. Cacti are plants that can survive and thrive and create beauty where there is little nourishment – who knows, feeling under a lot of parental pressure, along with being sent away to school, there was not a lot of ordinary nourishment around for me, but the cacti were part of that nourishment.

Nowadays I have reclaimed that magical child. He or she –

and you may have one of each gender, or maybe a gender-fluid one – is always with us, at the source of our creativity, the new life that is always bubbling away within is, this is what the East is about.

All ages remain within us as we age, we become a collection of selves.

The East at Different Ages

As an exercise we can look at what 'did' it for us at various ages, what gave us that sense of wonder: as children, as adolescents, as adults. And you may be able to discern a commonality, a magical thread of Spirit unfolding as you progress through life.

As a teenager, anything to do with the occult or unusual, psychic experiences came to fascinate me. There is a clear connection with the wizard of my early childhood. And as a young adult, there was a deep opening to those 'unusual' experiences in the form of a longing for Spirit and to make that the centre of my life.

The East is Always Present

Spirit, the East, is always feeding into our lives. There is always something we are dreaming towards, something that 'does it' for us, that gives meaning. Whether we actually live it, dare to live it, is another matter. It is the central question we can ask ourselves: what is it that gives my life meaning, and am I living it? I think there is always a way to live it, whatever our circumstances. Spirit takes care of us, and it is strange the way synchronicities and opportunities occur when we make the inner commitment to follow whatever it in us that calls us. It may only be hesitant steps, we may feel it is beyond us, we may be afraid of failing….. there are always 100 reasons for not doing things, and I know people who have turned this into a fine art. But the price is a lack of meaning, a small circle of life within which there is not much room for movement, and quite possibly some self-medication to keep the feelings of oppression at bay.

The East Requires Courage

It often requires courage to live the East, but what else is there to do but to follow that sense of meaning? All else, the rest of the Wheel, follows from that. There is a well-known quote by William Hutchison Murray (often wrongly attributed to Goethe):

> *"Until one is committed, there is hesitancy, the chance to draw back, always ineffectiveness. Concerning all acts of initiative and creation, there is one elementary truth the ignorance of which kills countless ideas and splendid plans: that the moment one definitely commits oneself, then providence moves too.*
>
> *All sorts of things occur to help one that would never otherwise have occurred. A whole stream of events issues from the decision, raising in one's favour all manner of unforeseen incidents, meetings and material assistance which no man could have dreamed would have come his way.*
>
> *Whatever you can do or dream you can, begin it. Boldness has genius, power and magic in it. Begin it now."*

The East is a demanding place to live from, because life itself is demanding. But when we respond to that call, there is joy and meaning to be found. The alternative, at best, is the stodgy quasi-contentment of an unlived life. If we are lucky, we will be plagued by our demons until we feel forced to do something!

There is an ongoing call from Spirit that will always guide us where to go next. And it can challenge comfy but limiting ideas of who we think we are, and it can mean living with the disapproval and ridicule, imagined or otherwise, of others. I have an artist friend who has a good reputation for her paintings, that are quite conventional in subject, though that is not a criticism. But she feels her strongest calling is to paint spirit guides and such like, and indeed she does this beautifully. But she has to some degree held back, for fear of what people might think.

The East is Transformative

The East is transformative, because it is always about something new wanting to come in. And if we observe the natural world, it is evident that this is the nature of life. Plants and animals are always moving on, always changing, usually slowly, but then at certain points there is dramatic change.

And the pattern of growth in the Spirit is generally the same, and why would it not be, for we are part of nature? There are relatively long periods where life does not seem to change very much, but there is usually some kind of slow and steady unfoldment occurring during such a period – maybe, for example, we are raising children, and a long period of stability is required for that, which nevertheless slowly changes us.

Times Of Major Change

And then there are the periods of major and sometimes dramatic change, where we move from one phase of our lives to the next or even, it can seem, from one whole life to another. And it is as if the long periods of gradual transformation build and build until a tipping point is reached.

These are often very difficult times for people, even times of crisis. And the difficulties are often caused because we resist the new, we fear it, and try to remain with what is known. But life, or the spirit, has an imperative that it must move on, and it can be ruthless in achieving this. We may get ill rather than embrace change, and Spirit is quite willing to bring us to death's door to get us to wake up. Sometimes major shocks are needed, and sometimes they are not enough, and death may be the outcome. But at least Spirit tried! Even with death, who knows what transformations people may go through as they pass from this world to the next?

I encounter these times of major change and even crisis regularly when I do astrology readings for people. The astrological language classically involves the idea of the outer planets – Uranus, Neptune and Pluto – impacting on the birth chart. This trio is invisible to the naked eye (which is why they were only discovered relatively recently), and are therefore seen as operating from outside of ordinary consciousness: from Spirit. Uranus is the creative and trickster aspect of Spirit, Neptune describes the re-imagining of our lives with new gifts of Spirit, and Pluto is the raw force of new life pushing through. With all three planets, there is often a destruction of the old to make way for the new, and this is what can be most difficult.

My job as an astrologer is to help create some kind of sense for the person at a time when life is no longer making sense. And how to *be* in these periods, when the old no longer works, and the new is not ready to be born. This ongoing uncertainty is difficult for most people, because we want certainty, we feel anxious without it (which is why conspiracy theories tend to arise at times of uncertainty: they give a kind of explanation and agency, to some people, for what is going on.)

And living with that uncertainty, that not-knowing, is very good practice for how to live anyway, beyond the times of crisis. If we can live with not-knowing, we become the 'hollow-bone' that the Native American traditions talk about, we are less in the way of Spirit and its designs. These periods also raise the question of how we are to value ourselves, if we can no longer do those things that, from the world's point of view at any rate, give us value?

The archetypal transition of this sort is the so-called mid-life crisis (I recommend *The Middle Passage* by James Hollis, a Jungian analyst, for a thorough and insightful exposition of this phenomenon.) Jung described it as the point at which we change from valuing ourselves according to our performance in the world, along with the recognition we are given for that, to finding a value that is more truly our own.

This transition is described well in the film *American Beauty*, in which the main character is a forty-something man who resigns from his executive job, and works instead in a fast-food restaurant while following his fantasies. The film follows the process of him re-finding who he is and what is of value to him. Meanwhile his wife, who is still a paid-up subscriber to the American Dream, thinks her husband has gone crazy. From a conventional viewpoint, he has indeed gone crazy, in the sense that he no longer subscribes to 'reality' in the form of society's values. But the viewer is led to see that it is really the husband who is the sane one, and the followers of the American Dream – including his homophobic military neighbour – who are the crazy ones. It is messy, but these transitions often are.

Psychosynthesis is a transpersonal psychology founded by Roberto Assagioli, a younger colleague of Jung's, and is akin to Jungian psychology. Psychosynthesis sees these crises as a time when a new element of the Self is wanting to emerge, and the whole personality has to re-arrange itself around this new element, which comes to preside within the psyche. Once that new element has been accepted, then the crisis can come to an end. And the outer world, which is not separate – we are, it must be recalled, relational – is rearranged accordingly, often with wondrous synchronicities, as though the universe responds to the new 'me'. Which I am sure it does. Money, opportunities, jobs, connections, homes often occur at just the right time, almost as though it had all been planned in advance. In a sense, I think it is. At these times of crisis and their resolution, it is often possible to discern a bigger pattern at work that has seen this coming for years.

There is a strange way in which we have choice, and yet the pattern of our lives is also laid out. There is both Fate and Free Will, they are both necessary and they do not contradict each other. They are only a problem if we insist on having everything nailed down and 'logical'.

The Shamanic Illness

This transition from living according to the values of the collective to following the call from within is crucial. It can occur at any point in life, and in phases. Shamanic cultures have the concept of the 'Shamanic Illness', in which the spirits call a person to become a Shaman, and they will not recover, in fact they may well die, unless they respond to that call. It is a similar process, except they put it in terms of 'spirits' which are external to oneself, and we put it in terms of a call from within. This reflects different notions of the self: the modern autonomous self (which is not in reality autonomous), in contrast to the indigenous relational self. This contrast will arise again when we consider our ancestors and our 'demons' in other directions of the Wheel.

Wherever we see the call of Spirit coming from, the principle remains the same: the ordinary life with its ordinary desires and concerns, lived according to collective values; versus the call to live by 'inner' values, that do not shy from the fundamentals of existence such as death, and that has a sense of service to others basic to its nature.

The Fire of Self-Doubt

It can require a lot of courage to make this transition. It can be halting, because we no longer have the old certainties, or the recognition of worth that comes from living by the same values as everybody else. There is a fire of self-doubt to be gone through. Why would we feel confident in this new Self, when we have not lived it yet?

Affirmations of one's own value are not, in my opinion, the answer to this kind of 'low self-esteem'. As Bill Gates puts it, self-worth needs to be earned by doing something. Self-doubt can be a great catalyst to action. But, I think, also in a less obvious sense than Bill Gates probably means. It is not so much about what you have to show for yourself to the world – which may not be much – but about doing that thing, however hesitantly and provisionally, that you feel pulled towards, and that is an expression of whatever it is that is deep within you. We shall return to this theme in the West, when we consider the Earth element and the adult.

Not Judging Ourselves

In any case, judgement needs to be taken out of the equation. It is natural to label ourselves as good or bad, and feel our value according to these labels. But Spirit is beyond good and bad. What matters is that we are true to ourselves, true to the call of Spirit within.

In his book *The Four Agreements**, Don Miguel Ruiz gives four Toltec principles to live by. (The Toltecs are an ancient indigenous culture in Mexico.) One of them is 'Always do your best', by which he means always acting from what is true, authentic within yourself. Then we have no grounds for criticising ourselves, whatever the outcomes may be. We will return to this idea of not judging ourselves when we consider the Shadow in the South.

*The four 'Agreements' are with oneself and they are: Be impeccable with your word; don't take anything personally; don't make assumptions; and always do your best.

My Mid-Life Crisis

I had my own 'mid-life crisis' bang on cue when I was about 40, but there had been a long run-up to it. The first crisis of this nature, which eventually led to the second, was in my early 20s. I felt under a lot of pressure to conform with what my father wanted me to do. As the eldest son, I particularly carried that need of his. But as described earlier, I had been through an initiation and an opening, and the life he wanted me to have held no meaning for me. I could put off the moment of reckoning while I was still at university (doing a degree that held no meaning for me either!) By the time I finished at university, I was well involved with Buddhist practice, which had helped place my metaphysical quest right at the centre of my life. I was surprised at how powerful it was. I had every intention of living in a Buddhist community and working in one of their businesses. But at the same time, it felt like I was doing the unthinkable. Not just my father, but my whole private education had been geared towards the outcome of a 'successful' career. But I acted on what was genuine in me. There was – and is – something obdurate in me that does not give way in this sort of situation. But it still took me some years to take myself seriously. The legacy of 'doing the unthinkable' needed to be healed, and that took many years. These crises and their aftermaths are often incremental and messy, even though there can be decisive events along the way.

Fast forward ten years and the Buddhist organisation, which had been a home for me to live out my calling, started to become a prison, as described earlier. It took me six years to finally find my way out. Something more metaphysically independent was emerging in me. Not that I hadn't had a good measure of that to start with, coming out of my earlier crisis. But it wasn't enough, I wasn't sure enough of myself, to be able to fully stand apart from a collective. And I was tricked by a dream into a kind of showdown. In early 1996 I had a dream pointing me to two things: following Shamanism (as symbolised in the dream by the colourful and ritual dressing gown I used to wear around the place in those days); and turning the Buddhist community I lived in into a public teaching centre. I did what the dream suggested. I think it is always a good idea to take up the suggestions of Spirit. I had a few years out of the teaching activities in order to make more of my own connections with them.

And it proved popular, because I was speaking from something substantial and genuine in myself. But it also provoked the distrust of people who considered themselves to be a higher authority within the organisation. I was not under their control, and could not be relied on to follow their guidelines. At the same time, I began coming out publicly with criticisms of the way the organisation was run. This was in on 1998, and I went through a lot of fear as I did this. How could I possibly be right and all these other people, many of whom had been practising Buddhism for many years longer than me, be wrong? It required a kind of chutzpah, but I had it. It was like gold had arisen in me, something deeply autonomous that could be its own guide on a metaphysical level. Eventually this crisis led me to leaving the whole life I had been leading for 15 years. I had claimed, I had honoured, this new level of Spirit that was pushing through into me. And that had begun with the dream-trick that suggested I do the teaching work, which in turn had led to exactly the crisis that was needed for me to move forward. Astrologically, this was the trickster planet Uranus at work. I also had Pluto, the raw power of new life, passing over the bottom of my chart, the foundations of my life, at the same time. It took me some years afterwards to catch up with myself.

But that inner guide has since remained with me, and gained in confidence. And it has showed me how to be an effective teacher: talk from experience, and guide people towards trusting their own inner guide, their own judgement, rather than that of the teacher. Teaching is not so much about transmitting particular ideas – though that can be part of it – as helping people move away from the idea that they even need a teacher, because their real teacher lies within, or with the spirits, depending on how you look at it. In this way a teacher is co-operating with the student's East, instead of trying to do it for them (an easy trap to fall into.)

Discerning Points of Transition

We each have points in our lives where something new comes into our consciousness and changes who we are. These times are often accompanied by some sort of crisis, and are pivotal. It is a good exercise to look back at your life and discern these times and reflect on them. Something new that we need to live by often emerges, and sometimes we forget that, we are not always true to it. That new element also unfolds over many years. I think there is always much to be gained from reflecting on these periods, because your perspective on it will change over time as the East in you unfolds over time.

The Shadow of The East: Gurus

Each direction has its shadow forms. And a shadow of the East is the guru, in the modern pejorative sense (that has occurred because so many gurus have shown themselves not to be up to the mark.) This shadow teacher is a kind of bully, needing his students to adore him unreservedly and never question him, and ideally bring in more students. The more worshipping students the shadow guru has, the better he feels about himself. And the reason that teachers become like this is because they have not done their own South work, they have not addressed the childish parts of themselves that are still needy. Any teacher will always have a shadow side: what they need to have done is not so much have transformed it but come into a good relationship with it, have a handle on it. Our dementors will always be with us, waking us up in the early hours: what we need is to know how to relate to them in a healthy way. We will come to this when we do the South.

What gets created is a sort of unholy, and certainly unconscious, alliance between the teachers and the students. There is something in it for each of them: the teacher gets to feel good about herself, and gradually compromises the genuine insight with which she often began teaching; and the students feel recognised and valued, they 'belong', they are 'higher beings' by association, and they avoid having to address in themselves that which needs addressing.

I don't want to damn this situation too much, because it is often a necessary phase that we go through. A good teacher will hand back, with kindness, attempts to turn her into a figure of perfection.

A good account of an extreme version of this situation is in the Netflix documentary *Wild, Wild Country*, about the rise and fall of the Osho movement in Oregon in the USA. At one point they had armed themselves with AK47 rifles, and some were subsequently convicted in court of trying to poison the local residents. Osho himself had started out with genuine teachings to offer. And what was interesting was that of the disciples who were interviewed decades later, many now in their seventies, some with hindsight were able to see, at least to some extent, the real nature of what had gone on and regretted their actions; whereas others, even after all this time, could not. They still had their East, their own potential, projected onto Osho.

Religion is a Natural Phase

I'm trying not to be too hard on people who are caught up in discipleship in this way. It is very natural, I think even necessary sometimes, to project a degree of our unrealised East onto a teacher figure. At least it shows that the East is an issue for us, we are not content just to be muggles! And we need to do something with that aspect of ourselves. It is what religion is for, and why it is so widespread. It fulfils a need. And during this lifetime, the path for some people is to make at least some headway in claiming their East for themselves. I have seen this with disciples in the Buddhist organisation I was part of. You see some people who have been 'good' disciples for many decades shifting a bit, opening up and questioning a bit. And that is maybe as far as they will get in this lifetime. But that is where they are, and judging them for that is not appropriate or helpful: when we judge, there is always something in it for ourselves, something we're probably not wanting to look at.

Catholics have their Pope to project their East onto. And Shamanic types have indigenous people to project onto! How many times have I heard it said that Shamanism is not a religion? Yet as soon as an indigenous person walks into the room, many people seem to become very reverential and give away their own authority. There are always a few who will not buy into this dynamic, and they have to be careful or they will be judged for being disrespectful. I made this point about not giving our power away to indigenous people in a couple of big Facebook groups, and I got blocked from the groups for saying so. It was an unwelcome truth.

No religion is a religion in its essence. But people who practice Shamanism are just as prone to religion as anyone else. Not having a holy book or a founder can help, but it is no guarantee. When I was involved with Buddhist practice, it was always being claimed that Buddhism was not a religion because it didn't have God. Yet it divided itself into leaders and believers, with hidden rules, just like most groups do, with most people in denial about the degree to which they were followers.

So let us not deny the fact that we project the East onto those who know, or appear to know, a bit more than we do and have a public presence. Projection is the first step in claiming a part of our psyche for ourselves. It is a natural thing. What we need are teachers who treat that projection humorously, who don't take themselves and 'their teaching' too seriously, and who aren't founding a 'school' (read religion) with apprentices, certificates etc. I am not saying there is no value in such institutions, but there are invariably rules, often unspoken, about who you can and cannot be, and what you can and cannot say, a hierarchy, and a fierce defensiveness of the teacher when criticisms are made. It is spiritual primary school, and it does some good, but the real learning is to claim your power back after you have surrendered it. This is a deep and transformative process.

The obvious, exoteric teachings can usually be found in books. I have sometimes come back from weekends that cost a fair bit of money, thinking I could have read what I'd learnt in a quarter of an hour. I sometimes say to people yes, go on these workshops, but take the teachings and run, don't get involved in the group dynamics around the teacher, because you will lose something of yourself.

The Teacher's Shadow

It can be difficult, because the teachers can be genuinely quite impressive, and you can learn quite deeply from what they have to offer. And yet there is always a shadow there, which you can spot after a while. And that is fine: there is only one thing worse than a teacher having a shadow, and that is them not having one! But spotting it can be tricky, because it can be hard to value someone for teachings that can change our life, and yet be critical of them at the same time. Our mind does not want to do that, and it can feel disloyal. So, it is a good exercise to practise relating to these teachers as ordinary human beings – which, of course, they are – as well as valuing their insights. And above all be honest with yourself about this, and be choosey about who you mention it to, because not many people are very honest with themselves in this respect, and will judge you.

And try not to judge the teacher for having a shadow. When we judge others, there is something in it for us, we feel better about ourselves for having put the other person 'below' us. It is more a matter of seeing the teacher's shadow, and asking yourself if you can live with it? Does the teacher have a sufficient handle on it that it is not affecting the group dynamics in too big a way? One shamanic teacher whose course I went on many years ago had such a big ego, was so inflated about his own gifts, that everyone could see it and was not going to be fooled by his own estimate of himself. Yet he had gifts, there was no mistaking that.

Animals of the Directions

With each direction comes an animal whose nature tells us something about that direction. It is difficult to be universal here, because animals tend to be fairly localised. This Wheel has come across from America with an Eagle in the East. Which is fine if you live in Scotland. In England, one could have for example a Buzzard. A bird of prey that soars high, symbolising the spirit vision of the East.

Shamanism as Local and as Universal

Personally, I do not mind using an animal from another culture. I am still able to connect with that animal over time, it acquires meaning and resonance and sacredness for me. And I view my Shamanism as both local and universal. Yes, it is important to let yourself be claimed by the natural world local to you (I live on Dartmoor, you couldn't ask for better), and let that relationship build over time. It is foundational to shamanic practice; it is where it begins.

But at the same time, we know ourselves to be inhabitants of this whole planet, of Gaia – the Earth as a living being – like never before. And I think our sense of local connection helps us make the global connection. Humans have 99.9% of their DNA in common with each other (we share a mere 96% with chimpanzees, and a tawdry 60% with chickens and bananas.) This wonderful scientific finding shows how much life on this planet is one thing, that we are all part of. So, I am happy to move between animals from another land, and ones from my own.

The Eagle

The point about the Eagle is that it soars high, yet has very accurate vision of what is down on the ground (you can work the symbolism yourself with these animals, and make your own connections.) The Eagle it brings Spirit, that which is universal, the bigger pattern that is behind our existence, into relationship with the specifics of our day-to-day life down on the ground.

I was reminded of this recently in a meditation I led with a Medicine Wheel group. I asked participants to bring a dream that they had, and to let it unfold further in the meditation, very like a shamanic journey. And I brought a dream from 40 years ago, in which I was an eagle on a very high white crag, with just the blue vault of the sky around me. Another eagle was with me, and it took off into the void. I followed suit, and spread my wings as I began to soar. Then I lost confidence and began to fall. That was the dream. So, I took this dream up all these years later. This time I was flying confidently (the dream was prophetic, it was showing me my path, what I needed to do, and it took nearly four decades.) And I was carried upwards by a powerful uprush of wind, that took me off the Earth, to a distant planet in another star system. And there was life there, rather like the fairy realm here, it was a parallel dimension, but just as real. And it was a colourful and joyful place.

This was part of the Spirit Vision of the Eagle (who has deep resonance for me, even though he does not live in my land.) He was showing me other worlds alongside this one.

We may put an Eagle or Buzzard as the animal of the East. And it is good to do so just because others do, so that there is a common language and tradition. But we may also have animals that appear to us personally in each direction, that illumine that direction for us, and help us when we are there. This was another meditation I have done with a Medicine Wheel group: face each direction in turn, and see what animals (or human guides, or plants, or whatever wants to come along) appear to you. It is a relationship that can be built over time. But don't assume it will be the same guides each time, that is not how

Spirit works. And don't assume the helper has to be visible to you: you may not be a 'visual' type, you may just sense them.

Chapter 3

The South – Emotional Awakening

Colour: Red
Element: Water
Season: Summer
Time: The Past
Stage of Life: Child
Animal: Mouse/Coyote
Some key words for the South: Trust, Innocence, Play, Emotion, Healing, the Shadow.

The Close-to Place

With the South we move to quite a different place, from the visionary to the 'close-to', to the personal. When I finished the first draft of the East section of this book, I came to a halt for a few days. It took me that time to understand that I needed to make that same shift in myself in order to write about the South. I had a revisitation from a feminine presence that hovers around me, who often wanders off when I am in my male linear trajectory. She is still there, and, of course, the female/feminine is what does the personal, not the male who often does anything but! Once she turned up, I realised I was ready to start writing. And with a better notion of how to keep her around me: by thinking of that close-to place in myself.

Paying Attention to Feeling

We are entering the Watery realm of feeling. As a man, it has taken me until the second half of my adult life to start to be properly initiated into my feeling life. We'll come to that second half of life process, for both men and women, when we do the West.

In the South we learn how to be with feeling, to care for it and to not judge it and to trust what it is telling us. There is something deep within ourselves that we are here to take care of. That is what we are here to do. Not to 'achieve' for its own sake, not to save the world, but to take care of and nourish and to be compassionate towards ourselves. Anything we do for others is a natural outpouring of that, a desire to be of service, rather than something that justifies our existence, that covers up a hole of self-doubt at our centre.

The Child

This personal centre in us is symbolised by the Child. Not the Magical Child of the East, that is outside of time, and unharmed by the vicissitudes of life. The South is the actual child, the historical child, the place of feeling in our body that is not usually as 'grown-up' as we might like to think, and just as well. Because we keep all ages in us. We continue to need the play and wonder of the child, the search for self of the teenager, the boldness of the young adult…

I drummed a Shamanic Journey for someone once who encountered a little girl who was being left out of her life amongst all the plans she had and all the things she was continually trying to achieve. This little girl was not happy at being left out, and the person said afterwards OK from now on I will include her in my plans. And I said no, it doesn't work like that. The little girl is not an add-on, to be included in the adult's plans. She is the source of your abundance and creativity and play, so she needs to be the ongoing heart of whatever it is you are doing. And she is probably not one for a lot of planning. Any plans you have need to be secondary to that ongoing sense of what the little girl wants, and flexible accordingly. This person was very embedded in 'proper' structures and achievements and plans, and because the little girl felt over-ridden, these plans never quite worked out as hoped. There was a lifetime of habit here, driven by feelings of unworthiness, as ambition often is. These processes are gradual, and the degree to which she will be willing and able to have the girl on board, in her rightful place, remains to be seen. This shows how our creative centre is easily over-ridden by the calls of the world, which can be very loud.

The qualities of play and trust and innocence are central to this direction. It is also the place for coming into relationship with the 'wounded' child, the shadow side. But that is difficult without at least a measure of the play and trust and innocence. If she is going to be judged and bossed around, why would the wounded child want to come into relationship with us in the first place?

The comic writer John Mortimer once commented that now he had reached a certain age, he no longer needed to pretend to be a responsible adult. Of course, he is not deriding the need to become responsible as an adult – to be able to 'respond' – but there is a way in which it becomes over-emphasised, an end-in-itself, it becomes who we are. And being child-like can seem the antithesis of being a 'proper' adult. In Northern Europe and North America particularly – the most economically successful parts of those continents – 'responsible' men do not wear colour. They wear 'sober' suits and ties that cut them off at the neck: the modern warrior uniform for doing battle with the world. Women too are being inducted into this colourless way of being as they compete on men's terms in the men's warrior-world.

Being child-like and being a responsible adult are not antithetical. It is certainly difficult to be a creative adult unless you can be child-like. So, play and be silly, honour the child within. Artists have not lost this quality, that is why we have the word 'Bohemian', which to a 'responsible' adult can read 'irresponsible and untrustworthy'.

If we are going to talk 'responsibility', then who is the more responsible in a real sense: the person who over-rides themselves in their desire to look good, to succeed, to do the right thing; or the person who takes care of themselves in this deeper sense? The child, paradoxically, leads us to our emotional depths. If you want to have depth, to know who you are, then be child-like. Look at the world with innocent eyes and follow your heart without judging it.

Winnie-the-Pooh

I read Pooh Bear occasionally and I delight in that child's world that has its own logic, and which with its simple eyes can see things that we adults cannot see.

Here is a quote from A.A. Milne, *The House at Pooh Corner,* likening this child-like quality to little streams in the forest:

> *"By the time it came to the edge of the Forest, the stream had grown up, so that it was almost a river, and, being grown-up, it did not run and jump and sparkle along as it used to do when it was younger, but moved more slowly. For it knew now where it was going, and it said to itself, "There is no hurry. We shall get there some day." But all the little streams higher up in the Forest went this way and that, quickly, eagerly, having so much to find out before it was too late."*

There is also a story in which Pooh goes to visit Rabbit down his burrow. And being a good host, Rabbit offers Pooh some bread, butter and honey. Thinking to appear polite and not greedy, Pooh decides to forego the bread, and just accepts the butter and honey. But being Pooh, he cannot help but overeat. When it comes to the time to leave, Pooh has grown so large from the food that he cannot squeeze out of the burrow. He gets stuck. So they call on Christopher Robin to come and help solve the problem. After thinking it over, Christopher Robin decides there is only one thing for it: Pooh will have to stay exactly where he is for a week, without eating, while he slims down. In the meantime,

Christopher Robin will read him stories. Meanwhile, Rabbit is faced with the back end of a bear sticking into his burrow for a week, and he thinks it would be a shame to let that go to waste, so would Pooh mind very much if Rabbit used his back end as a towel rail? Pooh agrees to this. And so, for the next week, Christopher Robin reads stories to the front end of Pooh that is sticking out of the hole, and rabbit uses Pooh's back end as a towel rail. At the end of the week, Pooh is indeed slim enough to wriggle out. How can one not love and delight in stories such as this, even without children to read them to?

I have some soft toys also: Tigger (who is always laughing), Pluto (the Disney Dog) and an Elephant. More recently I have acquired a knitted doll, and a Native American doll made of leather. The latter I have with me as I write this South direction, as inspiration. I think it is good to assume we all have both little boys and little girls in our psyches, dying to come out and play once we start to ignore society's strictures about not being 'childish' and about being rigidly just one gender. Play for me is a serious business!

In Rumer Godden's novel *Black Narcissus*, set in India, about a group of nuns, the children ask one of the nuns if they have ears. This is because the nuns' habits conceal the sides of their faces. And the nuns are foreign, so who knows what they are like? It comes out of the quality of innocence that does not make assumptions. This is a quality shared with the Wisdom of the North: the opposite directions are complementary (like the astrological opposite signs also are) and have much in common. How can the West (Body) be understood without the Spirit of the East? And how can the North (Mind) be understood without the Emotions of the South, that drive the thoughts of the North?

Innocence

A bit of bad etymology (courtesy of Leo Rutherford) helps here. Innocence sounds very like 'inner sense': what your being tells you when you remove the adult clutter and presuppositions.

Artists have the quality of innocence. That is why they see and paint the way they do: they are seeing what is really there, as if for the first time, by paying attention, rather than just allowing the brain to make lazy assumptions. And when you look at a colour, there is joy and delight to be had.

Innocence is a quality to be brought to our interactions with people, otherwise we cannot listen to them. We only think we are listening. To take it one step further, how can we listen to others if we do not know how to listen to ourselves, if we do not even know we are not listening to ourselves?

The Mouse

The South, the close-to place, is where we listen closely to ourselves. That is why the Mouse belongs in this direction. He is the opposite of the Eagle of the West who sees the vast spirit vision. The mouse is close to the ground and sees in detail. This is the sort of attention we need to pay to ourselves, all the time. What are you feeling in your heart, and in your stomach? You don't need words for it, you just need that felt awareness. And, as I have said and will say repeatedly, without judging it or pushing it away.

Being Honest with Ourselves

Being honest, at least to ourselves, is another way of putting it. Not trying to persuade ourselves that we are feeling what we are 'meant' to be feeling. That comes from the shadow side of the North: the mind and reason not as servant, but as ruler.

When my father died in 2015, a day or two later I said, while checking in to a group of people on a Psychosynthesis course I was on: "Thank god the old bastard is dead!" It felt a bit outrageous and disrespectful to be saying that, but it was true. It was how I felt. I did not, as it happens, say it with anger (though that might for some people be their honest feeling.)

Even though I had years before stopped wanting him to be other than he was, and by the same token I felt freer to be who I was, there was still a residual shadow, a sense of guilt that I was not the person I was 'supposed' to be. So, on an almost tectonic level, I felt free, and that was my honest response. I was a bit upset by him going, but not much. And is death such a terrible thing anyway? We will come to Death when we consider the West. When people close to us die, freedom often comes with that, and it is good to be honest about that feeling. Or we may be indifferent: be honest about that too. Be honest to yourself always, about everything. Then you have a solid basis in yourself, that is founded in reality. It gives strength. You cannot be manipulated (the shadow of the South) by, for example, guilt.

If you act on guilt, then you are doing something so that somebody will like you and accept you, and you are probably only half-aware at best that that is what you are doing. In fact, you will probably tell yourself you are doing whatever you are doing for all sorts of other reasons. Some people are expert rationalisers (a shadow of the North), not just to others, but to themselves too. I say 'expert', but you can always spot it in another if you are true to yourself: falsity becomes obvious in others (and then hopefully we try not to judge it!)

There is this pretending to ourselves and to others that we feel other than we do. Being honest in this respect can require standing outside the social norms, so can require courage. Of course, sometimes we need to be polite and not distress others. But at least to yourself, don't kid yourself that you are pleased to see someone when you are not.

Here is a common one: giving all sorts of reasons for not doing something, when at bottom it is simply that you don't want to do it, and you don't have a reason that can be put into words, and it sounds selfish to just say "I don't want to do it"; or you know that the other person is better with words than you are, and you fear they will make you look silly if you give the real reason.

And then there is ignoring or suppressing feelings, which is the same territory of not being honest with oneself. I know someone who announces proudly that when she has a difficult feeling, she simply puts it in a box and ties a ribbon on it and maybe brings it out at another time. This attitude can be characteristic of people who went to an English boarding school at an early age: you learn to be 'tough' and 'independent' and ignore your natural feelings of wanting to be at home with your parents. This can continue right through life. Of course, we often need to just get on with things even when we don't feel like it – that is part of being an adult – but there needs to be acknowledgement of the real feeling, or there is usually a terrible cost in depression, anger, alcoholism, dysfunctional relationships etc.

Trust What You Want

Coming back to what we want and don't want: this is very simple in the child. They know what they want and don't want. Adults will sometimes mistakenly try to persuade children otherwise, or make them feel wrong for what they are feeling/wanting. All the adult achieves is to start a process of taking the child away from who they are. That doesn't mean you have to go along with what the child wants or doesn't want. Or go along with the fact that they don't like their sister right now. But don't try to persuade them "Of course you like your sister." A classic is food, though I think in this respect there is less pressure put on children nowadays. But if a child doesn't like sprouts, then they don't like them. It is for real. In fact, it has recently been discovered that children's taste receptors respond negatively to a chemical in sprouts.

If you don't acknowledge what a child wants or doesn't want – and instead push what you want for them, or who you think they 'should' be – then the child can grow into an adult who does not think that what they want matters or is of value; they will lack drive, and can and will be pushed around by others.

So often as adults we are having to re-learn to trust and value what we want and don't want. It is not just parents who can do this. Society itself carries a very strong message about who we need to be if we want to be accepted and valued. The need to be accepted and valued, to belong, is so strong that some people will do or say almost anything in pursuit of it. This was why the most severe sanction among some indigenous people was exile, banishment from the tribe. We are relational beings, who we are is also our relationships and family. By banishing people, you are taking away their very selves, apart from the question of whether or not they could physically survive on their own.

What society does to us is a mixed thing, like most things are. Rarely is anything just 'good' or 'bad': not even early boarding school! Society makes demands on us to co-operate, to be responsible etc, and that is helpful. But it also demands we edit ourselves, the degree to which it demands that being dependent on the degree of rigidity and intolerance of the society, or that part of society in which you live or grew up.

It can take a lot of courage to be true to ourselves. We covered this in the East, in the context of being true to the call of our Spirit. From a South point of view, it can be expressed in terms of feeling and what we want and don't want. In a way it is artificial to divide our being into these four directions and elements: we are unitary. So really with the different directions, we are always looking at the same, whole person – yourself – but from different angles, through different qualities and functions.

Knowing and acting on what we want starts at the simple level of what we want for breakfast, but segues as we expand outwards into the deepest callings of the Spirit. But is not what we want for breakfast also Spirit? If it is not that, then what?

Sometimes people get in a tangle about what 'Spirit' wants

them to do, and maybe they want a spirit guide to turn up and tell them. And maybe, for some people, that is what will happen. (But then again, a message from a spirit guide always involves an element of our own interpretation.) And sure, we want to do that which will give most meaning to our lives, and that is the call of Spirit.

But Spirit generally comes out, in my experience, in what we want and don't want. It is quite simple. This is not something selfish, and maybe our Christian heritage can make us feel that it is. After all, Christianity at its worst told us that we are original sinners, and that the path to holiness lies in self-sacrifice and turning the other cheek, like Jesus did. In this context, living from what we want can feel sinful and selfish!

This is, of course, institutional Christianity. Like any religion, its mystical heart lies in finding the God, or Spirit, or the Buddha, within: we are originally (in a metaphysical sense) not sinners but pure. But any organised religion has an element of control, and the easiest way to control people is to make them trust the holy books and leaders, instead of trusting themselves. All large groups, religious or otherwise, do this. There is no point railing against it, it is just what happens. But that doesn't mean we can't sometimes upset a few of the rigidities.

So, trust your interest and likes, follow them. You don't need a grand plan of achievement to have a meaningful life. Such plans usually just get in the way, they are a compensation for a felt lack. And by following what you want and don't want, you will come to know yourself and to find meaning.

Trusting in Life

Trust is a quality of the child. A child doesn't worry about the basics of life: they know they will be looked after and loved and fed and sheltered (hopefully.) It comes naturally to the child to trust in life in this sort of way. And left to themselves, their life is a series of doing the things they want to do; they haven't yet learnt to doubt themselves in this respect.

When we address the South as an adult, we are often having to relearn that basic quality of trust, not just in what we want, but often in life itself. Probably after many years of brainwashing and betrayal – not just betrayal by others, but our own betrayal of ourself.

However, the innocence and trust of the child are not the same as those qualities we build as an adult. They are founded in the childhood attributes, and we would be damaged (as many unfortunately are) if they were compromised in childhood. As an adult, innocence and trust need to be qualified and integrated into the nature of life itself, which is not 'fair', which will betray our (naïve) expectations, and where s**t happens!

As a Chippewa Cree teacher explained it to me, the natural world has an observably benign aspect. All forms of life have the conditions they need in which to live, they are looked after by the natural world. And it is this fundamentally benign attribute of life which we re-learn to trust as adults. It doesn't mean that life will always go our way, and that horrible things won't sometimes happen; but alongside that we can build a sense that fundamentally the universe has our back. If we are true to who we are and have the courage to act on that, then there is a mysterious way in which the world seems to co-operate, in which events unfold around us in a way that helps and promotes whatever it is that we aiming to do. The natural world, Spirit (and I use these terms interchangeably) looks after not just our physical needs, but our interests at all levels. And why wouldn't it? Our spirit nature is not different to our physical nature, despite the spirit/body split of Christianity, and the mind/body split of modern science.

Trust and the Modern World

This building, through experience, of trust in life is a very different way of being in the world than we may be used to.

The modern attitude, at its worst, is that the Earth is a thing to be exploited and fought. We even treat other forms of life as 'things' too: think factory farming.

There is a balance to be found between trusting in nature and allowing events to unfold in their own way (South), and using our minds and acting decisively (North). The modern world is way out of balance in favour of the North over the South, Masculine over Feminine, if you like.

There is a story that Ffyona Campbell relates in her book *The Hunter Gatherer Way* that illustrates these different ways of being in the world. It involves some New Guinea tribespeople who gather honey. The bees make their nests high up in the trees, and it is a difficult and dangerous task to climb up and take the honey. So this job is undertaken by the men (as indeed most physically dangerous jobs are still undertaken by men). Meanwhile the women stay at the base of the tree, urging the men not to take all the honey, but to leave some for the bees so that they can continue to live.

Our whole ecological crisis is in that story. In our world, the masculine principle has come to dominate at the expense of the feminine. It is the feminine principle that is rooted in the natural world and trusts it and feels her to be the mother that takes care of us.

Ignoring the 'Shoulds'

The trust needs to begin with ourselves. Our large societies are built, to a large extent, on training young people to trust the voice of authority, the values of the collective, over the voice from within. Most of us no longer have the voice of religion telling us what to think and how to live. But we have its replacement, science, telling us what the universe is 'really' like, with little room for doubt (as if anyone knows where this whole dream of existence comes from.) There is also the collective need for physical and economic survival, and the training we receive to play our part in that, to be productive members of society. On its own that is fair enough, it is necessary. But this has become twisted and inflated in our materialistic world so that work and busyness have become ends in themselves: we often listen to the voice that tells us we 'should' remain active and busy, even when there is no need. These 'shoulds' are voices that are not our own, they control us (and so keep society itself controlled, which the majority are happy with, or it would not be happening.)

As long as we listen to the 'shoulds', we cannot to that extent listen to and trust the promptings from within. The modern collective is very keen to tell us who we should be, what will make us a 'good' person and what will make us a 'bad' person, just as religion was used in the same way in the past. There is no difference. We think we have become 'free' of 'superstition' and religion, but the basic way of living and thinking according to received opinion, and acquiring a sense of being 'good' from that, remains the same.

The adult trust of the South is fundamental. It turns us from a collective being into an individual being. All the wisdom we need is within, and it begins by paying attention to, and trusting what we are feeling in the moment, at all times. If you have a free day, trust what you want to do with it. If you want to do nothing and just potter in the moment, that can be an excellent way of building the trusting relationship with yourself. And I can almost guarantee that the day will surprise you, events and feelings can happen that can't when we interfere by planning. When, in other words, we play and stop being a 'responsible' adult who has everything worked out and makes 'good use' of the day. "Life is what happens to us while we are making other plans." (Incidentally, this saying is often attributed to John Lennon; in fact, the first instance of it was, prosaically, in *Readers Digest* in 1957.)

This attitude of trust is something we build not just with

ourselves, but with the world around us. From the point of view of Spirit, there is no difference. The spirit within us is outside of time and space, which are human categories for making sense of experience. We are not the separate selves that we imagine ourselves to be: look closely for this self and you will not find it. (That is one of the basic Buddhist insights.) It will elude your grasp.

To trust oneself is also to trust the world, because they are the same thing, they are not separate. That is why prayer works: when we speak our heartfelt wishes to the world, there is always a response, how could there not be? But because Spirit is infinite and we are tiny, we cannot know what that response will be. It is never quite what we imagine.

The Cultural Background

Trusting the world is something that is natural to us as children – trusting, without even thinking about it, that we will be loved and looked after. But, in our society, we are easily trained into the exact opposite way of thinking. It maybe goes back as far as the beginning of farming, when the natural world no longer simply provided, but had to be worked to do so. It certainly comes in with Christianity, where the world is seen as the creation of the Devil, and the natural world, according to some interpretations of the Old Testament, is ours to exploit.

It is not enough to say that we no longer believe in Christianity. It is a mythology that was central to our culture for a long time, and the underlying attitudes do not just disappear because on a rational level we have rejected that mythology. The unconscious, the imagination does not work like that. Why do you think people feel good about themselves when they have been working hard? It is not just the genuine satisfaction of a job well done, though it may include that. It is also the Protestant Work Ethic, which

> *"emphasizes that hard work, discipline, and frugality are a result of a person's subscription to the values espoused by the Protestant faith."* Wikipedia

We are still commonly driven by the feeling that hard work is, of itself, virtuous. In other words, we are still driven by some of the values of Christianity even though we may have consciously rejected them. And it is interesting that Northern Europe and the US tend to be Protestant, and richer, than their Southern often more Catholic, neighbours. What a wheeze, turning greed into a religious virtue!

This is what Eric Vuillard says about work on the first page of his novel *The Order of the Day*:

> *"... the great, decent fallacy of work, with its small gestures that enfold a silent, conventional truth and reduce the entire epic of our lives to a diligent pantomime."*

The mythological remnants of Christianity within us drive us to work hard. (However, it is said that on their deathbeds, no one expresses regret that they did not spend more time at the office!) And by the same token, we have inherited the feeling that the world is ultimately not a good place, it is the work of the devil. It needs therefore to be opposed and fought rather than trusted.

How else is one to view, say, large scale open-cast mining, that ravages the Earth on a vast scale, to force her to give up her treasures? Or modern agri-business, that kills everything alive over large areas in order to grow the one crop that is desired, and that also destroys the organic, living quality soil, turns it into mere dirt? I recommend the documentary *Kiss the Ground*, that explores what modern farming does, and shows how it could be done very differently and still feed us. What comes through in the documentary is an attitude of love for the planet, rather than the indifference or worse that modern farming is expressive of.

Science is our modern religion. I will return to this in the North, but I maintain it is at bottom, for most of us, just another belief system that tells us how the universe and life came about. Science is the offspring of medieval Christianity. It inherited the basic attitude that there is only one truth, one reality; and instead of the world being the work of the devil, it is now just a thing, it is not alive, which is a horrifying idea from an indigenous perspective.

So why would we trust something that is just a thing? It has, rather, to be worked and fought to make it behave in the way that we want it to.

Richard Dawkins, Emeritus Professor for the Public Understanding of Science at Oxford University has this to say:

> *"The universe that we observe has precisely the properties we should expect if there is, at bottom, no design, no purpose, no evil, no good, nothing but pitiless indifference."*

I would argue in response that you often find what you are looking for, that the universe becomes what you imagine it to be. If you have decided that a certain class of people are less than human, that is probably what you will observe in their behaviour. Similarly, if you have decided that the universe is just a thing (which sounds very similar to saying it is the work of the devil) than that is what you will probably observe. I quote Dawkins, because he has a large following and is taken seriously as a thinker. I find the term 'pitiless indifference' chilling. It is not the ostensibly neutral term that it purports to be. If you treat a person with indifference, then you are not treating them with respect, it is an act of hostility. Dawkins is saying here that the universe is a hostile place. It is not a place to be trusted.

We carry a lot of cultural baggage when it comes to trusting the universe. The people we are often taught to admire are those dark warriors who are successful in shaping the world-as-thing to their own ends. I am not saying they are evil people – but more on that in the North.

Trusting the Natural World

A good place to start is by forming a relationship with the natural world, and feeling that you are a part of her. Why would we trust the natural world if we do not feel ourselves to be an intimate part of her? And why would we not trust the world if we feel that intimacy? It is a very natural thing. Lie face down on the Earth, feel your heart, and feel the massive heart of Mother Earth beneath you. Her heart is beating with your heart, she loves you because you are her, you are nothing but her. All the healing you will ever need is in Mother Earth. Bring all your sorrows to her, and let her absorb them and take them away. Bring your prayers to her. And visit the same places in nature regularly, get to know them, enjoy them. All this will help heal the divide in ourselves that has been growing in Western consciousness since the time of Plato.

Having a relationship with the natural world, and realising that we are nothing but her, we can begin to trust that we are taken care of on all levels. The natural world is integral to our metaphysical quest, our 'spirituality'. Unconsciously we can feel they are different things, that 'spirituality' is 'higher' than the natural world. This is a legacy, a hangover from Christianity, and it will come up again later in this section when we look at 'spiritual bypass.' We are nothing but the natural world in human form, with a human nature to live out while we are here. Just as a fox has fox nature. And it is the mind which puts one 'above' the other, that humans are somehow 'more than' nature. The mind in proper balance does not even think to judge like this. It is just the human ego flattering itself! We will return to this when we look at the trickster.

Trust What is and What isn't Happening

Spirit does not make a distinction between you 'in there' and the world 'out there'. It is all one pattern. When you have a heartfelt intention, you will find events have a tendency to co-operate. And when they don't, trust that too. Trust what is not happening, as well as what is happening. Trust everything, everything is Spirit. If something isn't happening that you want to happen, it is worth looking at. Is your mind in the way, are you specifying an outcome too much? Or is there something in the situation you cannot see? I have experienced getting the exact opposite of something I had prayed for. I wanted a situation to go a particular way, but I wasn't taking properly into account the nature of some of the people involved, their limitations even, and very quickly I found myself outside of the situation. My prayers catalysed that outcome, they speeded it up. And I learnt from it.

Something else I have learnt to trust from, is that I ever advertise my services – astrological or shamanic – in a formal way, there is very little response. Some other people seem to manage to advertise their wares successfully in this way, but not me. On the other hand, if I do these things informally, people come my way. With astrology, I write blogs about whatever I want to write about – and often I don't know what that is until I am doing it – and I put them out there, and people then approach me for readings. And the same has applied with shamanism: if I just stay natural and don't plan too much, then people come my way and productive things happen. Of course, there are places where proper planning and advertising are needed. And some teachers can 'do' shamanism that way. And it's as if Spirit has its own way with each of us. And if no-one is coming my way, I trust that too. There is some other way of being for me right now, or something else to do. And what 'Spirit' wants, if I am honest, always corresponds to how I am feeling deep down. And if something is not happening that I want to happen, it usually means I am not paying sufficient attention to what is happening within me. What I want and what Spirit wants are not different, and why would they be if I am paying proper attention?

Trusting Spirit with Money

Money is often a big trust area for people, particularly if they are spending a fair bit of time on something vocational, and living on the shoestring that that usually seems to require. And magically, they so often seem to get just the right amount of work and income to keep going, but they don't know how it will be next week, and that creates anxiety, because it is hard to have that level of trust around survival issues. But then they keep surviving, year in and year out, and gradually trust builds. This is a tough lesson, but I think if you can develop trust on this basic, survival level, you can have trust almost anywhere.

The Universe is on your Side

There is a basic attitude to cultivate that the universe is on your side. That can be very hard if circumstances are difficult, or if you weren't taken care of properly in childhood. But whatever our circumstances, Spirit is there in the centre of our lives, if we choose to pay attention to that. And if we can trust that, favourable things will happen that probably surprise us, or we will find ourselves feeling abundant and joyful in a place that many might experience as lack. Which, as mentioned earlier, is what cactuses do.

There is an Islamic saying "Put your trust in God and keep your camel tethered." There is an ongoing art to playing our human part in events (the North-South Road of mind and emotion, where we have choice) and letting Spirit play its part (the East-West Road of Spirit and Body.) There are extremes in both directions. We need to balance these two roads along the Wheel.

It is not always obvious. Do I just let events unfold in their own way, or is it the 'responsible' thing to intervene? Or is being 'responsible' in this instance just trying to control? This is where the wisdom of the North is needed alongside the Trust of the South. It comes from experience.

When I was younger, I was on the side of trying to control events. And this can come from feeling that the universe is not on your side, even that it is against you, and unless you make something happen, it won't happen. It is also the one-sided male warrior energy of the North. (There is a masculine-feminine balance to be struck between North and South.) I made a lot of progress in my forties through being around someone who was quite attuned to letting events unfold and not getting in the way of them. This person was, however, at the other extreme, and was reluctant to take action when it was time to take action. But she did, all the same, have that sensitive attunement to events, which can almost appear 'psychic', but which I think we all have, it is natural: it comes through listening in that place which begins with ourselves, but is also connected to the world around us. It is, in a way, about remembering to be conscious, something we all slip in and out of. When we trust and listen in this way, it always becomes clear what to do. If it is not clear, do nothing until it is. All the wisdom we need is within. We are all connected to the entire universe and its wisdom. This sounds a bit high falutin', but it can be everyday experience, albeit subtle.

There is a Native American tradition that if someone is asked to make an important decision, they will wait four days before doing so. This is something that I try to practise, and I can find it excruciating. If I want to do something, I can be very impulsive, it can feel very urgent: though when I sit back and reflect, there is usually no good reason it cannot wait. (This is the positive side of the North, the Mind, and its ability to be objective, not to be swamped by feeling.) And invariably, if I wait, my perspective will change in ways I could not have foreseen, and I will do a better job. This is why we have the saying that we will 'sleep on' something. The Unconscious, Spirit, Life gets to work and brings in its own, wiser perspective.

Developing Trust, attuning to Spirit, is an ongoing task of the South: it occurs as the Spirit of the East feeds into the Emotion of the South. This exploration of the Wheel is also a cumulative journey as we go round it. That is why Wisdom is in the North: it takes the longest.

The Wounded Child and the Shadow

The other crucial task of the South is coming into relationship with the shadow. Note I don't say 'transforming' it, for that is to judge it and to want to change it. It is for Spirit, not for us, to change it, if Spirit wants to.

The area of ourselves we are talking about here is all those things that don't seem to work and that torment us. Not just what we feel inside: the anger, self-doubt, self-loathing, anxiety, self-pity, envy and so on. But also, the behaviours: the self-medications with drugs and alcohol and sugar, the inability to do the things we feel called to do, harsh and angry words towards others, manipulating or being manipulated, giving in to others, not standing up for ourselves….. I'm sure you can add to the list!

This is the aspect that is sometimes called the wounded child. The one who no longer trusts and plays, and has erected defences, in order to survive. It is maybe slightly over-egging it to say it is always 'wounded'. There is a natural process in 'civilised' life where we adapt to the norms around us, and put aside aspects that don't fit. For some people, that doesn't matter too much. They may have a bit of artistic talent, and that is seen as effeminate by their male society, so they never go there. As a result, they are less of a person than they might have been, but it doesn't cause them huge problems. For others, the talent is too powerful to be put to one side, and they will become dysfunctional and cranky unless they live it.

The Gold in the Shadow

The shadow isn't just the 'dark' stuff. It is also the gold. That too gets repressed. And they can sometimes be two sides of the same coin. Hence the line 'the crack where the light gets in'. It is why we find our soul when we allow the shadow side to breathe, and stop fighting it and judging it. I knew someone who was an alcoholic. She could down a bottle of sherry in one go. This went on for years. But as soon as she left her husband, and felt free to have an independent life, she stopped drinking. What appeared as a demon was just something needing to be lived. The shadow is a complex thing. And it often provides exactly the impetus we need to unfold into who we are.

Take Compliments on the Chin

There is a saying by Marianne Williamson that,

> *"Our deepest fear is not that we are inadequate. Our deepest fear is that we are powerful beyond measure. It is our light, not our darkness that most frightens us."*

I don't know how true this oft-quoted statement is, though it certainly sounds good. But there is truth in it. Have you noticed how if you compliment someone, they will brush it off, or make a little joke of it, or even deny it? Their response is presented as modesty, but really it is because to think of ourselves in that new way is unfamiliar, it is outside of our comfort zone. If someone compliments me, I try to make a point of taking it on the chin and thanking them, and I have no hesitation in telling others also to take it on the chin when I see them trying to brush off a compliment.

It can be a tricky area, because the ego likes to get involved and inflate itself. But I have a tentative notion that boasting sessions could be good Medicine, done with humour and a bit of obvious exaggeration to keep the ego out of the way. Boasting is something that children naturally do, and it is healthy. I once overheard my young son, trying to keep up with the boasts of some new-found older friends, saying somewhat desperately, "There's something I'm really good at, but I can't remember what it is!" Humour aside, what it reveals is the natural desire of a child to think well of himself and to be thought well of. If you are English, you are almost obliged as an adult to be self-deprecating, to turn yourself into a bit of a joke, and this is not good for us. It is false, and it tends to leak out in less straightforward ways. The English also do this to themselves as a nation. As George Orwell said many decades ago,

> *"England is perhaps the only great country whose intellectuals are ashamed of their own nationality."*

I think it is important and it is natural to appreciate what is good in one's own culture. Why wouldn't anyone?

The Origin of the Shadow

The origin of these difficult and tormenting sides of ourselves can be a bit imponderable. If you take the materialist viewpoint that we are extinguished at death, along with the political viewpoint that all people are born 'equal', then differences become mainly due to nurture, and you may tend to attribute your various dysfunctionalities to what went wrong in your childhood. On the other hand, long-term genetic research has shown that we are much more a product of nature, of our genes than was previously thought (see *Blueprint* by Professor Robert Plomin.) Nurture still plays a major part, though. So maybe some of our 'shadow' is genetic?

And then there is the viewpoint of who we are, that is a logical corollary of the observation that this reality that seems so tangible is manufactured by the brain (see *The Man Who Mistook His Wife for a Hat* by Oliver Sacks.) In other words, it is dreamed up. We are dreamed into being. So, what are we? It is imponderable, it is profound mystery, the 'Great Mystery' as it is known in Native American traditions. It is a beautiful thing to feel that mystery, and it doesn't take much reflection to get a sense of it. And at death, all we know for certain is that the physical body dissolves.

It is possible that we have been here before, and that some of our patterns are the product of choices in previous lives. We do not know; this is a mystery also. For some people, past lives are a reality because they have memories to support it. For others, it is a belief, it is not based on experience. I tell people I believe in past lives on Tuesdays, Wednesdays and Fridays.

What I am getting at is that yes, we have these difficult sides of ourselves, and to a certain extent we can explain them through what happened in childhood, but I think only up to a point. Their origin is also imponderable. All we know is that they are there, and they are ours to be responsible for. A disadvantage of an over-emphasis on the 'wounded child' perspective is that we can subtly end up not feeling responsible, because we are blaming who we are on our parents and others. To that extent we are a victim, maybe with a polished hard-luck story to tell! The childhood explanations *are* important, and they are helpful to investigate. But sometimes we can never know, we cannot remember that far back, and it is good to hold such explanations with a measure of provisionality: they are just one perspective, and as with any perspective, ultimately behind it lies the unknowability of the Great Mystery.

Demons as Visitors

A traditional Native American perspective is that our 'demons' are not our own, they are visiting us from the outside. In his book *Healing the Soul Wound,* Eduardo Duran, a Native American therapist, describes how he introduces this way of seeing to his clients, who are mainly Native American, often with alcohol issues, and beset by problems that are the outcome of being psychologically colonised by the white people over centuries. So here we have the idea of generational trauma, of healing ancestral wounds. And also, the idea that we are visited by 'spirits'. In these cases, it is often the spirit of alcohol, which can be a Medicine as well as a poison, and we need to form a relationship with that spirit.

This is very different to the AA approach of saying 'I am an alcoholic' repeatedly. Naming is a powerful thing, it can fix us, and while not wanting to take away from the genuine help organisations such as AA offer, I think it is worth a second look at what we do when we name ourselves something. I am an angry person, I am an anxious person, a depressive person. Or maybe even worse, I am a bi-polar person, I am schizophrenic. When the medical establishment gives us a syndrome, on the one hand that can help, because our suffering is recognised; but on the other hand, it can fix us, there is something chemically and inherently wrong with us, and only pharmaceuticals, taken long-term, can help.

I don't want to oppose the medical establishment. It has a way of seeing that world that also does a lot of good. And it is outside of its worldview to be able to see symptoms as spirits visiting.

Bringing in the Sacred

When he sees a new client, Duran usually begins with a bit of ceremony. This is how I like to work. You drum or you rattle, you burn some herbs, and in so doing you invoke the 'sacred', the sense that what matters most has entered the room, Spirit is present. In our terms, the Unconscious has been activated: not the unconscious in an autonomous, isolated sense, but in its broader, collective, transpersonal meaning.

Duran does this with Indians (as they call themselves) who have become completely dissociated from their old ways. But nevertheless, it evokes an ancestral memory. It is the same for us when we do some ceremony. We may have adopted the rational, scientific worldview, but that is superficial. The greater part of our being does not work in this rational way. You are reading this book not because it seemed like a logical exercise, but because something pulled you towards it. You get involved in a relationship with someone not because you have worked it all out, but because you feel pulled. And the Unconscious, Spirit, knows exactly what it is doing. It already knows that person you are getting involved with, and it probably knows the gist of this book without you having even opened it. It may have made it fall off the bookshelf and into your hands!

Psychotherapy as Ceremony

So, before we do any work with our woundings, with our shadows, give it a sacred context. Invoke Spirit, bring in a bit of ceremony. This work is not about technique, it is about soul and heart. Even psychotherapy, which can sometimes seem a bit desperate not to appear unscientific, develops its own ritual, mythological context, which is where the most powerful healing happens. Spirit is the best healer. In a way, all you need do is invoke Spirit and then leave it up to Spirit.

Psychotherapy usually takes place in a specially designated room, with furniture and decoration and other effects carefully chosen. It happens often at the same time every week. It is not unlike a confessional in church. Indeed, Freud's practice of the patient not looking at the therapist almost turns the session into a conversation between the client and God, or her Soul. Or the therapy room is an alembic, the vessel in which the alchemical transformation occurs. The therapist is in the role of priest or priestess, conducting the religious rite in a non-personal way: the archetype of the healer is working through them.

The Unconscious soon turns the situation into this mythological setting in which old archetypes, with all their power, are invoked. This is what happens when we simply wave some herbs and ask for help: old and powerful forces that are found universally enter the room. I think it would be good for psychotherapists to make this dimension of their work more overt: the fear of seeming religious or irrational runs deep in our culture, but it is happening anyway, so better to go with the stream instead of attempting to against it. It is the same with astrology: it is a divinatory art, but some astrologers seem almost desperate to prove it is a science, to make it respectable. But it isn't. There is no scientific reason it should work. We need to fully own the powers working through us. The desire to make everything rational is simply the shadow of the North, the mind wanting to dominate, instead of being the servant (See *The Master and His Emissary* by Iain McGilchrist for a fuller exploration of this theme, based on the workings of the brain.)

Introducing Yourself to the Spirit

Eduardo Duran begins with a bit of ceremony, which immediately connects the dislocated Indian back to the forgotten old ways. And, if alcohol is the problem, he will invite the spirit of alcohol into the room, and ask the client to introduce himself to the spirit. And this includes telling the spirit who your parents are, and your grandparents and so on. This is the relational self that was mentioned earlier. A modern delusion is that we are purely autonomous, lone warriors up against the universe. But really, we are integral to a community – not just of friends and family, but spirit family too, ancestors, guides, animals and so on. Whoever it is that we feel is helping us.

Introducing yourself in this way is the respectful thing to do. It is treating the spirit of alcohol with respect. And then that spirit is asked, in turn, to introduce itself. Now that is going to work in different ways for different people, but if you listen with your whole being, you will get a sense of who that spirit is and what it wants. Included in this ceremony is some offering of tobacco to the spirit.

What Eduardo Duran has observed is that by this simple ceremony, the client's relationship with the bottle is immediately changed. They do not find it so easy to go and get wasted. The sacred, that which is of highest value, has been brought in, along with a spirit that needs treating with respect.

When it comes to your shadow work, make it sacred, hang loose, do not over-identify with these things, get to know them, see what they have to teach you. They are not essentially you. What you are essentially is pure Spirit. This is also a Buddhist view: they have a term that translates as 'adventitious defilements', meaning that our demons, our impurities come in from the outside, they are not inherent.

Projecting the Shadow

I have been calling this aspect of the South 'shadow' work. The reason these spirits are called 'shadow' is that they can be difficult to acknowledge: we don't like to see ourselves as that sort of person. What we tend to do instead is see others as having those characteristics, as being the ones who are angry, intolerant, callous etc. And then we judge them and dislike them for it, and that is the key to our own shadow.

When we judge someone, we are not being truly discerning – it is very important to be discerning, which is different from judgement, and we may have to learn it, painfully – but rather we are getting a sense of satisfaction from our criticism of the other person. That satisfaction lies in us feeling better because we have put the other person down. We are now 'above' them, we feel good about ourselves, because they are carrying that 'reprehensible' quality.

This is a good place to start in addressing the woundings of the South, because they will come out in our attitudes and behaviours, they become part of who we are, they don't just lie there doing nothing. Most of us like to think of ourselves as nice people, probably with a liberal conscience: we care about those in society who are disadvantaged or suffering. We are probably 'spiritual' too. And that is usually genuine. But it is usually also a mixed thing.

Foxhunting, Donald Trump and the Shadow

If you mention foxhunting, many of these good people (in the UK, at any rate) practically start foaming at the mouth. I was slightly shocked when I saw an anti-foxhunting post (which in itself is fair enough) on Facebook, below which people I knew were being savage about the foxhunters. They felt it was OK, that it was justified to express anger and hatred, to be abusive about these foxhunting people. And I know that if I were to step in and say something about this, I would be misunderstood: people would think I must be defending foxhunting, maybe in a covert way, because they feel so justified in the way they are being.

This is a classic way that the shadow comes out. And because it is the shadow, we cannot see it. Donald Trump was a perfect shadow figure while he was President of the US. He was in so many ways a person who embodied qualities that we would not like to think we have ourselves. He was, for example, a 'narcissist'. Now I am sure there is considerable truth in that. But isn't that something we all embody to some extent? We feel we are special; we feel we are right (and often feel we are miserable worms at the same time.)

It is about the way we make these observations. That is often the difficult and subtle thing to see. It requires honesty with ourselves, catching that feeling of separation from 'the other', of feeling good about ourselves, when we call Donald Trump a narcissist and in-so-doing damn him. Of course, he does seem to display narcissistic traits and it is quite extreme and almost comical. I am not denying that, and I think it is important to see that. But even the phrase, "he is a narcissist" names him, with all the power that naming has. It fixes him, it makes him essentially that. And that satisfies the part of us that wants to damn him, but it takes us away from our own humanity when we do that, that is the point. Hang loose to Donald Trump's narcissism, and by the same token hang loose to your own. We often don't want to admit these things about ourselves because it feels humiliating, it feels like an awful judgement of ourselves. It means we are not the nice, conscious, advanced person we imagined ourselves to be.

Beyond Good and Evil

There is a whole mindset here. As long as we think in terms of 'good' and 'bad', 'better' and 'worse', 'evolved' and 'unevolved', 'spiritual' and 'unspiritual', we can't become conscious. All we can do is become a more or less acceptable member of whatever groups we belong to. This is why the philosopher Nietzsche wrote a book called *Beyond Good and Evil*. Thinking of ourselves as having any identity – 'liberal' or 'spiritual' being classic examples – immediately creates an 'other' who is not (in our minds) that.

This is very common, very normal. It is how humanity works, because it is uncomfortable and threatening to stand outside the usual identity props we give ourselves. That is why, for example, the debate around EU membership in the UK was so intense and so polarising. It was based around (broadly speaking) two different ideas of what the UK was, and people were often very identified with one or the other idea, to such an extent that their idea was 'right' and the other idea was 'wrong'. That is why nationalism is such a powerful force: our ideas of who we are, are deeply identified with the peoples we feel we belong to. With the EU referendum, it was at bottom one nationalism versus another nationalism. And that is not to judge it, it is just to observe what happened.

To start to do shadow work, to start to address the 'wounded child', we need to begin to hang loose to our ideas around who we are, and stop dividing the world into 'good' and 'bad'. If you can stop dividing political figures into 'good' and 'bad', and judging them (often on the basis of little knowledge) you will, in my opinion, have made great strides towards becoming self-aware. If you are able not to judge in the political arena, you can probably do this anywhere. And that, in my experience, is a rare quality.

There is Nothing we are not Capable of

It is worth watching Jordan Peterson on YouTube on the subject of the Shadow (and on many other subjects). He says if you imagine yourself back in Nazi Germany, it is extremely unlikely you would have been one of those exceptional people risking their lives rescuing Jews. He said it is far more likely you would have been a concentration camp guard, had circumstances led you there. Not only would you have been a guard, but you would at times got enjoyment out of it. He says that unless we can imagine ourselves in those circumstances, we have not understood our shadow.

This can seem like an extreme and horrifying thing to say. But the historical record backs it up. There is a book called *Ordinary Men* by Christopher Browning, in which the author traces the genesis of a Nazi killing squad. They were regular policemen who were gradually led into this work. They were given the option of transfer, so it wasn't that they had no choice. The commandant spent time in his room getting drunk while the killings took place, it was so difficult for him. But gradually that is what these ordinary guys, just like you or I, became.

As the Roman playwright, Terence said,

"I am human, and I think nothing human is alien to me"

We are also Fundamentally Good

Before this gets too depressing, I want to mention another book, *Humankind* by Rutger Bregman (2020), which I recommend. His central point is that we have been led to believe that humans are basically a bad lot, that civilisation is just a veneer, and that if we remove it, we will quickly revert to barbarism. Bregman extensively documents why the opposite is the case. In the Blitz in London during WWII, people showed great goodwill and solidarity amidst the destruction. The same happened in German cities when they were bombed. And in New Orleans in 2003 when it flooded. The list goes on. Yet *Lord of the Flies* is a work of fiction whose author won the Nobel Prize. It shows a bunch of children turning savage and beastly when isolated on an island. There was a real-life incident of this, and the opposite happened. William Golding has a lot to answer for!

Mythologically, we have inherited a view of ourselves as 'bad'. It began with the Original Sin of Christianity. Encouraging people to feel bad about themselves, to doubt themselves, is one of the first things you do if you want to control them, and this is what religions often do. Tibetan Buddhism is not necessarily much better: its texts document the hell realms in ghastly ways that would do a Catholic proud, the suffering they portray is beyond imagining, and all one can do (if one believes it) is to shrink away in terror.

Christianity may have withered in the West, but Original Sin is still there influencing us unconsciously. That is part of how mythologies work: they don't just go away because we have disavowed them. I think Original Sin has found continuity through the Theory of Evolution, whereby modern 'civilised' humans have only just emerged from a barbaric and ignorant past: this is who we are, therefore, just below the surface.

This view is quickly seen to be false from only a cursory examination of living indigenous cultures, which have been living their ways for millennia. These indigenous ways have

Spirit, which is benign, at their centres, and they know how to live in balance with the natural world, whereas we have largely forgotten. Like Rutger Bregman, indigenous cultures also affirm that we are basically good and kind and caring.

I think we are a lot better than we tend to think we are. That is the context which we need for shadow work, for coming into relationship with all those problematic sides. If you already have a fragile view of yourself, if your confidence is easily knocked, it can make it much harder to own the shadow, for it can just seem to confirm our view of ourselves as a 'bad' person.

A while back I got angry over something in a way that I hadn't for a long time – it was the child in me convinced that somebody was not listening to me, and it was a piece of nonsense on my part. I then compounded this by feeling bad about myself, judging myself, for having got angry. And it took me a while to be aware of the judging, because it felt appropriate. I had just done a 'bad' thing, so it felt like the 'responsible' thing to do was to damn myself for it.

However stable you are, it is still a big ask to fully own the shadow: the idea that, as human beings, we have the potential to do all those ghastly things that other people have done. There is an upside to this realisation, however: it means we feel our brotherhood and sisterhood with all of humanity, instead of dividing off the people we strongly disapprove of into separate categories. The key is to stop judging, but that ain't easy.

Have No Views of Yourself

What we are here to do is to align ourselves with Spirit. That is the journey of the Medicine Wheel. We begin with the Spirit inspiration and initiation of the East, and that then works its way through feeling, body and mind. Of course, that is schematic, and it is never quite like that, it is more of a jumble.

Spirit is beyond all views, it just is, and it is infinite. Views of who we are, are like dams in the river of Spirit. These views belong in the North, the Mind, but they have strong emotional foundations, which is why we are looking at them from the South.

One of the things to do is just to observe your reactions and responses without judging them, at least not too much! Progress lies not in making our 'bad' emotions 'good', but simply in becoming aware of them. We are not attempting, with the Medicine Wheel, to become 'higher' beings, but whole beings, balanced beings.

At the Coal-Face

Every time you get anxious, and instead of being consumed by it, you are able to stand apart and note that you are feeling anxious; and are able to note further that it is probably an exaggerated response to whatever it is that occasioned (not caused) the feeling, then you become more whole. You will probably still be consumed by it to some extent, but not entirely. That is real progress. This is the coal-face, where in a sense the real work of the Wheel happens. In that sense, the Mouse of the South, the tiniest of the animals, is also the most powerful, as he helps us pay attention to the nuances and complexities of our personal responses. And that is where the real transformation happens: if we can pay attention, if we can get a grip, at this level, then it can almost be like everything else will take care of itself.

When you are having a hard time, and it is seeming too much, and you just want to reach for that bottle or those chocolates, call on the Mouse to help you. Over time, you will build a relationship with him (or her) and you will feel an active helping power with you.

For myself, anxiety, anger and self-doubt have been big ones that torment me, and continue to do so up to a point. I try to be disidentified (a North quality) when they arise, and sometimes I succeed. Disidentification, or disinterest in this sense is not a cold or alienated quality. This is important. We are still with the feeling, we are in it, but it is no longer entirely who we are.

And just be 'everyday' about it. Whatever we are feeling is no big deal, people feel like this all the time. You may also have acted on that feeling in ways you weren't happy about. Expressing anger, or letting someone push you around. Catch yourself making the judgment of yourself, starting to feel bad and beating yourself up. Note that too. Just note everything, like it is something of interest rather than something to feel bad about. This is tremendously freeing. As I said, actually changing those troubling sides is not our job, they may even have their uses, we do not know the full Spirit picture. But what we can do is to change our relationship with them. And in doing that we change our orientation towards our whole lives: we step outside of the conventional, respectable way that sees in terms of good and bad, we step outside the safety of that and into our own life, maybe for the first time. It is radical.

And then you can come back to the spirit work. Get to know that spirit of anxiety, make offerings to it, ask it what it wants. In that way a rich alchemy develops, and you are no longer limiting yourself by thinking of yourself as an 'anxious' person. No, you are fundamentally Spirit in all its joyful unknowability, and you sometimes have these troubling spirits coming in your door, and you give them a cup of tea and talk with them for a while, you develop sympathy. But you don't lecture them or judge them or try to change them, let Spirit do that. Maybe it is not polite to ask spirits to be other than they are! But you can ask them if there is anything they want, that can help.

Soul Retrieval

There is a parallel approach in the idea of Soul Retrieval, which is taught in the 'Core Shamanism' courses (see Chapter 1 A Note on the Word Shamanism for my comment on the word 'core'.) The idea here is that when traumatic events occur, a part of us may flee to the Spirit World, which in Core Shamanism is divided into Lower, Middle and Upper Worlds: this structuring is not absolute, and it may or may not correspond to individual experience when we journey to the Otherworld (as Celtic Shamanism terms it.) Fleeing to the Spirit World protects this soul part, but also leaves us disempowered, lacking in our full complement of soul. The process of healing involves locating that missing soul part, often with the help of guides, and classically it is someone else doing the work for you, with their guides persuading the soul part to come back: it often takes the form of a young child at the age at which the traumatic event occurred. It may take a bit of persuasion, but generally it is very happy to come back.

It has its parallel in Western psychotherapy in the language of repression in the unconscious. And you can see here the difference in the idea of the self: for the modern Westerner, trauma leads to repression in the personal unconscious, so it is still part of 'me'. The shamanic viewpoint does not have this rigid separation into self and other, the self is relational, so that soul parts flee to a common Spirit World. During the shamanic healing work, other people can, with the help of their guides, find your soul-part and help bring it back. Which to me proves that the modern separate self, on which is founded a whole political system of rights and freedoms (as opposed to say responsibilities and relationships), is illusory – or, at least, the degree of emphasis on the separateness is the issue, because obviously it has its practical uses.

But either way works, and that is what matters. "If it works, it's real." We can talk to a psychotherapist and gradually make the unconscious conscious. We can have some shamanic work done, and have lost soul-parts brought back. We can do the shamanic work ourselves – go and meet our own soul parts, and ask them to come back. When I first took up shamanic journeying in 1997, I had several months where all sorts of healing journeys for myself took place. I could never have put into words what was happening, but I felt deeply changed by the end of that period. This amounted to Soul Retrieval, but with the help of my own guides, rather than via an intervention.

Soul Retrieval is also something that can happen spontaneously, during the natural course of life, particularly if we are open to changing. If we are sympathetic to our troubled sides, the soul-parts will feel welcome and are more likely to return. If we are judging ourselves, and fighting ourselves, trying to become a 'better' person (by our own lights), then why would they want to come back?

Psychotherapeutic Boundaries

Psychotherapy is probably our most widely known and accepted method of addressing the South issues. It too can be very effective. It demands a lot of the therapist in terms of having done their own work. This isn't the place for an exploration of this topic. But I think it is worth a comment on the subject of 'boundaries'. Eduardo Duran, who works with Native Americans, and has that ancestry himself, says that anything less than a full human relationship will not work with his people, they do not understand it. This reflects an observation I have also made: unless both people are fully present and open about who they are, there is not a full relationship, and that limits what can happen, because healing is 'energetic' as much as it is about words. I have observed further that sometimes the 'boundaries' in fact serve the therapist and their need to keep sides of themselves hidden, rather than the client, whom the boundaries are ostensibly there to serve. Because psychotherapy has become a profession, with its own rules and certifications and codes of conduct, dogmas easily arise, and this is often the case with the issue of 'boundaries': I have learnt to tread carefully if I venture to critique them, because I soon find myself being told I do not 'understand', and treated to a lengthy explanation as to their purpose.

In Jan Van Ysslestyne's book *Spirits from the Edge of the World,* it is clear that the healers in the village do not have the luxury of 'boundaries', for everybody knows everything about everybody! And this makes it incumbent on them to be generally careful about how they behave. But it also means a full human relationship is there. I think it is worth considering whether it is somehow symptomatic of modern culture that our healers compartmentalise themselves in a way that other professionals do. Of course, you don't expect to know much that is personal about your lawyer or accountant. But when dealing with the soul, that changes, it has to be soul meeting soul for the alchemy to happen. You don't need to know the intimate details of the therapist's life, and no doubt that wouldn't be helpful: but it frequently gets taken much further than this, so that you don't fully meet them in an ordinary kind of way. A healer is not a 'professional' in the way that word is usually used to denote a compartmentalised skill-set.

Healing Crises

The healing of the South can come in the form of crises. Points at which our lives cannot go on as before. Times when the defences that we constructed as children just to survive – when a soul-part left for the Otherworld – no longer serve us. The East is that principle of life that is always unfolding, always wanting to move on, so we will tend to reach points in life when those wounds, which we are probably at best only half-aware of, need to be addressed. They may be from childhood. We maybe see things one-sidedly in that way, for they may also be ancestral, or cultural. They may be something which we brought in with us. Analysis of these things is helpful up to a point. But at the end of the day there is an energy that needs healing, something that needs to be lived that is not being lived. At this point we are involving the West, Earth, also, in the healing process: the need to incarnate, to live.

As I said earlier, the four Directions are not truly separate, they are four ways of looking at the same unitary thing – ourselves, and the whole universe. The healing process, which brings so much else with it in terms of our perspective on life, is rooted in the woundings of the South; but it is propelled forwards by the impetus to new life of the East; the need to incarnate, to fully live, of the West; and the understanding, analysis and perspective of the North. We will complete this discussion of healing crises in the next section, the West, the Earth.

Trickster Coyote of the South

Along with the Mouse, Coyote is also an animal of the South in some of the Native American traditions. He has a trickster quality. There is a story about the Coyote, that an attempt was made to eliminate him from the South West of the US, where he lived, and the result was that he spread all over the US. Sometimes if we push on blindly, fixated narrowly on what we want, the universe will push back and we will get the opposite result.

Maybe the Fox is our own trickster in Europe. There is a grisly story about a fox who had eluded the huntsmen over many hunts. He was known for being wily. Eventually, with the hounds hot on his heels, the fox came to a railway line. He ran parallel to it until a train came. Just at the right moment he popped across the tracks. The hounds, in blind pursuit and not very smart, crossed the tracks as the train came, and a large number were killed.

I have a picture of a Coyote by the South of my Wheel. But it is a small picture, and that is out of respect for, and wariness of Coyote. It can be helpful to invoke Coyote when a situation is particularly intractable. But you may get more than you bargained for. I think we need to be particularly clear that the outcome we are looking for is a Spirit outcome, and not just something we want, however laudable or worthy.

A reason Coyote is in the South is because we are creatures of emotional habit, and these habits are often our defences against what appears to be a threatening reality. These defences can go back to childhood. We are not going to give up our habits, our comfort zones, willingly. And it's as if the universe conspires sometimes to lead us by the nose into a situation where we will meet ourselves. I talked in Chapter 2 under My Mid-Life Crisis about a dream that tricked me into a crisis. That dream in early on1996 suggested I run the Buddhist community I was living in as a public teaching centre. It went swimmingly, but put me at odds with 'higher' authorities, who did not want me going my own way. And I was left with a choice: do I go for an easy life and conform, or do I stick with my daemon, who was becoming increasingly confident? I chose the latter course, and it completely changed my life. But I could not have foreseen those consequences when I innocently followed that dream.

You see this sometimes too with relationships. They are ideal territory for the trickster, because here we are so easily led by the nose. And that wonderful person we got involved with – or at least, they appeared wonderful – turns out to be someone quite different, and we have an awful time, but hopefully we learn something. Coyote is perfectly willing to put us through extremely painful and long-lasting situations in the hope that we might wake up. Astrologically, he could be said to be the planet Uranus, who is associated with sudden and unpredictable change that will, hopefully, awaken us. Mercury too, in his own way, has this function.

Clowns and Fools are also this trickster archetype. And so is the boy in the story of the emperor's new clothes: the only person who, with his innocent eyes, can see that the emperor is naked. In a way, the trickster only appears to be a trickster because we are so convinced by conventionally agreed realities. Tricksters can appear like people who are being wilfully contrary, and what is their issue with just being like everyone else? But the trickster is simply looking with fresh eyes, he is not taken in by the collective collusions that appear so real to those living in them. The trickster does not care what other people think of her – at least, not to the degree that most of us care. And that makes her free to see and say things as they are. You will not get very far on this journey of transformation around the Wheel if you care too much what other people think of you, or rather what you imagine they think of you. It requires courage. Fitting your life around what other people think and value is comfortable and secure, in a way, and many people are happy to live like that, and they don't even know they are doing it. But if you are fortunate, you will find that uncomfortable, you will feel edited, oppressed and like you are in a cage.

Education

Education belongs in the South, the place of the Child. Our system, though, is very North (the Mind) oriented, which immediately suggests an imbalance. We have a mass education system, whose purpose is to create economically productive, conforming members of society. It is not, and cannot be, especially tailored to the needs of the individual. There are not the resources for that, and its aims are primarily collective rather than individual, even though the teachers, who are often there for vocational reasons, may feel otherwise.

The Medicine Wheel, even though it can be used for collective ceremonies, is really geared towards the individual finding her own values and her own balance, outside of the voices of society, which may be telling her otherwise. In considering the Wheel in relation to society, there will always be this tension. And no less so in the education system.

For many children and adolescents, the education system works. They maybe want nothing other than a straightforward career, home and family, at least for now. So that works for them, even though the process of putting children under pressure to pass lots of exams that will determine the future course of their lives, at just the age when they don't know who they are any more, seems insane. The qualifications obtained are North-oriented for the purposes of the West (becoming economically productive). It is about intellectual performance as a measure of who you are. Children are taught to perform in a very narrow way from a young age, and to judge themselves accordingly. The South, the play and the emotional engagement, and the imaginative development of the East, are not prioritised.

I have never been able to see what the hurry is about. The knowledge and skills necessary for a career are soon picked up in the doing, and probably remembered far more quickly and effectively for being used, rather than merely being learnt from a book. Children are pushed into the West, the Adult, before they are ready, and it stunts their more rounded development. The university system is equally insane: young adults find themselves under pressure to learn a specialised subject in a purely intellectual way, gaining knowledge that they will probably never use, and may well not have a deep interest in, in order to prove they are employable at a level that will eventually be highly remunerative. And in earning their degree, they acquire high levels of debt that will keep them in 'the system' until at least middle age, by which time it can be hard to do anything else. This has the effect of tying young people into 'the system' for life.

In recent decades what are known as the Big Five Personality Traits have been broadly agreed on by the psychology community. The first two are Openness and Conscientiousness. These two tend not to go together. Put simply, people tend to be either imaginative and 'lazy', or hard-working and a bit boring! East and West respectively. You probably recognise these different types of character from people you know. The education system is quite suited to 'conscientious' types, who value hard work, and who do not require a deep interest in what it is they are studying. The system probably makes them narrower and more boring than they might otherwise have been, but there is maybe no great harm done, as the system is broadly in line with who they are. It is less likely to suit the East types, however. Though even then, some may stay happily at the bottom of the class, ignoring the whole thing; while others, being intellectually very capable, may spend the lessons dreaming out the window, yet still absorb the lesson and come top in the tests.

Speaking personally, the system took me years to recover from, because I was good at pressurising myself to learn, and ignoring what I was actually interested in, because that was how I was brought up from a young age. However, once I finished my A-Levels, something in me switched off, and I was no longer able to study in the way I had trained myself to. It meant that I didn't go to the university that I might have gone to, and even then, I only scraped through with a third class degree. It was not for want of trying. But however hard I stared at the page, very little would go in. At one point, I tried hard to 'pull myself together', because finals were coming up; the only result was that I felt awful, and had a dream of being in an exam room with glowing heads placed on pillars around the room. That said it all: something in me, beyond my control, had decided that I was not going to be a glowing head any more, in fact had decided that four years before, but I did not understand that. My acquired conscientiousness had fallen away, and I had become very open.

In the 40 plus years since I left university, I have had a recurring dream in which I am back there at the start of the first term, scrabbling hopefully to find a subject that I would be sufficiently interested in to study. Sometimes in the dream I think I've succeeded in finding such a subject, but it never works out, if only because I can't find the lecture hall. And somewhere I have always felt wrong-footed, second class, because I was not able to go to the top university that I might have done, nor even get a decent degree, when before I had had those abilities, and they had been the principal way in which I felt my own worth.

In reality, something had gone right, not wrong, in my inability to study, because it reflected a spontaneous broadening of my personality, which 'the system' no longer suited. From that point on, I took over my own education, and it has been lifelong. I gradually learned to think originally, which the system was never going to teach me, and I have always read widely and thoughtfully. But I still have that recurring dream, because I have not yet fully come to terms with what happened at that age: the appearance of failure where I had hitherto been successful, and the sense of intellectual inferiority (and as ever, what is needed is simply to acknowledge the feeling, not to hide from it or 'make it better'); versus the real meaning of those events, which was a moving forward, the opening up of a much deeper interest in life than could be satisfied by a narrow curriculum and its aims. That conflict has for me been one of those edges in life that are uncomfortable; it has broadened into a conflict between valuing my life in conventional career-terms (loser!) versus what I find to be of worth for myself (this slow burn path that has taken decades, in which I have managed to make some deep changes to myself.) Society will never see, let alone value the latter.

This is where the path of the Medicine Wheel can make such deep demands. We are herd animals, in which we find so much of our personal value in contingent ways, through conforming and fitting in and doing well by comparison to others. When that is taken away – and for me it was taken away not by outside agencies, but by virtue of who I was – you have to find something within instead that is your own, that in reality gives you a much surer base than the collective fitting-in ever could. It takes courage, and many years in the furnace to forge, and even now, as the recurring dream shows me, the process is not yet complete.

Having said all that about the education system and its one-sidedly North emphasis, I don't want to deny that for some the university can be a genuine education. I was listening to a Canadian journalist who won a Rhodes scholarship to Oxford to study law for a year. He did the law studies, but spent nearly all his time reading English literature. If you have the desire and the capacity, which most of us don't, the university can be a tremendous opportunity to pursue learning for its own sake, in a way that is enriching and transformative and even initiatory. It is an opportunity that has been gradually eroded for some decades now in, for example, literature, where the emphasis has shifted from appreciation of the great writers to 'deconstructing' them and pulling them down. The American academic Camille Paglia is particularly good at describing, and denouncing, this change.

Learning by Mercury Placement

In astrology, the placement of the planet Mercury shows us how our mind works and how we best learn. That is one of the great things about astrology, in that it shows how each of us is individually built: we are anything but one-size fits all. Some people's Mercury will show, for example, that they learn best through a systematic course of study; others will need a strong imaginative stimulus to get them interested enough to learn; others need it to be practical; others cannot learn unless they can first find their own original take on the subject on which to hang everything (that is me.) And those are just a few of the Mercury placements. We can end up feeling inadequate, or lacking in intelligence, if we don't do well at school, and that can plague us our whole lives (as I showed in the example of myself.) But seeing how we personally learn best can cast a different light on the subject, especially when we can see that it does not fit well with the way we were expected to learn at school. Mercury shows that there is a great range of types of intelligence. It is not so much a matter of whether or not someone is intelligent, but discerning how it is that our intelligence works.

It is time now to move on to the West, where we can begin to fully resolve those sometimes very intense demands and conflicts that occur when Spirit from the East meets the defences of the South.

Chapter 4

The West – Incarnation

Colour: Black
Element: Earth
Season: Autumn
Time: The Present
Stage of Life: Adult
Animal: Bear
Some key words for the West: Incarnation, the Physical, the Dream, Responsibility, the Inner Opposite, Death, Ceremony.

Spirit and the Adult

We have visited the timeless place of the East, where Spirit and inspiration is eternally present, and then the childhood place of the South, the Past, where Spirit and our early circumstances shaped us. And now we arrive in the Present, the Adult, a demanding place in which we not only have often consuming day-to-day responsibilities, but also our deeper self, which is a mystery and often problematic, to take care of.

Traditionally children and old people were seen as closest to Spirit (see *The Circle of Life* by James David Audlin for a thorough exposition of traditional Native American attitudes to the world). Children, raised in a natural and balanced way, see the world from a basis of trust and with fresh, innocent eyes, in which their imaginations are also very real to them. Old people have less day-to-day responsibilities (usually) and their bodies aren't quite so vigorous as they once were. This doesn't mean they are not full of zest for life, but they are closer to, more informed by, the Spirit world, in a way that is more lived and understood than with children.

It is the adults for whom ceremonies like the Sweatlodge

are necessary, to bring them back to what matters, to their connection with mother Earth and the gratitude we have for this wonderful life and the ways in which we are looked after. We rightly complain about the one-sided materialism of the modern world, but humans have always had a tendency to become out of balance in this way. The difference is that in a traditional society, people would be more embedded in the mother, the natural world, and the elders would be listened to. In our society, that imbalance has been turned into a philosophy of life, and our 'elders', the people many look up to (even though they may not admit it to themselves) are the guys who have made a lot of money, or who have power, or who are famous. At the same time, we love it when they fall, for we are also envious of them.

Our societies are so huge that they are governed by impersonal rules rather than by relationships, and I think that is the key problem. What chance does a genuine elder have of being heard? These vast collectives are a relatively new phenomenon in human history. Maybe we will eventually find a new balance. It is hard to know.

Incarnation vs Transcendence

Incarnation is a key word for the West: arriving here on the planet, being fully alive and present in Spirit, Heart, Body and Mind (the four directions.) Our religious background through Christianity gives us a model of *transcendence* which is very different: that being 'spiritual' involves getting away from, being above the world, the devil's creation. The form of Buddhism I was involved with for many years also had the transcendent model: we were exhorted to ignore the merely 'psychological' and concentrate on the 'spiritual'. Eventually, if you practised hard enough and for long enough, you would not be re-born. In the modern atheistic world, that split persists in the form of reason versus nature: we have elevated reason to the place of

God, and look down on the world from that cold height. For an indigenous person, this world and this life are precious, it is a joyful privilege, albeit demanding and difficult at times, to be here.

It is not too difficult to steer many young people, full of idealism and from backgrounds that have maybe damaged them and that deny that idealism, in this imbalanced direction, towards 'the light'. It creates a big shadow of all the things in ourselves that we ignore, that we don't want to know about. I recently watched a New Age teacher talking on YouTube in a very assured way about how he and his audience were on the side of the light, which would inevitably win through against the dark forces that rule the world. It seemed to me to be medieval Christianity in another form, and a huge projection of everything he didn't like about himself onto the world. Why judge the world as a bad place: who does that serve, and were people ever any different, fundamentally?

After the Ecstasy, the Laundry

There is a book by Buddhist practitioner Jack Kornfield called *After the Ecstasy, the Laundry*, in which he tells his story of heading out to the East as a young man and becoming a Buddhist monk, involving himself in the renunciative life with its emphasis on discipline, meditation and higher states of consciousness. He eventually returned home to the US, with the intention of teaching Buddhism. But what he found was that he was not able to, it all fell apart and he ended up working as a taxi driver. Eventually he did end up teaching Buddhism, but from quite a different basis, involving

> *"the honest development of the wise heart within the cycles of day-to-day life; for instance amid all the Western masters and teachers I know, some idealistic perfection is not apparent. Times of great wisdom, deep compassion, and a real knowing of freedom alternate*

with periods of fear, confusion, neurosis, and struggle. Most teachers will readily admit this." Wikipedia

The point of the title of Kornfield's book is that yes, our path can begin with visionary experiences, this is quite common, even normal and necessary. But they are 'otherwordly', they are a guide to living, and not life itself. After those experiences, like the initiate returning from his Vision Quest, that vision needs to be lived in the nitty-gritty of the everyday to become integrated, to become real.

The Teacher Owning her Shadow

Kornfeld also refers to teachers readily admitting to their struggles. I try to do that myself. I don't just talk about acknowledging my shadow, I try to talk about specific and recent examples of it. The students can feel the reality of that, and it keeps everyone on a level. It is, paradoxically, inspiring rather than discouraging for the student to experience that the teacher is just like him or her.

I was watching another 'new age' teacher recently, and to start with I was impressed as he talked about the great event he was going to be running and the wonderful sense of community that would be there. It wasn't just hot air, because he has been running such events successfully for years. He has a genuine gift, as most teachers, however imbalanced, do have. And I was wrong-footed for a moment, as well as impressed. I sometimes lose a measure of my own confidence when I see someone who is good at the sort of thing I do. That can then very easily turn into envy and trying to knock the other person down by fault-finding. Most of us do this; as always, don't judge it, just accept it, it is no big deal, it is 'normal' to experience envy. I try to catch myself, and to stay with the uncomfortable feeling. I did this recently with a shamanic book: I had not written one, and this guy who had been younger than me had done so, and I found that uncomfortable, a bit threatening to my own confidence. I was reluctant to go near his book. So, on principle I made myself do so. This is the warrior path: it is about facing, rather than compensating for, the places in which you feel uncomfortable. There is a cartoon in which a businessman is saying that eight minutes meditation a day gives him the focus to conquer the world. In the background there is a monk saying an hour a day and you wouldn't need to. If we can just stay with ourselves, tolerate ourselves, the inner emptiness starts to fill, and the need to compensate recedes. Think Donald Trump and Trump Tower.

Anyway, back to the 'new age' teacher who was impressing me in talking up his coming gathering. He was also mentioning the shadow, and he was gracious enough to admit more than once, that he 'of course' has one. He was giving a nod to being humble and being like the rest of us. But he was not specific about his shadow, and to even say it like that suggests that there might be some doubt in the first place as to whether he had a shadow. And then what I noticed, after about five minutes, was that everything he was saying was designed to create an impression of onward and upward into the light, it was this big, loving, happy and certainly very 'special' event (as I am sure all his events are 'special') that was going to be created. I was being drawn into this 'happy' space, and I realised that I didn't want to go there, because it was also drawing me away from myself. And if I had been more unconscious of my own shadow and reluctant to encounter it, then I would happily have gone there with him, and probably attributed any blissful feelings I had to that teacher. This was what happened to me in my early twenties: I was drawn into Buddhism in an 'onward and upward' sort of way. I never felt entirely comfortable with that, but it was many years before I felt confident in the side that wasn't comfortable (rather than judging it as a fault to be overcome), and then I left.

Note Your Authentic Responses to Teachers

We are back with our discussion of gurus of the East, but with the emphasis on the shadow, rather than the projection of Spirit onto the teacher. And what happens is that the teacher has a particular shadow, certain things about herself that she does not want to look at, and if that fits with what the student doesn't (unconsciously) want to look at, then an unholy alliance is created, and those unacceptable sides are projected out onto the world, which becomes a 'bad' place, and the spiritual group becomes a 'good' place, a superior kind of place that is a remedy for the world's ills.

Watch out for teachers with this 'onwards and upwards' kind of feel, where everything becomes 'special'. As I say, it doesn't mean they don't also have some wisdom you can learn from. But you learn just as much, I would say even more, by paying attention to your emotional responses and honouring them, rather than doubting them because everyone else holds the teacher in special regard. You get to know yourself, and what was your shadow now becomes an important and discerning part of you; you get to know the world and people and what really goes on, because so much of what happens in the world is based on unconscious projection, and we stop being part of that.

If you have a significant experience when you are with a teacher, it is natural to attribute that experience, to some extent at least, to the teacher. And in that way, we give away some of our power, and become addicted to that teacher. Any significant experiences you have are yours and yours alone, it is Spirit working through you, and they need to be owned.

What a Good Teacher Does

A good teacher is not leading you 'upwards' into a glittering and special experience. Good teaching has the quality of the 'normal', of the everyday, it is grounded. Again, examine your emotional response: around this person, do you feel freer to be who you are in an ordinary kind of way? If so, whatever the content of the teaching, they are the real deal. A genuine path is not about 'higher' states, it is about becoming whole and balanced, just as the Medicine Wheel is about that. It may not seem very 'powerful' at first glance. We may be seeking a teacher who offers a 'powerful' initiation (some Tibetan Lamas offer this), and we in turn acquire a sense of power (we imagine) by being around that teacher, who probably has the 'authentic' teachings, the 'pure' teachings. But in simply being true to yourself in a down-to-earth way lies all the power you will ever need, because it is real. And something of how the teacher is with themselves will rub off on you. I think that is the real meaning of the 'initiation' that is sometimes offered. It is another level of teaching that is unspoken, it is 'esoteric', which simply means inner and implicit, as opposed to 'exoteric', which is outer and explicit.

Don't Demonise the 'New Age'

I used the term 'new age' about certain teachers. It is a vague term that has its uses. I think it points at best to the freedom we have in the modern world to follow our Spirit authentically, and not feel beholden to tradition in a rigid or narrow way (which, it has to be said, some indigenous people do, and it is important to see that and not be drawn into their fundamentalisms.) 'New age', however, is also associated with a superficial eclecticism in which nothing is followed through deeply over time, and certainly nothing which will challenge, rather than flatter, us. And it is also associated with 'ascension', the one-sided path towards the light. 'Light workers' often have this imbalance. Again, pay attention to your responses to people and don't feel too easily that there is something 'wrong' with you. Your feelings are always telling you something!

The term 'new age', however, easily becomes one more shadow projection by people wanting to bolster their own path.

I have seen it within Shamanism quite a lot. I have seen the 'new age' dismissed as everything Shamanism is not, as though Shamanism is this real, 'muscular' path, and the new age is just for drippy hippies. In fact, it seems accepted by many that 'new age' is a pejorative and contemptuous term and can be used as such, without the term ever being defined (a bit of a give-away). If you feel this contempt for the new age, you are fortunate: there is self-knowledge for you here. What is it you look down on in the new age? Maybe there is some useful quality in yourself that you are not aware of that you are projecting onto these 'hippies'? Maybe you are a bit rigid, a bit over-identified with your own path, and you need to let go a bit, soften, be more open – just like the new agers!

Incarnation is Difficult

So back to the theme of incarnation. We have just been looking at ways in which spiritual paths can be about the opposite of this, they can lead us away from an experience of wholeness and balance and into fantasies of 'higher' states of consciousness and of saving the world. And the reason this occurs is because incarnation is difficult. We may feel a genuine metaphysical quest, we may want to find deeper meanings in life than the collective has presented to us. But we may not yet feel ready for that fuller encounter. I see it a lot: people who have formed a sense of who they are via an identification with one set of ideals or another, whether it is Buddhist or Shamanic, or just a general sense that they are a 'higher being', and from the outside I can see there is something in themselves they are protecting through this identification: their Buddhism or Shamanism contains a significant element of defence. This can be part of the motive for joining religious orders: in the joining, you are accepted by an authority as being a 'spiritual' person, above the general run of humanity, and there is inflation and complacency in this.

Spiritual Bypass

It seems to be a stage that many people go through, to one degree or another. It gets given the term 'spiritual bypass' defined as

> *"a tendency to use spiritual ideas and practices to sidestep or avoid facing unresolved emotional issues, psychological wounds, and unfinished developmental tasks."* Wikipedia

When you get large numbers of people doing this together, in a sense colluding in the avoidance of psychic material, then you have religion.

As I said earlier, I don't think it is something to be judged, as though there is something wrong. You never know what it is that people need to learn, and how long it is going to take, and what choices they are going to make along the way. These deeper learnings of the psyche can take a long time. Maybe there is only time for one or two in a lifetime. And religion can sometimes be exactly the learning ground that is needed. It was for me, in what I jokingly refer to as my 'misspent youth.' And sometimes the bypass is just ordinary life with its collective values, which is the same as religion if you take its values too rigidly. In these contexts, the contradictions between the authentic urge to become whole and complete, and the collective denial of aspects of the psyche can act as a pressure cooker, until eventually there is some kind of explosion or meltdown or reckoning, and it may well be messy as these things often are; and then we may backtrack for a while, back to the comfort zone of the familiar but inauthentic. And then the conflict returns.

I'll Be Back!

Spirit can be rather like Arnold Schwarzenegger's Terminator: "I'll be back." It can take a long time. 20 years ago, a friend had an awakening to the restrictive nature of the Buddhism he was involved with. But to live with that was too much for him at the time, so he retreated back into the acceptance of the collective. 20 years later, and it is still as if it never happened. And you just never know. What choices will he make? You can't push people, all we can do is to continue to be true to ourselves, which is a powerful thing, it rubs off osmotically on other people.

The Terminator turned up in my life when it was time to leave a long-term relationship that had become restrictive for me. It was like an enormous force banging at the front door, demanding entry. And sometimes I would let him in for a bit, and then I would persuade myself it wasn't real: my self-doubt, my lack of trust in myself would kick in. And then maybe a few months, or a year later, Arnie would be back, hammering at the door, even louder. Eventually, after much persuasion, I let him in permanently. It took Arnie five years to get me out of that situation.

Saturn and Incarnation

We have been circling around this idea of Incarnation as a key theme of the West. This is because the West is the Earth element, it is about solidity, embodiment, physicality: making the vision real. And there are ways we avoid or resist that, because it is difficult.

I am going to bring in some astrology at this point, because the attributes of the planet Saturn describe this process well. Saturn is the outermost of the visible planets, so he 'contains' the solar system, he provides the underlying structure, and the laws of that structure, by which we live. He stands for that need to incarnate, as well as that resistance to incarnating which we all experience at one time or another, but which is also by the same token a very creative point, in which something new is brought into life.

What happens for everyone is that between the ages of approx. 28-30, Saturn returns to the position it was in when we were born. And that is often a difficult time for people, because

Saturn makes the sort of demands that young people, who like to play, resist: Saturn requires qualities like discipline, patience, responsibility, finding your place in the world, earning a living, using your talents, being serious about your life. It is as if (schematically) we spend our twenties exploring one avenue and now another, and we get to 29 and Saturn says OK, what does all that add up to? Pull all those threads together and make something of them.

It is almost like clockwork for most people at this age, in that they acquire some new responsibility in the world: they get married, or they start a family, or they get promoted at work. Or some, having done the regular 9-to-5 routine for some years, decide they have a calling to follow instead. And there are, of course, all sorts of permutations. For some, the Saturn Return means getting serious about their calling/vocation, but putting off and maybe even looking down on ordinary life. But usually, sooner or later, that has to be come back to.

And then there is the second Saturn Return, aged about 58. Schematically, we have been doing the 'adult' thing of the West for 30 years, we have now incarnated in that sort of way, we are at ease with material existence (which a lot of 'spiritual' people avoid, for mixed reasons.) And Saturn now says OK, you have arrived, now you can afford to let go a bit, let the next generation do the hard work, it is time to let Spirit in more. And it is often around this time that people will do their best work, because they are ready to, and there is no longer anything to achieve, anything to prove, and Spirit can have its way.

The Protestant Work Ethic

As I say, this is very schematic. And to come back to an earlier theme, it's as if we no longer have to pretend to be an adult, we can let go of so much responsibility and learn to play again. And this is a serious consideration in our society, with its Protestant Work Ethic. I have seen people retire, who in the early stages of their retirement keep themselves busy all day, because that is what they are used to, that is what gives them a sense of value. It is bad enough in the UK, and seems to be even more intense in the USA (which has a challenging Saturn in its national chart). And then gradually you see the wheel slowing down, people who have retired start to feel OK about pottering and listening to themselves. (I have to say I know one guy in his 90s who has still not stopped, he is compelled to keep busy: habits do not necessarily stop of their own accord.) As long as we are busy because we are driven to it, because we feel valueless without it, then to that extent we cannot listen to ourselves.

In reality, we are our own value, we do not need to justify it through anything. Everything starts from that, it is the centre of the Wheel (which is also the whole universe, just to remind you!) That push to be busy for its own sake knocks us off centre, and we cannot listen or be properly at peace. It goes very deep in our culture, it is fundamental, which is why I am going on about it, and why I went on about it earlier. We cannot listen properly to Spirit as long as we feel guilty about being 'idle'.

For indigenous people, when there was work to be done, they did it. And when there wasn't, they did other things. A story I heard from the horse's mouth illustrates this. The white people decided to help out the Indians on the reservation by creating some work for them. They created a project to build a dam nearby for a hydroelectric power plant, and they reserved many of the jobs for the Indians. So, they turn up at the reservation and start explaining their generous offer to the Indians, and the Indians are not interested. The white people are perplexed by these ungrateful Indians. They try explaining to them that it is for their own good, it will help them develop self-respect etc. But the Indians aren't buying it, and eventually the exchange becomes heated, and an argument begins. At that point, one of the Indian Elders steps in and says: "You white people, you invented work, you do it!"

When my mother was in her early 60s, and newly living on her own, a friend asked her at a party about her day. And my mother replied by saying her day usually began at about 11am, when she got up. The friend, trying to be 'helpful' replied "But don't you ever wake up at about 8am with a zest to get up and start the new day?" To which my mother replied in the affirmative. "So, what do you do?" asked the friend. "I roll over and wait for the feeling to go away," replied my mother. Which, of course, was exactly the wrong answer from the helpful friend's point of view, but exactly the right answer from a Spirit point of view!

The Protestant Work Ethic is Saturn in his negative form, it is one of the shadows of the West of the Wheel, saying only that which is observable and measurable is of value, and you personally are only of value if you achieve in this way. He becomes the denier of not just the value, but the very existence, of the inner life and of Spirit. People with a challenging Saturn are often driven to achieve in the world, and they can be impressive, it is not 'all bad'. The USA, with its challenging Saturn, throws up skyscrapers and puts men on the Moon and has been the world's wealthiest country for over 100 years. But can it look after its own people properly? Not really, because that is not sufficiently high on its system of values. It is far more important to them to put a man on the Moon. At the outset of my 'spiritual' career I was told by my father, who had the same sort of Saturn as the US, and was similarly an 'achiever' that, "People who look into themselves are boring." We are not here to 'achieve'; we are not here to be 'useful'. We are here to take care of that thing deep within that gives meaning to life and which, I suspect, is the one thing we can take with us when we die.

Balancing Spirit and Matter

'Spiritual' people often swing to the opposite extreme to the materialistic culture around them. So big business becomes the Great Satan, with no redeeming qualities. The tendency to spiritual bypass is exacerbated by this opposition to the world, which is natural, in a way (I was like that myself for many years, as a sort of survival mechanism.) But eventually we need to make our peace with the world, and not treat it with exaggerated mistrust and suspicion.

This is about balancing East and West, Spirit and Matter. It is about finding one's own authority – the Emperor Card in the Tarot – where we feel sure both of our connection to Spirit and of our ability to engage with the world. As we complete the West in this way, so do we start to move towards the North, the Elder – schematically, at aged 58, after the second Saturn Return.

The wider culture does not support the validity, the 'authority' of those of us who have a metaphysical quest. Rather, we feel the pressure to succeed on the terms of the world alone. It is important, however, that we are able to engage with the world on its terms, at least to some extent, to avoid some aspects of spiritual bypass: to 'grow up' in that provisional kind of way.

Exaggerated Mistrust of Authority

But finding that deeper centre within, where we are sure of ourselves in an open-minded kind of way, is a long process. And one of the first steps often lies in taking a good look at our mistrust of authority. An exaggerated mistrust of authority is very common, and I think it always points to a lack of confidence in one's own authority. Authority – control, if you like – is projected outwards and therefore takes shadow form. That can go either way, into idealising gurus, or damning to hell anyone with worldly authority, from politicians to bankers to CEOs to police. In reality, most of these people in 'authority' are just ordinary people trying to do a good job, and they are in their positions not because they are power-crazed, but because they are competent: that is why things don't fall apart. The statement 'the police are, by and large, trying to protect the public' can seem outrageous to some people. Or even worse 'Politicians of whatever party are by and large trying to serve the interests of the country.'

Many people are so caught up in an exaggerated mistrust of these figures, and supported by many others who see in the same way, that they cannot see that they are damning these figures on the basis of very little evidence. And it is the damning of them which is a bit of a giveaway: whenever we damn someone, there is something in it for us, it is shadow material, it is pointing to something in ourselves we are not comfortable with. And part of it in this case is that we feel we are being controlled by the government, and we resist that, we kick against it.

No-one is in Control

But actually, they are not controlling us, not in any fundamental way. Our soul remains our own. As Dr Johnson said,

> *"How small, of all that human hearts endure, that part which laws or kings can cause or cure."*

Paradoxically, the idea that no-one is in control is a threatening one for many people, even though they kick against the 'controllers'. There is an ambivalent response: the secret, unowned response of feeling reassured that the government – or the king, or the Pope, or the guru – is in control and providing certainty; and the more conscious kicking against that alleged affront to one's autonomy. The teenage rebellion does not stop when we are twenty, it continues, almost inevitably, for as long as we cannot be honest with ourselves about our lack of genuine autonomy. Pride gets in the way.

When the government is seen not to be in control – when there is a major terrorist attack, for example, or a pandemic –

people club together and invent a dark force that is 'really' in control. The Covid pandemic, for some, was planned in advance by governments to fulfil some other agenda. That way you know again who is in control and can continue, as before, to kick against it. But because such beliefs do not have a genuine foundation – mere facts play little part – it is always fragile, and there is a need therefore to bring others on board, like a religion, to make it appear more solid, and to call people 'sheeple' who do not think as you do.

Don't Judge Authorities

There was a degree to which I used to prop myself up through denigrating people in authority right up until my mid-50s. And one day I recognised what I was doing, and how it made me spout some strange critiques of people, and I made a decision to stop doing it. Just like that. It began with my father, who always had a low opinion of me because I did not share his values. I decided in my own mind to stop wanting him to be other than he was, and just let him be. He had been the primary authority figure I was fighting against (though it had considerably attenuated anyway by this time.) What I immediately noticed was that in allowing myself to let my father be who he was, I became happier with who I was. I accepted that he would never be able to understand my point of view (though I was able to understand his, as well as my own – that is the thing about spending years attempting to be conscious.) And I moved outwards from there. And in a way it is about assuming basic good faith on the part of other people: that if they are a policeman or a parking attendant or an MP or a government minister, they are probably just trying to do their job, unless there is obvious evidence to the contrary.

I think it is easier to see this with people with whom we are in physical contact. A finding from wars (see *Humankind* by Rutger Bregman Chapter 1) is that it is the people at home who hate the enemy the most, rather than the soldiers at the front, who will at times meet these human beings who happen to be on the opposite side. It is the same with 'authority' figures: it is far easier to despise politicians who are on the national stage, with whom we have no experience of as human beings.

It is, in a way, natural for people to do this, particularly when there is a collective, a mob mentality, at work. It has always happened, and it would be foolish to expect otherwise.

But on an individual level, we have a choice to step out of this projection of what is our own authority onto those in power, and then despising them, and finding it within.

Crises (continued)

We looked at crises in the East, from the point of view of times when new elements enter our consciousness, and create a new centre to who we are, and everything needs to be re-arranged around that. It can take some years. Shedding a skin, like a snake, can be a slow and uncomfortable process, and we can end up with a completely new life at the end of it. These times don't occur very often, because we need years afterwards to absorb and live out the ramifications. When it happens to me, I think who am I going to have left in my life after this? Because my friends are often the ones who felt comfortable with the old me.

And these crises tend not to be just about the East moving in on us; they often tend also to involve our painful sides being addressed. And that can sometimes be very difficult, and go on for some years. But it is also 'the crack where the light gets in'.

Sometimes these things can seem to come to us from the outside, and that can be because we don't want to listen, we want our life to carry on as it is and 'make it work'. That is very natural. But if something has to be 'made to work', then it may well not be the right thing. Sometimes when I am doing astrology readings, I can see that someone's relationship area is up for serious change, and if they don't leave, the other person will, and it will be like something bad happened 'to' them. I have to tread delicately. But we are often unconscious agents in the things that happen 'to' us.

We looked at the 'shamanic illness' in the East, the times when Spirit comes calling and makes you an offer you can't refuse! There is something new and deep and life-giving to be listened to at these times. The other side of this is the illness itself, which being bodily is a West consideration.

Spirit and Physical Illness

Probably all illness has a spirit dimension to it. It is not just a physical, biological, biochemical phenomenon. Nothing is. It is well-known that people who want to be well, who have something to live for, tend to recover more quickly. In recent decades there has been a slew of hard-to-diagnose and hard to treat illnesses, that often become permanent conditions, like ME, chronic fatigue, irritable bowel syndrome, fibromyalgia, multiple sclerosis and various auto-immune conditions. And this does not include the various mental health conditions such as depression that can also have a spirit component.

The entertainer Stephen Fry did a couple of programmes about his manic-depression, or what is nowadays called being bi-polar. And he spoke very movingly and openly about his condition, and explored it in others. But at the end of the day, it was for him a biochemical imbalance, a fault in his engineering, in his genes. And I am not denying there can be that dimension to it. What was standing out for me was that the guy drives himself very hard, he has a packed schedule, when there is no objective need for him to do so. He has plenty of money and fame, there will always be work for him. Aside from his abundant talents, there seems to be an insecurity driving him too. And when we let ourselves be driven in this way, there are other parts we do not listen to. And those soul parts will make their voice heard, one way or another. I can't prove it, but the connection seemed fairly obvious to me. More than that, saying it is just biochemistry fixes it, there is no way out, there is indeed something inherently wrong with us. It names it, with the power that comes with naming. And yes, it gives a certain relief: it is not 'me' after all, I'm not crazy, it's my biochemistry. But then there is no way out, and Fry decided reluctantly to take the Lithium medication. I would say to him it is you, you are probably responsible for much of these manic and depressive states, but that doesn't make you 'crazy': it means that Spirit is sending you a message to stop and to listen to yourself.

When we get out-of-sorts in one way or another, mentally or physically, and it seems intractable, I think there is a perspective in which this may be fortunate. It may be Spirit saying no, I'm not going to let you carry on in that same old way. Spirit brings about a crisis, in which our old life no longer works, but we often cannot see the way forward.

Clinging on to the Familiar

I encounter this regularly in astrology readings. People often come to me at times of major change, and this is usually reflected in the movements of the outer planets: Uranus, Neptune and Pluto. These planets are not visible to the naked eye, and so describe currents from beyond the ordinary personality: from Spirit, from the unconscious, from the collective. Uranus brings in new paradigms, often quite abruptly, that shake us out of our comfort zones; Neptune leaves us floundering as the old dissolves and more soulful, connected ways of being present themselves; while Pluto is the raw power of life that wants us to die in order that the new can be re-born.

It can be very confusing, very difficult, as we hang on to the old and desperately try to make it work. We looked at these crises in the East, from the point of view of Spirit trying to move life forward, of something new entering our consciousness. From the South, the emphasis, or the lens, in these crises is the wounded problematic parts of ourselves becoming highlighted. The two seem to go together. The times in our lives that have been the most difficult and painful are often also associated with the times when we went through the greatest transformations. And from the West, it involves going deep within and incarnating the new self.

Looks Within and the Bear

The West is also the 'looks within' place, where we find our deepest dreaming. In the same way that the East is associated with the sunrise and new life, so is the West associated with sunset and looking within, and the 'dark night of the soul' that can entail. The Bear, who hibernates in winter, and goes to the deep dreaming place, is associated with the West. Because he eats honey, he is also associated with the sweetness of life: let us not forget that in our talk of dark nights of the soul! Out of these difficult places – the stings of the bees – comes new life with a new sweetness.

The Underworld Journey

These are Underworld Journeys. Coleridge's ancient mariner shot an albatross – a bad omen – and from then on, his ship encountered bad luck, to put it mildly. It became stranded, everyone died, and the mariner was taken to hell and back. Ever afterwards, he was driven to tell his story to whoever he felt could listen. He had a look in his eye:

> *"By thy long grey beard and glittering eye,*
> *Now wherefore stoppst thou me?"*

asks the wedding guest that the mariner has buttonholed on the way in to the wedding. But the guest was soon gripped, and missed the ordinary celebrations of life that were going on as he heard this darker tale.

There is also this quote from Goethe:

"And so long as you haven't experienced this: to die and so to grow, you are only a troubled guest on the dark Earth."

When we are truly in the Underworld, we are dismembered. Nothing in our life seems to work anymore. It is TS Eliot's *The Waste Land*, which refers to our collective underworld journey post-Christianity:

"What are the roots that clutch, what branches grow
Out of this stony rubbish? Son of man,
You cannot say, or guess, for you know only
A heap of broken images."

The Underworld is a time both personally and collectively when the old meanings have broken down, and the new has yet to be born. This is not something we choose, for generally we hang on for dear life to what currently gives our life meaning.

Pluto's Abduction of Proserpina

Astrologers use a story about the planet/God Pluto as the archetypal description of this process. Pluto was Lord of the Underworld, and one day he abducted Proserpina (Greek Persephone), young daughter of the fertility goddess Ceres. Ceres was left distraught, unable to find her daughter and not knowing what had happened to her. In her distress, the permanent state of summer that had existed on the Earth came to an end, the leaves fell from the trees, the Sun cooled and life withdrew. Eventually, Helios, the Sun, who sees everything, came to Ceres' aid and told him what had happened to Proserpina, who had been forcibly married to, and in some versions raped by, Pluto.

After some negotiation, it was agreed that Proserpina would

return for six months of the year to be with her mother, and for the other six months she would return to be with her husband. And so, for six months of the year, Ceres rejoiced while her daughter was with her, and summer returned to the Earth. And for the six months she was with Pluto, winter returned. And this is how the seasons came about.

It is just the same with the individual human life: there are periods of activity and expansion, and periods of withdrawal and re-dreaming of who we are. It is when we resist those natural cycles (as we often do) that the trouble starts.

In the case of Ceres, Jupiter, king of the gods, had given Pluto permission to abduct Proserpina, because he understood that Ceres would never let her daughter go willingly. This reflects a sometimes brutal law of life, that it must move on. Proserpina was inducted forcibly into the next stage of life – from girl to woman – because her mother was not going to let that happen. And because of her resistance, the Earth turned to a wasteland.

Life has to Move Forward

It is the same with these crises, that can cost us our health. We are like Ceres, wanting things back as they were, and mourning their loss. Meanwhile new life is gestating within, Proserpina is in the Underworld, and that is something we can tune into. It is not under our control, it is a new imagining of who we are, given to us by Spirit. It is a time when old traumas start to spontaneously heal, a time of Soul Retrieval, as well as time for a new stage of life to unfold. These things often go together. The sense renewal at the end of these periods can be deep and joyful.

My Own Underworld Journey (One of Them!)

For myself, I was smitten with chronic fatigue in 1992. I was 34, and had just spent ten years working for a Buddhist organisation, rising to the top of a local branch that had residential communities, businesses, a country retreat centre and an urban teaching centre. I was mainly concerned with heading off a collapse that had been threatening it when I took the job that nobody else wanted. After three years, we succeeded, and instead it was me that collapsed. I did not believe in the institutions we were trying to reshape and to save. But I was young and had something to prove. It gave me a certain kind of practical confidence. It was, however, at the cost of listening to myself. It was an old conflict in me coming to a head: my early upbringing, which said I must visibly 'achieve'; and the Bear in me that wanted to dream and live authentically from that dream, with no thought as to how it measured up by other people's criteria.

It was a mixed thing, as these things often are. The project that had compounded my tendency to be wilful, to be ruled by my head and 'worthy' ideals, had also given me that confidence that I could run an organisation. The fatigue deepened, and there was very little I could do for several years. It wasn't tiredness, it was more like the plug had been pulled on my life-force, which up till then I had taken for granted as mine to do with as I wished. One of the first things I started to learn was that I was not in control in the way that I thought I was. Something bigger or deeper was calling the shots, and always had been, and at a certain point it said we're not going to let you carry on treating yourself like this.

And what I found was that when I listened to the things that really 'did it' for me – shamanism and astrology – I had plenty of energy. Apart from that, I was 'given' just enough to keep life going. And after about a year of this, I felt I had been taken somewhere deep, as though I was on a long journey to a distant realm; and at the same time, I felt like I had had a major operation on my abdomen, psychically speaking. All this didn't stop me trying to carry on in the old way, dreaming up practical projects to prove to myself that I was a 'valid' person, then finding I did not have the energy to continue them. Nothing I tried in that sort of way worked. It probably took me about another 15 years to finally knock that one on the head. Even now, I will get the odd twinge of fatigue when I start putting my ideas of what I want to happen before what my feelings are telling me. You could say I was being taken out of a one-sidedly masculine approach, which was how I had been raised, and what the wider culture tends to value, and into a more listening, less goal-oriented, feminine approach.

As I listened more, so was Spirit able to trust me more, trust that I wouldn't head off – at least too much – in that one-sided way. And so, I was given a dream, that I related earlier, suggesting I follow Shamanism and establish the Buddhist community I was now living in as a public Buddhist centre. This was the beginning of the actualisation, the living, of that deep dream place I had now been in for several years (a dream place which has remained ongoing). And it was because I was operating in a new way, speaking more from my heart and less from the teachings that I was 'supposed' to be transmitting, that there was a strong response, both from people who came along, who connected, and with the 'authorities', who felt they had lost control of me. But that's religion for you.

So that was me slowly emerging from the Underworld Journey, being me in a very different way, with a new element of Spirit that was gradually re-arranging everything in my life, and which would a couple of years later take me into a completely new life that had its own set of gifts and challenges.

What has Authority in Your Life?

What was occurring was also what I described earlier as a Psychosynthesis, and which I have also put in terms of the Shamanic Illness: I had felt deeply out of sorts, no longer able to function, and it was only when I learned to listen to the voice of Spirit – which is essentially a solitary journey, and often unsupported in our culture – that I could be re-born. It is also a question of what has authority in your life: the voices of the collective around you, urging you to conform, and offering you recognition and belonging in return; or the voice within, the voice from the universe, offering you your very soul, and the fulfilment that comes from living that?

That is a modern way of putting the crisis that the proto-Shaman may have to go through, of becoming ill until she heeds the call of the Spirits. It is so much easier to live the life of everyone around us, and so much harder to live with the exacting demands of the Spirit, which needs us to be a clear channel, a hollow bone, to do her work; and that means encountering and forming a relationship with our demons, all those sides that are normally kept unconscious, left unlived, and where necessary projected onto others. These 'demons', this shadow side, is not just the troubling, tormented aspects – it is also the gifts. It is no surprise that many of the proto-shamans become ill first, because the life they are being called to is so much more demanding. Not just in terms of the healings they are asked to do, on top of the demands of day-to-day living, but the extra inner task of being truly with themselves – with the Spirits – and the demands that makes, and the courage it requires. If you read accounts of them, they are usually fallible human beings with plenty of faults, and they don't always measure up, and neither do we.

Spears of Twilight is an anthropological field study by Philippe D'Escola of the Achuar people in the Amazon, who had had little contact with modern people. The Shamans within the tribe had rivalries (as do writers and other professions nowadays), and many of them frequently did 'bad magic' to each other. I'm sure we can do better than that!

Shamans are also Regular People

An important West point to note is that traditional shamans and healers still had regular lives and had to earn a living. They were not split off into a separate 'holy' category and materially supported by the community as such. And this is good for many reasons. *Rolling Thunder* is an account by Doug Boyd of the modern Medicine man of the same name. He worked on the railways during the week, and did his healing and ceremonial work at the weekends, for which he was widely known and respected. Someone of his calibre could probably have done a lot more healing work if he hadn't had such a demanding day-job. But the ways of Spirit need to be trusted. There would have been good reasons for it, and those reasons may never be known.

Leave Space to Dream

A lot of good healing and teaching work can be accomplished in a short space of time. What matters is the dreaming in between, so that we have the deeper resources of Spirit to do the work. This is how I work with astrology. I do at most one or two readings a week (usually over the internet) and I am fully present for them, and I give deeply of myself, and I love doing it, and it seems to give a lot to the astrologee (what else shall I call them? 'Client' makes it sound like essentially a business transaction, which is certainly isn't, though I think it is important that the person having the reading gives something.) If I do more readings than that, I quickly start to notice myself becoming 'thinner', that what I say is not so fresh and can seem repetitive. Again, we never know the whys and wherefores of the Spirit – God moves in mysterious ways! – and some people may feel called to earn their living full time from healing and teaching work, and to develop the trust that Spirit will provide in what is often a hand-to-mouth existence.

Burn-out

But for others, working in this way leads to 'burn-out', a West imbalance, fuelled by unacknowledged needs from the South. Again, let us not judge: sometimes that is people's path, sometimes that is precisely how they learn. The chronic fatigue of my early thirties was precisely a case of this sort of burn-out, where I put my drives for recognition and achievement before the authentic yearnings from within, because I did not take them seriously enough, did not think they mattered enough. But how else would I have learnt this? I needed to be cracked open in order to listen.

Healing is not a Profession

This work is deep, it takes a lot of our resources. It is not a 'profession' in the sense of something that is done 9-to-5, and which gives a good living and an identity. Let Spirit run it, don't go seeking people to heal and to teach. Don't make it your identity, find some other description of yourself at parties! If you get out of the way, that leaves Spirit more room to send the people your way who you particularly can help. If someone comes your way, trust it. If no-one is coming your way, trust it. Really, we are moving on to the North now, the place of the Elder and Wisdom. But first we need to learn the lessons of the West as we journey round the Wheel, and here it is about how to be with that Spirit calling in the physical world as it travels across from the East and into material existence.

Living with the Shamanic Illness

If we find ourselves in the 'Shamanic illness', it can be a very difficult time, partly because in our society there is little understanding of its real nature. Our lives no longer seem to work, we may not be able to earn a living or easily join in social or family activities. You may require disability benefits for a while, and for that the illness has to be seen as 'real' and not merely 'psychological'. Because these ailments are not always obvious, the sufferers can expend a lot of energy proving to others that their symptoms are real, and feeling worthless because they are not able to earn a living and because the state is providing for them. What I would say is do not let the illness define who you are. People sometimes have an opposite reaction where the illness becomes a get-out clause from living, from incarnating; their lives centre around it, and they become very sensitive to any discussion around the subject that might seem to threaten its centrality. They come to identify with being ill.

And like most things, it is a mixed affair. I can usually see some gift that is calling out to be lived when people have these illnesses, and the person may indeed be taking some tentative steps towards that, while at the same time getting over-identified with the illness. And I don't blame them for that, it is not an easy situation.

Spirit has a ruthless aspect. Spirit is not taking us on a fluffy journey towards the light. That is new age (in its pejorative sense!) wishful thinking. Spirit, like Pluto, is not interested in life being nice, but rather in life being real, being lived. With these illnesses, there is usually some side of us that is not being lived, as well as some trauma or damage that we need to find relationship with (and not be defined by), a spirit to welcome in and get to know.

The doctors do not always help. I was told I had 'post-viral fatigue', and I knew I hadn't had a virus, and that the doctor was just giving it a name to make it something 'real' in the language of modern medicine. I could have clung onto that, and said look there really is something wrong with me, the doctor has even given it a name! And remember the power of naming to fix things and make them hard to change. What I knew for myself was that my lack of energy was real, but there was probably not a physical cause to be found in a medical sense. In the mindset of our culture, that makes it 'merely' psychological, which is not far off saying that you are a malingerer. And we feel these cultural judgements strongly. It takes quite a lot to over-ride them. You can see why people would want to hang on to a doctor's diagnosis. But that then closes down the field of possibilities, and to that extent closes us off to the root cause, which is Spirit. I call these conditions 'soul ailments', to avoid that split into mind and body, and that insistence that we have to find a purely bodily cause, that the conventional medical establishment leads us into.

Shamanic Illness and the Medical Establishment

We are up against the imbalanced worldview of our age, and we get to engage with and understand that imbalance more deeply when these ailments occur. In calling them 'soul ailments', I am in a way calling them 'psychological'. However, the word 'psyche' is an ancient Greek word that originally meant something like 'soul'. When the medical establishment calls an ailment psychological or psychosomatic, there is an implication that it is all in your head, so it is natural to rush to the opposite extreme and become desperate to prove it is in the body. I am saying do not enter the debate on their terms. Do not be disempowered by the cultural prejudices and judgements of our time. Maybe say yes, my ailment *is* psychological! But the psyche is not just the head, it is something way bigger than even the body, and there is a level of causality that comes from there, that is the ultimate level of causality. It is what continually dreams us (another West theme) into being, and it is sending a strong message, that has a physical component, that we need to relate to ourselves in a different way. It may be a long and gradual process, these things often are, the Shamanic Path itself is slow-burn; progress, finding that new balance, is incremental.

Spirit Means Business

Spirit means business. Just as the proto-Shaman could die from their illness if they were not willing to heed the call of the Spirits – which, in a broader sense, is themselves too – so too can these soul ailments take over our lives and make us sicker and sicker and give us an early death if we are not sufficiently willing to rise to their call. Death is a minor event from the point of view of Spirit, and if we die, so be it, but at least Spirit tried. Because that is what we are here to do: to answer the calls of embodied existence, and if we are not willing to do that, then what is the point of being here?

These Soul Ailments, these Shamanic Illnesses, call for a deep journey into who we are, and a willingness to live out our gifts, however much self-doubt we have, and to make friends with, and to stop judging, all our 'faults'. It is very much the Underworld Journey, from which we return with gold, something that is truly our own to live by. And begin to transition to the North of the Wheel, for we now have some hard-won wisdom that is our own.

The Real Qualification

It is this Journey that is the real qualification to be a teacher or healer. You can learn the basics of the Medicine Wheel – with your head at any rate – in half an hour. Similarly, with any of these things like Pipe Ceremonies or Shamanic Journeying or Sweatlodges. But it is our relationship to these things that matter, and that comes back to our relationship to ourself and to the spirits. Like I said, it is not a 'profession' where you attend a course and get a certificate and that is your qualification to be a shamanic healer or whatever it is (though you may find it offered in that form.) This 'real' qualification may take decades, and it is something you know for yourself. You don't teach because somebody else 'authorises' you, only you can do that.

I observed the lack of this process in my old Buddhist teacher. He was English, and spent 20 years in the East practising and studying Buddhism. He had a measure of insight come to him aged 16 while reading one of the Scriptures, and that was both the best and the worst thing that ever happened to him. He began writing about and teaching Buddhism in his early twenties, based on that measure of insight. But what he had to say never moved on in a big way, he just elaborated on his original insight which, though there could be a certain brilliance at times, was one-sidedly intellectual. He was very identified with this intellectual capacity, and needed those around him to see the world as he did. In a way, his disciples ended up like him: a certain kind of clarity about Buddhism, but emotionally arrested. This lack of emotional development, and lack of encounter with the shadow, was also manifest in the mess of casual sexual liaisons the teacher entered into with dozens of his students – for their benefit, naturally. He never went on the Underworld Journey, never allowed himself to be dismembered and to come back renewed, with that gleam of the ancient mariner in his eye.

The Vision Alone is not Enough

It is not enough, in other words, to have the vision alone. Many people have epiphanies in this way. The East needs to meet the South, the underlying emotional nature, through which it becomes conscious (if we choose) and we are no longer blindly run by it. The West is where we live this new synergy, it is how we become the Adult in a deeper sense, rather than the outwardly responsible, but inwardly conformist individual, which is the conventional conception of the Adult.

Death

Death, being the dissolution of the physical body, is also found in the West, where the sun sets. Our whole life is, in a way, a preparation for death. Death is something that most of us are afraid of. It is natural to be afraid of death, because it is the unknown in every possible way. Everything we know, everything that makes us feel solid – our body, our name, our relationships, our property, this world itself – is taken away from us. This prospect can be terrifying.

Someone I know was dying in his late 80s and made a terrible fuss about it. When he was off the morphine and knew what was going on, he was even crying, he was so upset and afraid, which men of his generation did not do. He had a gift for playing, which he continued to do right up until he got ill, and he just wanted to carry on playing. Eventually he died, and a friend encountered him after the event, looking rather sheepish after all the fuss he had made, because he was fine!

The Fear of Change

We have the natural fear of death, which is simply the logical corollary of the resistance to change that many of us put up during life itself. We may think we are open to change, but look for example at the 2016 EU referendum in the UK. The country voted narrowly to leave the EU, and many people who wanted to remain in the EU were exhibiting some of the symptoms of trauma. I am not taking sides on this one, in my opinion both views had their merits. It was fundamentally about two different ideas of what the UK is, two different nationalisms in a way. But it showed how fragile many of us are, that we have to prop ourselves up with an idea of a collective that we belong to. This is very different to an appreciation of the merits of that collective – I think it is important that we have a healthy appreciation in that respect, and the disappointment of those of us who appreciated the merits of the EU was very understandable. But it went way beyond that, and was visible in the lashing out, that seemed to go on for years, against those that voted differently. Now I am not saying that those who voted Leave are any less fragile in their sense of identity, I don't think they are, it was just that their fragility was not exposed. I am doing my best to keep politics out of a very politically loaded subject, and I am only raising it because it provides such a good example of the way we cling on to ideas of who we are, as a way of resisting the flow of change that is simply the nature of things.

You see it too in the US in the way many people are furiously identified with being either Republican or Democrat, and demonise those of the other party. We will explore this very human tendency to polarise in our views when we do the North. But for now, it is enough to note that Death asks of us the very opposite of this (often unconscious) clinging to an identity. And hopefully the process of living gradually softens and loosens us in this respect, so that by the time we become to die, it is no longer so scary, it will become something we look forward to. A friend was telling me how when his father was dying, he was animated and excited, looking forward to the adventure. Now that is the way to go.

Another friend was present when her father, who was over 100, died. And his spirit began to shine strongly as he withdrew from the body. And when he went, she rung up her brother and told him excitedly about their father dying. She was so moved and thrilled by the experience, she forgot that it would be rather different for her brother.

Religion and the Fear of Death

The natural fear we experience at the prospect of death has become exaggerated in our culture. The fear of what might happen after death if you were not 'good' was used by the church as a way of controlling people. I think it is important to remember that the church was not simply an external oppressor: that sense of certainty and control that the church gave was reassuring for people, the church was also an expression of what the collective wanted. To get a sense of that, just look at the modern-day allegiances we have to political parties and nationality – as outlined above – and how strong that can be. And how crazy it can make us when it is threatened.

The church offered eternity in hell for those who were 'bad' and outlined in elaborate detail the awful tortures people would be subject to. For ever. It is beyond our grasp; it is too awful to imagine. It wasn't just the Catholic Church that behaved in this way. Tibetan Buddhism also has scriptures that outline the various types of hell that you can go to after death if you haven't been 'good', and again these descriptions are awful. Tibetan Buddhism has a get-out clause in that these tortures are not for ever; things can eventually change. But all the same, the timescales can be eons, so they may as well be for ever. We often idealise Tibetan Buddhism in the West, because it is a foreign culture that appears to have a spirituality that we have lost. Indigenous cultures get idealised for the same reasons. But people are people wherever you go, with the same failings. And these Tibetan scriptures point to the attempted level of control on in its institutionalised side.

So, we have this cultural baggage from the past, which we may be unconscious of, but it is still operative, just as are notions of spirit versus the body, which has been inherited by science in the mind-body split. Death as the Grim Reaper is still floating around in the collective.

Death the Modern Way: Extinction

There is also baggage from the present, in the notion that material reality is all that there is, and death means extinction. This position is firstly a logical fallacy: science itself will tell you that the apparently solid reality in which we seem so enmeshed is a creation of the brain, even the brain itself is an image created by the brain! What is 'out there' is unknowable, the Great Mystery. So how can we know what happens after death? Secondly, it is wilfully ignorant not to take into account the numerous documented experiences of people who have died for a short while. (Netflix does a good documentary series on this called *Surviving Death.*) Not only are they sometimes given new perspectives on life through the dead relatives they meet (which could be argued away as a creation of the brain), but they sometimes also have out of body experiences in which they can see, for example, what is going on in the operating theatre in ways that are theoretically impossible.

Death and Existentialism

I have read several books by the well-known psychotherapist Irvin Yalom, who is based in California. He has a novelist's gift for telling tales from the psychotherapy room, and they are both entertaining and instructive. However, where I differ from him is that he takes an 'existential' approach, which is pretty bleak: it asserts that we are essentially alone in a meaningless universe, that any meaning in life has to be manufactured by ourselves, and that death is an extinction. I disagree with all of these positions. We are not alone, we are cared for intimately by Mother Earth, of whom we are a part. Meaning is something we discover simply by being true to ourselves, revealing a broader Spirit picture that is outside of space and time (which are constructions of the brain), in which life is replete with meaning. For reasons given, death is not an extinction; as I say, it seems wilfully ignorant to assert this in the face of so much documented evidence to the contrary. Just as, according to the psychologist Jung, it is for the same reason wilfully ignorant to deny the existence of 'psychic' abilities. It shows the 'rationalist' position to be just as susceptible to dogma as is 'superstitious' religion.

In his therapy sessions, Yalom does his best to lead his clients away from any notion of continuity after death. He sees this as a false comfort, a rationalisation of one's natural terror of extinction: his job, as he sees it, is to lead his clients towards accepting his existential positions. Personally, I find those positions somewhat horrifying. It is also bad therapy, for it is not his job to get his clients to adopt his own viewpoints, however certain he might be of them. One indigenous teacher said to me that she would ask what happened to Yalom in his childhood that he has such a bleak view of existence? And indeed, Yalom's parents were first generation Russian refugees in New York, having escaped the holocaust. There is a Jewish position that asks how can God exist after the Shoah, the Holocaust? This is understandable in the context of such unimaginable trauma. And it perhaps makes some sense of Yalom's existentialism.

Extinction as a Simple Certainty

What Yalom is also peddling is a simple certainty about death, and there is a lot to be said for simple certainties, however wrong-headed. They give comfort, in that we think we know where we stand. Of course, really, we stand nowhere, that is the true existential position, which has the Great Mystery underlying it. In medieval times there were the simple certainties of heaven and hell. Nowadays it is the certainty of extinction. Maybe there is not much to choose between them in terms of their psychological functions.

But doesn't it constitute yet another certainty to say, as I am, that life does continue after death? It all comes down to rigidity versus openness in underlying emotional attitude. I don't think it unreasonable to have a sense of the Spirit as something bigger than us, that we sometimes see out of the corner of our eye, so to speak, and that also has a sense of being outside of the usual categories of time and space. With that sort of perspective, it makes no sense to talk about death as extinction. It is a perspective we profoundly need to become full human beings, with abundant life flowing through us. It is more about experience than it is about intellectual position.

As I was writing the above, I thought what might be a remedy to our ancestral fear of heaven and hell, and our modern fear of extinction? And it came to me: have yourself buried underground for the night (See Victor Sanchez, *The Teachings of Don Carlos* p219 for details.) Feel your Mother the Earth close to you, caring for you, and reflect that it is to her that you will return after death, not to some medieval horror fantasy, nor to some modern bleak nothingness. Know that there is nothing to fear about the return to the Mother, it is rather something to be welcomed. And if you can't get yourself buried, just lie flat on the Earth from time to time and feel and reflect in the same way. She is your home.

Normalising Death

Compounding our exaggerated fears around death is a culture of not talking about it. If someone has a close relative die, we may avoid them, because we do not know what to say to them, or how to be around them. Death is indeed painful for those close to someone, because we get attached and tend not to have the vast Spirit perspective. But for the person who died, we have the sentiment that it is a bad thing, an unfortunate thing. Where did that idea come from? It suggests that the dead person has gone to a bad place. But if you look at the Medicine Wheel, what has happened is that the West, the bodily existence, has dissolved, and the person has withdrawn into the East, Spirit. Life was only ever the dreaming of the East, and dreams come to an end, as does life. As the philosopher Francis Bacon said

"It is as natural to die as to be born."

I had a dream not too long before I wrote this in which I was shown that death, from the point of view of death itself, is only a minor occurrence in the bigger scheme of things, there are thousands of lives ending all the time. I guess it is like passengers arriving at an airport and departing. From the point of view of the staff it is an everyday occurrence.

Death needs normalising. If your view of death is extinction, and there is the feeling of the grim reaper there somewhere too, then death becomes something to be avoided at all costs. Sure, this life is to be treasured, and one of the first steps in a healing process is to ask if the person wants to be well, wants to live? And they don't necessarily, even though it is in all of us to want to live, which is healthy. But that is not the same thing as desperately avoiding death. Think of the 'brave battle against cancer' that so many people have in the run-up to death, as if to show that the now-dead person wasn't some kind of loser. Sure, life can be worth fighting for, and that fight can change us profoundly, bringing us to see and value our life in ways we never did before. But within that struggle there needs to be a hanging loose, it is not a fight to be 'won', it is simply putting our desire for life centre-stage, and if it becomes obvious that Spirit has other plans, well we go with that joyfully and trustingly instead. Death is not the end of the world; it is a tiny event in a much bigger picture.

Stephen Jenkinson, author of *Die Wise*, recounts the story of when he was working in a hospice, and a 28 year-old woman was terminally ill with cancer. She did not have long to go. The woman, talking to Jenkinson, referred to her illness. Jenkinson thought no, you are in denial, your life is now your death, and you need to be with that. An illness is something you hope to recover from, and you know that's not going to happen. And then the woman's mother turned up, and referred in her daughter's presence to her fight against the illness. And Jenkinson thought well you are colluding in your daughter's denial, and that is not helping her at this time.

Meeting death joyfully is about trust. Not the natural trust we have as children, but the deeper trust we earn as adults, where we learn what to trust and what not to trust, and where behind it all is Spirit that we can always trust, a trust that deepens with time.

Grieving

For those left behind, it is important to be able to grieve. In traditional cultures, it seems that people did not have a problem with wailing loudly and expressing grief. In many modern cultures, particularly perhaps Northern European and American, we have forgotten how to grieve, and this is not good for us. It would be hugely embarrassing and awkward for many of us if someone did start to grieve in a traditional loud and heartfelt way. Grieving is something that needs to be part of everyday life, of which death is a special instance. Life is always burdening us with troubles, it seems to be its nature, and to be able to regularly speak those troubles to Spirit is a relief and a blessing.

Tear Quotas at Funerals

There is a book by social anthropologist Kate Fox called *Watching the English,* a very thorough, readable and humorous account of what the English are like in nearly every respect. And here (pp376-7) is Kate Fox talking with humour, but also a wicked accuracy, about funerals, which the English find particularly difficult. It illustrates the problem that needs addressing, which I am sure is not confined to the English:

> *"The English do not measure grief in tears. Too many tears are regarded as somewhat self-indulgent, even a bit selfish and unfair. Grief-stricken relatives who do not cry, or who cry only briefly, at a funeral are likely to be seen as showing great courtesy and consideration for others, putting on a brave face to reassure their guests, rather than demanding attention and comfort for themselves. To be more precise, and at the risk of getting into pea-counting mode again, my calculations indicate that the optimum tear-quota at an average English funeral is as follows:*
>
> *Adult males (close relatives or very close friends of the deceased): one or two brief 'eye-fillings' during the service, brusquely brushed away. Brave smiles.*
>
> *Adult Males (other): None. But maintain sombre/sympathetic expression. Sad/concerned smiles.*

Adult females (close relatives or very close friends): one or two short weeps during the service, with optional sniffles; occasional eye-filling, apologetically dabbed with hanky, in response to condolences. Brave smiles.

Adult females (other): None, or one eye-filling during service. Maintain sad/sympathetic expression. Sad/concerned smiles.

Male children (close relatives/friends): Unlimited if very young (under ten, say); older boys one weep during service. Brave smiles.

Male children (other): Same as for adult males (other).

Female children (close relatives/friends): Unlimited if very young; older girls roughly double adult female tear quota. Brave smiles.

Female children (other): None required, but brief eye-filling/sniffing during service allowed.

Quite apart from any genuine grief we may be experiencing, the prohibition on humour, the suspension of the earnestness taboo and the tear-quotas make English funerals a highly unpleasant business. We are required to switch off our humour reflex, express emotions we do not feel, and suppress most of those we do feel. On top of all this, the English regard death as rather embarrassing and unseemly, something we prefer not to think or talk about. Our instinctive response to death is a form of denial – we try to ignore it and pretend it is not happening, but this is rather hard to do at a funeral. Not surprisingly, we tend to become tongue-tied, stiff and uncomfortable... we don't know what to say to each other or what to do with our hands, resulting in a lot of mumbled so sorries, very sads *and* what can I says *– and awkward embraces or little wooden arm-pats... references to God or the afterlife are inappropriate unless one is absolutely sure of someone's faith."*

Trusting in Death

The processes of major change, the deaths and rebirths within life, build trust in what is coming next. And particularly, maybe those few times in our lives where some new element comes in, and where the old life has to go. This can be incredibly difficult and drawn out, with all sorts of painful endings along the way – people die, relationships end, jobs go, health gets lost, homes get burned down (yes, I have seen this one happen) and so on. Sometimes all this is necessary, so convulsive is our clinging on to the familiar. And out of all that, eventually, something new is born, and you say through gritted teeth that you are thankful for all that has happened, because of what came out of it, but you would never have agreed to it in advance, given the choice.

I'm not sure we can take too many of these sorts of periods in life, besides which they need many years afterwards to absorb and live out, before they tip over into the next change. What we learn on our pulses, in our bones, from these periods is that within all the difficulties there is something at bottom that can be trusted, there is a reason behind it all. Life teaches us in this way to trust the challenging times when we seem to lose so much that we hold dear, that has hitherto given us our sense of our life, because there is some new stage to come. And this is precisely how these crises not only make way for the new, but also prepare us for death, because death, more than any other transition in our lives, asks that we let go and trust, because nothing of what we know is going to be left, not even our bodies.

In particular, when close family members die, that changes us. It can be hard to put into words what it does. Both my parents died within a few years of each other, and afterwards it felt like a slow tectonic shift was taking place. The first to go was my father, and the night after he died, I dreamed about a young polar bear lying on the ground outside the caravan I was living in, like he had just been born. That was a clear sign of something new coming, but even now it is hard to say exactly what. Eighteen months after my mother died, a woman who had been turning up in dreams for some years finally appeared in my psyche, making me more whole. And, naturally, we are brought closer to death when parents die, because it is our turn next. And that is a big shift in perspective. I think these deaths, if we are not too young when they happen, are all to the good in the long-term.

Some time ago I was given some LSD (I do not generally seek these things out, I can take them or leave them.) It kept me occupied one day early in the Covid lockdown. It was a joyful experience, very different to the darker experiences I used to have decades ago on psilocybin mushrooms, and probably testament to the amount of time I have spent at my own personal coal-face. Anyway, at one point I was seeing through the gates of death, as it were, and it was the same as life, there was no difference, and both places were essentially abundant and joyful.

The image we have of death is that of the Grim Reaper. In reality, death is a benign friend at our shoulder, ready to welcome us home when the time comes. She is a constant reminder of the bigger perspective of Spirit, in relation to which all our troubles and woes are as nothing, temporary bubbles in this temporary dream called life. This is my recommendation: keep recalling death, do not avoid her, and imagine her, experience her as the benign friend at your shoulder.

And remember also that you have choice as to how you die. If you do not exercise that level of choice in how you live, then you will likely die in the same sort of way as your family members. How did they die? Do you choose to go that way? Remember that the fear of death is largely a culturally conditioned phenomenon, and in treading this path of the Medicine Wheel, we are stepping outside of those kinds of conditionings. We can make a choice to drop them, and to experience each moment afresh, without preconceptions, death included.

Finding the Inner Opposite

The West is the place where we go within and find the inner opposite, which usually means female if we are male, and vice versa. And in-so-doing we find completeness. As Jim Tree says in *The Way of the Sacred Pipe* p54,

> *"It is only when we attain a balance of both male and female sides that we can be the fullest expression of whatever it is we have been called to do."*

This coming together of masculine and feminine is symbolised in the Pipe Ceremony by the stem (male) and the bowl (female, which receives the stem). The ceremony is begun when bowl and stem are joined, and this balance of male and female stands for the balanced universe, and the new balance we are trying to find in ourselves through the ceremony.

This balancing seems to be something that happens naturally with age, at least to a degree. It involves living from the inner opposite. In Jungian terms, we are talking about the anima in a man, and the animus in a woman. It is, if you like, our soul, and for a man the soul is experienced as feminine, and vice-versa. I don't know how true this is, it is certainly not going to be true for everybody, it never is. But it is a good schema to start from.

And, schematically, it is also part of the 'mid-life crisis', the point when we stop living by the received values of the world, and turn within to find our own.

Astrology, Mid-life and the Inner Opposite

I encounter this process regularly in astrology readings. Most of the people who come to me are women, and it happens almost like clockwork: they are in the second half of life, and there are issues around knowing what they want, being willing to go for it even if it doesn't suit others, and no longer feeling obliged to take care of everyone around them. If you are raising young children, you probably need to be able to put others first and be kind, or the job would be unbearable and you probably wouldn't do it very well. One friend in her early 50s told me she welcomed the menopause, that she felt like she was being re-wired, and no longer felt she had to take care of everyone else. She felt freer to live her own life. I'm a bit wary of speaking too much for women here, being a man, but it is what I have encountered in astrology readings.

By the same token, men are likely to start to feel more readily and more deeply, and to be more connected to others, in the second half of life. This has certainly been true for myself. Maybe the receding of the testosterone, which makes you an effective warrior, is one explanation. Another one is that men stop over-riding their sensitivity. It is not just about something waking up. The culture tells us it is not 'manly' to be sensitive (although less so than it used to.) There can be a wilfulness, an ignoring of one's innate sensibility, in masculine one-sidedness.

It has become a cliché to say that men are from Mars and women are from Venus, but like a lot of cliches it has become one because there is enough truth in it. Not true for everyone, by any means, but true enough. The trouble with generalisations is that they then get applied unthinkingly to every member of a group, and those people become characterised according to, for example, their gender or some minority trait, rather than as an individual, but that is not what I am doing. Let us be able to use generalisations, they often have wisdom and observation, and not shy away from them just because they also get used unthinkingly.

Mars is the planet that means we know what we want and are prepared to fight for it and be disagreeable if necessary; Venus is the planet that values feeling beauty and connectedness and good relationship. The idea is that at mid-life, men start to embody Venus, and women Mars. Hopefully. One friend, whose husband is in his sixties, finds the fact that she still can't get close to him, that he is emotionally unavailable, a source of considerable distress. Venus is not happening for him – or, more likely, he is choosing not to let her in.

This mid-life process can be pretty minimal for some people. The rigid cultural stereotypes of what genders 'should' be like does not help. For men, the polarised stereotype is that they should be out there successfully fighting the world, and any display of feeling is weak and unmanly, it is 'gay'. There has been a considerable softening of this rigid stereotype in recent decades, and men generally feel freer to experience, and display, feeling. And that may well mean that more can happen at mid-life.

There has been a parallel opening up for women as they have gradually been taken more seriously in the workplace, the traditional male world, and allowed (if that is their temperament) to become the warrior-archetype that was hitherto the preserve of the men. It also means that at mid-life there is significantly more cultural freedom to do their own balancing.

In some respects, however, it has swung in the opposite direction, as collective movements often do. 60 years ago, it was seen as shameful for the husband if his wife had to go out to work, because it meant he was not the provider he could be. Nowadays it can be experienced as shameful for women if they don't want to go out to work, but want to stay at home and take care of the children, which is a very natural thing to do, and no doubt good for the children. The warrior archetype predominates in our commercial world, and that suits some women – think Margaret Thatcher. But it will only ever suit a minority of women (and maybe men too), yet they can feel under pressure to feel that that unless they are living that warrior archetype, they are not measuring up. For a discussion of some of the different archetypes available to women, see Chapter 8 Amazon-Medial-Maternal-Hetaira.

This is where the Medicine Wheel can come in useful, because we are each different mixtures of the elements, and those mixtures will often change over time, or even on different days of the week. Someone who functions strongly from the South, from Water, is likely to be very feeling and related to others. This is their particular strength, and they are unlikely to be the sort who sees their life in terms of going out and fighting for a top spot in the world. This sort of analysis is where the Wheel can help us see the individual we are, and help us resist the cultural or familial pressures to be a particular type of person. For more on this type of analysis see Chapter 8 Jung's Typology.

The Two-Spirits

Amongst the Native Americans there are people known as Two-Spirits. This is a term of recent creation, but it describes a long tradition of people who are both male and female, not in a biological sense (though when they occur, hermaphrodites are seen as sacred) but in terms of their characters and how they live. These Two-Spirits were always held in high regard, and looked to as chiefs and healers and teachers. The reason for this is that they have both perspectives, male and female; not only that, but each perspective is developed to a high degree.

The equivalent in our culture is 'gay', but for the Native Americans, that term focuses too narrowly on sexuality, and Two-Spirit refers to something much broader than this, even though it seems most of them are what we would term 'gay'. If you search Two-Spirits on the internet, there are a number of documentaries and interviews available, which are very informative and interesting.

The reason they are called 'Two-Spirit' is because it is as if they have two spirits, male and female: it is a way of helping others understand their natures. In themselves, however, they are not two spirits but one spirit, just like the rest of us. The Two-Spirits embody what the 'inner opposite' aspect of the West is really getting at. There is no prescribed way in which they dress or live. Some are women living as men, some are men living as women, some are men living as men but with feminine attributes to the way they dress, some appear to be simply their biological gender. And I am sure they change according to the day of the week. They cannot be rigidly characterised in the way we usually do with gender.

We use the terms masculine and feminine to describe two different sets of qualities, two perspectives. That is because they are usually emphasised in the biological genders, and whether that is because of biology or culture or both is a matter of debate. Maybe it doesn't matter. And you can see how each grouping of characteristics, masculine and feminine, hang well together: the classic masculine attributes of assertion, can-do, risk, warrior, will and logical thinking; and the classic feminine attributes of feeling, relationship, sensitivity, trust in spirit and nature. And you can see how they split into different roles. Like the earlier example of the men collecting the honey high in the trees, and the women standing at the bottom urging them to leave some for the bees.

Some might say that this sort of division is due to biology, some say culture, some say it is to do with oppression of women by men. I don't want to get into what has become a politicised debate. In a way, it doesn't matter, from the point of view of our individual journey around the Medicine Wheel: the point is that in the West we are finding that other half of the split that both biology and culture have divided us into.

Some people are born with less of that divide, and in the Native American tradition they are the Two-Spirits. The rest of us, hopefully, move towards something more encompassing with age. Perhaps we need to re-evaluate gay people in modern culture. We were only recently able to accept them as full human beings, so maybe it is asking a lot to recognise that they may have added qualities of wisdom and leadership.

We humans like to think in simple, rigid categories (which we will look at more in the North.) Then we know where we stand – or we think we do – and we know what is what, what is right and what is wrong. And of course, somebody being gay is not 'natural', as we see it. Somebody being outside of the rigid categories threatens our sense of who we are, even though that person may not be actually harming us, and that can be enough to make us aggressive. That is why transgender people attract abuse, from women as well as men. Maybe it is not just that they are 'different': maybe, embodying both genders, they are more real, and that is also a threat. As the poet Rilke said

"Every angel is terrible",

for they embody a greater reality than us mortals.

As I say, the Two-Spirits were held in high regard. But not always. The young warrior men were capable of laughing at them for not being 'real' men. That tendency towards rigid boxes is perennial, and a healthy culture will have a way of dealing with it. Not so European culture. When the Spanish arrived in the New World, there were instances where they arranged for Two-Spirits to be torn apart by dogs, so offensive did they find these people. It would also have been a political move, removing people in positions of leadership.

Nowadays there is more room for the West as inner opposite. Not just in terms of the culture allowing men to be softer, and women to have careers. But also, the acceptability of transgender and gender-fluid people, our equivalent of the Two-Spirits.

Incidentally, the Native Americans have made it clear that 'Two-Spirit' is a term that they have coined to describe a tradition in their own cultures (which took different forms and had different names among all the different peoples.) They do not want people from white culture using the term to describe their own people. This seems fair enough, but in a way, it is also a pity, because I think it is such a great term, it is so descriptive.

Transgender or No Gender?

Though being transgender is now more acceptable – and not

seen as a mental illness, which would have been the case not so long ago – I think it still tends to exist within the rigid categories of male and female, which I think misses the point. The case of Jan Morris is illustrative. Born James Morris, as a young man he was well known as a journalist, and was with the team that first climbed Everest in on1953, ensuring that the news of the successful attempt got back to his newspaper without the others finding out. He was exhibiting masculine qualities to a high degree. He had known as a young child that he was in the 'wrong' body, and James Morris, who became Jan Morris, details her journey towards becoming a woman in her memoir *Conundrum*. She was one of the earliest to make the full surgical transition in her forties, and described the outcome in transcendent, ecstatic terms. Finally, she was in the 'right' body. I don't want to comment on that – I can't. As a woman, Jan Morris wrote many books – including one about the Italian city of Trieste – exhibiting the high level of feminine sensibility we would expect in one who, in the Native American context, would probably be classed as a Two-Spirit.

Forty years after her transition, in an interview, she said she realised that the point wasn't to be one gender or the other, but to be both, or even neither. She didn't express any regret for the transition she had made, and I am sure it was an important part of her whole journey.

I think it is her statement that the point is to be both or neither that is key. That is something that, hopefully, comes with age to all of us as we live the West of the Wheel. And I think it gives an interesting perspective on the transgender issue. A lot of young people who transition are determined to be one gender rather than the other, and it can be a source of considerable distress to them that they are in the 'wrong' body.

The medical establishment, inevitably, gives it a name, gender dysphoria, to 'prove' there is something wrong with you and are therefore entitled to treatment. The fancy term also makes it sound like they understand what is happening; they probably fool themselves as well as others in this sort of way. I don't think there are any easy answers here. But if there was a different culture, where it was recognised that some women live as men and vice-versa, and that the eventual aim is to be both, at least inwardly, it could considerably alleviate their suffering. It might still be the right thing to transition surgically, I really don't know and wouldn't want to say; but what I will say is that I think it is the rigidity that needs softening, where it can seem so vital that you are one gender rather than the other. It is understandable and maybe even necessary in younger people, who may well need for the present just to explore one gender. But I think the point of the transgender issue is, for many, to eventually be both. Or to not particularly have a gender inwardly – that comes to be seen as one more rigid box. It is about gradually letting go of all identities to become the 'hollow bone' for Spirit. But that is a long and difficult process, with usually a few crises along the way.

Trusting Spirit with Your Body

There is also the matter of trusting in Spirit, rather than moving too quickly to the conclusion that there is something 'wrong' with you that needs surgical intervention. By whose lights is there something 'wrong' with you? What you know is that you have been, say, born biologically female but you feel yourself to be a man and wish to live like a man. How interesting, what are the designs of Spirit in this situation? There is I think the potential for a lifetime of fruitful contemplation here. I am by no means saying that full transition is not the answer: what I am saying is that, as with many things that are not 'normal', the first port of call may be to see what Spirit has to say, rather than the medical establishment, which is easily inclined to find something 'wrong' with nature that needs 'correcting'.

Relationships – What is Love?

Relationships are one of the major things we 'do' as adults. They are a huge area. And one of the reasons they are so significant is that we can, and do, project just about any unlived quality in our psyche onto the partner. When we get involved with someone in the usual unconscious way, there is a process of editing ourselves that goes on, to become the person that the other (unconsciously) needs us to be. Meanwhile the other person also edits themselves to become who we need them to be, and at that point both people are comfortable, they feel like they have met someone who completes them, their 'soulmate', and it gets called 'love'. Being 'in love' is a kind of madness, there is no way we can see the other in a straight kind of way in that state – no doubt, however, we think we have a special insight into that person, we see all sort of wonderful qualities that others cannot see.

So frequently you have two young people in this state of madness, who decide on that basis to commit themselves to spending the rest of their lives with that other person, their 'other half'. Is it any wonder that so many marriages come to an end? I am reluctant to use the word 'fail' because an ending is just that, an ending, it doesn't help to judge it. No wonder parents and family used to have a say in who one married. Of course, they might well have had their own considerations too around wealth and social connections that could muddy the water. But they might also have brought some common sense to the matter.

Navajo Love

Here is an extract from *Coyote Medicine* (p 227-8) by Lewis Mehl-Madrona. This was Lewis in his younger days, talking to his old Navajo teacher about relationships:

> *"Hosteen Begay didn't know how old he was exactly, but his*

memories stretched back at least 83 years, and he could easily have been 90. I asked his advice about a woman I had been dating. I wanted a companion badly. He put on his glasses and stared me directly in the eyes. Then he smiled and laughed. My ears turned red and my face flushed. "It must be the bellagana in you", Hosteen said, still laughing, but not without compassion. 'Bellagana' means 'white person' in the Dineh language. "Because I doubt you will listen to me. You must stop looking for love. When the spirits want you to have love, they will bring it to you. You must devote your life to your work and children. And though it won't win them back, it will bring you peace within yourself. Shake my hand so I can feel your resolve."

He stood up and took my hand in his. We did not really shake, but rather he held on to my hand and studied me carefully. "You will not change. For all the other things you have learned, this is the one area where you prefer to remain stupid."

"But Grandfather", I said, "I need a companion, a half-side."

Finally Hosteen Begay let go of my hand. He took off his glasses. "You have watched too many of those Hollywood movies, the kind my granddaughter acts in." To him the matter was closed. But I needed to hear more. "Is it not right that a man and a woman come together in this way? Is this not what the elders teach us in the ancient stories and songs?"

"Only young men speak so stupidly and without wisdom." He smiled at me gently. "Do not even bother to answer me," he said. "I will be gone soon, before you see the wisdom of my words. You will keep trying to find this thing you call love, like a crazy teenager, until it bites you in the ass. Then maybe you will grow up."

Relationship as Crucible

I am painting a bit of a one-sided picture here to make a point. Of course, there can be genuine compatibility as well, it is not just about projection. But it is precisely the projection element that is often the growth point. It may be possible within the relationship, or it may need to come to an end. And often it seems to be that the relationship, with all its projection and all its mess at the end, and all the years that it has lasted, has provided exactly the crucible necessary for us to start to reclaim those unconscious elements.

What seems to happen most frequently is that one person starts to wake up and the other doesn't. One person is happy to carry on as they are, with the other person carrying a load of psychic contents for them – unacknowledged, of course. And the other person starts to feel trapped: their psyche is starting to open up, they are starting to want to be and to do things they haven't done before, and they maybe need to start talking about who they now are, and the other person isn't interested. In relationship, we aren't necessarily that interested in who the other actually person is, but rather in what we need them to be.

It is classic for the other person to be carrying our childhood stuff for us, ways in which we are not yet adults, either because we were damaged or not taken care of properly in childhood, or just because! It isn't necessarily very sexy to own up to the fact that to some extent your partner is Mum, that you need to someone to love you in an unconditional way because you can't love yourself: yet this is often behind the façade of the 'big, strong man'. In fact, it is why he needs to be macho in this way, precisely because behind it all he doesn't feel very secure in himself. And why he gets so jealous: he doesn't want to lose Mum's love. And by the same token, the partner may also be Dad. The world can seem like a big scary place, in which it is difficult to survive. So, you want a protector, someone who will be out there fighting in the world and bringing home the bread. Of course, the partner may be a mixture of Mum and Dad for you, and it is not gender specific either. There are ways in which we are all not sure of ourselves, it is part of being human, and we let the partner carry some of that for us. Probably not all of it: our actual parents probably carry some of it, maybe the boss too, maybe a spiritual teacher. And then our poor children have to carry all our unlived aspects. As Jung said, children are fated to live out the unlived lives of their parents.

So, there is all the parental stuff that the partner usually carries for us. I say 'usually' because I think it is the norm not to be a psychological adult when we reach physical adulthood. We may be on the way to it, but it usually takes many years, it is precisely our path. Ongoing practical responsibilities are obviously part of that process. And a sense of the sacred, of Spirit: without that, the deeper centre around which the four directions come into balance cannot properly form. We remain stunted. Capable and successful, maybe, with an ability to project authority. But without that inner connection, over-identified with our place in the world. A hospital consultant with his bow-tie, at the top of the hierarchy, too important to explain to you what is actually wrong with you, comes to mind.

And then there is the anima/animus content that the partner carries. Our very soul. Female if we are male, male if we are female. The partner doesn't just fill the psychological gaps: they carry our deeper unlived potential too. At all points, remember I am being schematic, that we don't always divide into male and female so simply. And that there is no neat dividing line between 'psychological' and our deeper potentials. To not need some kind of father-figure, for example, we need to find that metaphysical, autonomous centre within, and that is a long and deep process, with usually a few crises along the way. Projection is nothing to be ashamed of. It is necessary, for it helps identify what is unlived in our own psyches.

Marriages often start to become rocky when one partner starts to wake up and needs to start to live, for example, that father side that the other person carried. They may be the wife who has prioritised taking care of the children and the home at the expense of a career. And this is a perfectly natural process. There is nothing 'wrong' with starting out by living just one side of the psyche, it is how humans are, what we need to do usually, to start with. And then the children reach a certain age (and having children is usually a very good way of incarnating, of arriving on the planet) and the wife starts to feel there are other things she wants to do, sides that need to be lived out. In some marriages, this will be great, and the husband will support that, and maybe feel relieved that it is not just him being the provider. But for other husbands this will be a threat, not just to his role as sole provider, which makes him feel 'strong', but also because his wife is no longer the soft, gentle mothering figure that he (unconsciously) needs. If he is willing to look at that, he can change and become more whole himself. But he may not be: he may want to just carry on as he was. That is not something to judge, however frustrating it may be for the other person: there is no law saying that we have to become conscious, that we have to start listening to ourselves.

The arising of that desire to become conscious is a mysterious thing. People may carry on in the same old habitual way for decades, and then suddenly something changes. You never know if, or when it is going to happen.

Ideally, both partners will begin to withdraw the unconscious projections as life goes on. This might be unspoken; it might be quite natural. Or it can be a dynamic interchange, each helping the other see their 'stuff'. It's not always going to be a comfortable process, and a lot of honesty is required. But if each partner is secure enough in who they are, so that they can live with the other person no longer being who they used to be, then it can work, and it can be very creative.

This doesn't seem to be the norm, however. It is usually just one partner becoming conscious, and it usually becomes messy, and it provokes a crisis that is not over until the relationship is over. At which point, the unconscious 'ex' will find themselves a replacement, so that they can carry on in the same way as before (albeit maybe slightly awoken and changed by the shock of what has occurred); the conscious partner may well then need some years on their own, to get to know the new them, to be with themselves in a way they have never been before: the more whole, more balanced person that is the goal of the West.

Relationship Crises

A relationship crisis can be huge, it can be one of the few big turning points in life. A relationship can have become pivotal to who we are, with all other aspects of life – career, home, money, children, social life – intimately involved. Everything can be threatened by its ending, or possibly ending. It easily, therefore, becomes a long drawn-out process that we back into, with maybe affairs along the way. It can require a lot of courage. The process of leaving itself means affirming and valuing the new way that we are, something we may have always denied or brushed under the carpet. Because when you look back, there may have been something you were not easy about in the first place. An extreme example was Princess Diana, who said that at her wedding, she felt like 'a lamb to the slaughter'. But the pressure of our unconscious needs – what the other person is prepared to carry for us psychically, maybe also the desire to have children – can mean we over-ride that thing in us that is saying no. This seems to be quite common. And maybe the time just hasn't come yet, there is something to be lived first.

But when something is denied, it will eventually come back to bite us, hard. There is a price for putting sides of the psyche on hold. The new element of consciousness that the East brings is usually something we have always known about or sensed, but not given sufficient importance to: and suddenly here it is, demanding to be centre stage, and 'wrecking' our old life in the process. That is what the Underworld journey is about: the dismembering of our old life in order to make way for a new psychic centre. The reason we have to go to that dark, bleak place, that can seem to go on and on, is that it is hard for us to recognise that the old needs to go, that its time is up, for it has become who we are, and that is a deep thing. These crises are not easy, they are often the most difficult things we have to do in this life.

And then, maybe, you finally become certain that leaving is the right thing to do. No more going back, trying to make the old work, and denying something in yourself in the process. Clarity finally arrives. You may not have it all clearly worked out. You may not have the words for why you are doing what you are doing. You may just know that this is what you have to do. Not having the words, the reasons, can feel disempowering, it is one way the masculine can dominate the feminine. But the feminine needs to own its own power, to trust its instincts, and that opposition by 'reason' can be exactly what it needs to find and claim that power. There is the idea of the 'worthy opponent': sometimes that which opposes us, however difficult and maddening, is exactly what we need to find and claim ourselves.

The 'Crazy' Ex

Then there is the aftermath. People become deeply and energetically entangled with each other, and that can take some years to pull clear from, so that the new can be fully born. There is the "my ex is a sociopath, psychopath and a narcissist" stage that many of us go through (these were someone's exact words, but I have heard it plenty.) I think these psychological terms can become just another way of fixing and demonising someone. That is why I am wary of them. As I wrote earlier when dealing with our own 'demons', it is best not to fix ourselves by naming: the 'I am an alcoholic, or 'I am bi-polar' statements. It is the same with other people. It is not just strategy: I don't think it is fair or accurate to fix other people in this way. We are doing something to them with our minds, and that is transmissible, it is how magic works, whether dark or light.

Chances are that the ex is no better and no worse than most people, it's just that you, by virtue of your intimacy, have come up against their shadow side, and your own, and it's all got a bit tangled. OK, there will be early stages where there is strong feeling involved. But fuelling the naming is generally a need to see the ex in this sort of way. How many people have told me that their exes are 'nuts' (which is perhaps more honest than the psychological terminology)? It is a shadow projection (just as they are probably also doing to us, these things are usually two-way.) We need them to be the 'bad guy' so we can hang on to our fragile sense of ourselves as the 'good guy'. Some people can spend the rest of their lives going on about how awful one or more of their exes were.

As ever with shadow work, we need to step out of that paradigm altogether, or it is endless. It is about standing away from the fragile self (the self will always be fragile, for it is contingent) and simply observing and noting. There is a sense of richness and meaning in that, it is not the cold place that it can sound like. To put it simply, once you can stand back and let the ex be who they are, without 'awfulizing' them, you then become freer to be who you are. Then you can be fully reborn. And free, maybe, to start exploring relationship in a different kind of way, where each person is able to listen to themselves and to the other, and to be honest. That is a completely different paradigm, and not very common.

Let Spirit Send Someone Your Way

As Lewis Mehl-Madrona's Navajo teacher advocates, let Spirit send someone your way. Don't go searching. How do we know who is suitable? It is such a big area, so much can happen in it, so much alchemy, that the mere rational mind has little chance of working this one out, finding boxes to tick, as people do on dating sites. Spirit works through our instincts, our intuition, it is spontaneous. So, leave it alone. And if you find yourself strongly attracted, pay attention.

Spirit probably has something in mind. It may be long-term, it may be short-term, where each person is changed in some way and then moves on. So much more becomes possible once we become happy just to be with ourselves and not compelled to be with someone, anyone, anything apart from the scary prospect of being on our own, and the judgement as 'loser' or 'left on the shelf' that we think we might attract. There is so much judgement around relationship, and it skews everything. If you get involved with someone, no it doesn't have to last forever or it has failed, with one person being the 'bad guy' for it 'failing'. Let yourself be used by Spirit, yes be passionate, yes love, but also hang a bit loose, as we need to with everything in this temporary dream called life. Then Spirit can do its work, and you will be continually surprised.

But be prepared for Spirit tricksiness, that is often how he works. There is a shift we often need to make from that compelling, romantic impulse that can consume us, to the ability to just be collected and true to ourselves. Spirit may send you some lessons in that along the way.

You could say there are two principles, or archetypes at work here: the Spouse, who belongs in the West and who has the Earth qualities of being dependable, reliable, supportive and family oriented; and the Lover, who comes from the East and is inspirational, connected in a very personal way, otherworldly, mercurial. (They are related to the archetypes of Senex and Puer, see Chapter 8 Correlations.) The Spouse is more functional, it is about being with someone who will do the practical things necessary to raise a family. It is not particularly personal in essence. Which is why someone with a strong Lover archetype running through them will end up feeling trapped, put in a box and not listened to. I think it is rare that someone is strongly both of these archetypes. And there may be movement between these principles at different stages of life. Most of us probably begin as Lover. Then maybe we become Spouse. And maybe, when we've done that, the Lover comes back. Who knows? But it can be a useful way of looking at why relationships do or do not work in your life. Each of these can, as ever, judge the other. But if you can keep your judgement out, as well as other people's judgement of how you 'should' be in relationship, it can maybe help clarify a few things.

This does not mean that the Spouse relationship does not feel intensely and personally connected. It inevitably will do so if you are 'in love'. They may well feel like a 'soulmate'. I think it can be difficult to get perspective on this until the projections start to crumble, maybe years later, and you realise that the person you are with is not the person you thought you had married. That doesn't have to mean that the relationship cannot continue in a new way. And maybe the Lover can appear, in which it is the actual person you feel connected to, including that which is East/Otherworldly about them, rather than a projection.

You've probably noticed I have said nothing about gay relationships. I expect that a certain amount of what I have already said holds true: I can't imagine two people, of whatever orientation, not wanting the other person to carry certain parts of their psyche for them, and I would imagine similar sorts of crises when that deal starts to fragment. But beyond that I am not going to comment, as I am not qualified.

I will close this section with Kahlil Gibran's lines:

"Let there be spaces in your togetherness,
And let the winds of the heavens dance between you.
Love one another but make not a bond of love."

And William Blake's lines:

"He who binds to himself a joy
Does the wingéd life destroy;

But he who kisses the joy as it flies
Lives in eternity's Sunrise."

Sex

Sex comes with a pile of medieval baggage that we are still recovering from. The fact that the church tried to control it, in the same way that it controlled that other natural bodily activity, dancing (see Dancing in the Streets, later in the West) is a surefire indicator that sex is a way of experiencing Spirit through the body. Otherwise, why try to control it?

The counter-culture of the 1960s was a time when this repressed Dionysian spirit burst back into consciousness on a collective level. Sex was re-invented. Nowadays we have a culture in which sex is becoming controlled again, through fear of abusive or inappropriate behaviour. There is a new Puritanism. 20 years ago, people went into Sweatlodges naked. That rarely happens now. One elderly man told me that you can no longer put your grandchildren on your knee. Of course, it is right that abusive behaviour is brought to notice and curtailed. But collectives always swing to extremes, just as the counter-culture itself did. It is particularly male sexuality that has come under fire. As I say, it has in many ways been necessary. But with that has come a fear of sex.

And because we humans like to turn everything into rules, sex itself has also become a performance, the aim of which is for both partners to have an orgasm, and if one of them doesn't, then the sex has failed.

In what is known as Tantric sex, the point is not orgasms, but the experience in the moment of the flow of feeling and energy between the two partners. Now that is more like it. Anything that brings us into the present serves the designs of Spirit. Can you have sex if you are not present to yourself and the other person, but worrying about orgasms instead? Not in the Tantric sense. It is different, however, when we are young, and there is that biological imperative to reproduce fuelling the drive to have sex, even if it is just at the back of our minds. Maybe Tantric sex becomes more possible as we get older.

The reason sex can be ecstatic is because there is, at least for a while, a forgetting of self in the merging with another. When we forget ourselves, consciousness alters. It is when we are present to ourselves that, paradoxically, we can put down the burden of self. It is similar in this sense to Trance Dance (see later in the West). In both, we become present to ourselves through the Body, in a way we abandon ourselves to the Body, and when we do that, Spirit can take over. I have had experiences of Spirit presences turning up in quite profound ways in both situations.

Key to this, in both Trance Dance and Sex, is the ability to surrender to Spirit. Some people have a natural gift for this. I began to be able to, through the dance, in my early 40s. It wasn't something I could have engineered; it began to happen spontaneously. It is a gift from the East, experienced through the West, for which we provide the fertile ground through our ongoing North-South work, but we cannot directly cause it to happen.

Sex is something natural. In all aspects of life, we 'civilised' humans easily become distanced from what is natural, and become guided by ideas and moral judgements. My recommendation is to put aside all ideas of success and failure, any insecurities as to how the other person may be judging you, and simply enjoy being present with that other person.

Celibacy

It is also natural not to have sex. We have been brainwashed into thinking there is something wrong, that we are missing out, that we are undesirable, if sex isn't happening. But as with relationships, trust it if it isn't happening. It is like fasting: once you get used to it, other things can happen, you can slip into a slower, contemplative, altered consciousness in which the digestive system gets a break from being continually worked, and maybe has a chance to perform other functions.

I find when I am at my most whole, the desire for sex recedes. It is certainly not there as a hunger wanting satisfaction. This is the point about Tantric sex: it is changing the sexual act from the satisfaction of a hunger, to a blissful experience of flow of feeling and energy between two people. A heart-based, rather than genital-based, emphasis. My own experience suggests that the hunger for sex is tied to a hunger for completion that is really something that we need to find for ourselves. The deep process of the integration of masculine and feminine, that is the task of the later stages of the West.

So where does this leave celibacy? It has developed a bad reputation because of the church. How could an institution not mess up something as subtle as this, and use it for its own ends? By making sex sinful – and just about tolerable within the confines of 'holy matrimony' – people are left feeling permanently guilty by virtue of a natural impulse, and that guilt is something the church can use against people, it keeps them cowed, which is where it wants them. Celibacy itself is only required for the priests, and that is just in the Roman Catholic Church since the 12th century. It is presented as a spiritual ideal, and there is enough truth in that for them to get away with it. But really it is about economics: it is much cheaper to support a priest who does not have a family, and when he dies, any possessions he may have go to the church rather than to the family.

Because it is carried out for the wrong reasons, and insisted upon for the trainee boys at the seminaries, priests are let loose on the world who suffer from arrested emotional development. Hence the terrible problems with paedophilia. Once the church admitted this problem – and that was only because it was forced to – its response was to attempt to stamp down blindly on it, instead of addressing the training that has contributed to it: presumably because the training comes from God, so cannot be questioned.

Celibacy has a bad name, not just because of its association with repression in the church, but because nowadays we have swung to the opposite extreme (as collectives always do, about everything) so that you can feel there is something wrong if you are not having sex. But truly, celibacy is not about an absence, but about the blissful experience of union within oneself, it is the androgynous state that we associate with angels. It is not something that can be forced. As ever, it is about where the Spirit is taking us, rather than about an idea of where we would like to be. If you find yourself going in that direction, welcome it, nurture it. It can happen in the context of a relationship, for all the right reasons. Usually, it means the relationship is over, bar the shouting, which may take some years. But it can also represent a natural deepening: this is maybe another brainwashing, that sex has to be happening, that we need to find our way out of.

I was told in a dream some years ago that I would not be in another relationship until I was happy not being in one. And I had a cheetah on a leash, that kept bounding away from me, trying to chase prey. It has felt like a big ask that Spirit is making of me. But what can one do? I am honoured that Spirit is asking this, because it is not easy. And I think that paradoxically what I am being offered is freedom: the cheetah is not currently free. Once I can find this self-containment, then I will also contain the power and beauty of the natural world. And I will be free around sex and relationships, in that it will not be something I feel I have to have, but something in which I have complete choice. Sometimes I have that containment, and sometimes I don't, and when I don't, I easily forget that it is possible. It happens in fits and starts, like the rest of my relationship to myself: sometimes I am more conscious, and truly at the coalface, so to speak. A lot of the time I am sort of there, and sometimes not at all. But I try not to judge myself for this, because I think it is how we all work. Progress, wholeness, balance proceeds for us in this slightly haphazard way.

Ceremony

The line travelling from East to West across the Medicine Wheel is known as the Blue Road. It is the route by which Spirit (the East) enters this physical reality (the West). Spirit cannot be 'caused' to enter this reality: it is beyond our mere human machinations. The Blue Road is the non-ordinary aspect of existence, the sacred. It is the Red Road, running from North to South and back again, that is the work of the everyday, where we have choice and control about how we think, feel and act.

Ceremony is all those means whereby we create conditions to give thanks to and talk to Spirit, and for Spirit to speak to us and act on behalf of ourselves or others. Whether Spirit will or not, is up to Spirit. But done with good intent, Spirit does turn up, it is a presence we can feel, everything takes a shift, and everything that happens in that space is of significance and needs to be noted.

Creativity

Creativity is a form of Ceremony in that we are giving form to an impulse from Spirit. It is, you could say, the fullest expression of the West. It is when we incarnate the most. We are here so that Spirit can show up in this physical reality. When we create, we are taking something from the depths of our Spirit, something from our Centre that is most who we are, and giving form to it. Anything can be a creative act if we give ourselves fully to it. It can take years of preparation, and is an expression of where our being has got to, now. The actual act of creation may not take long, but there may be a whole life experience behind it. A Zen painter may spend 15 years looking at bamboos. He absorbs the bamboos; he becomes the bamboos. Then maybe, after all that time, and with a few deft strokes, he paints the bamboos. And in-so-doing he captures the spirit of the bamboo, and anyone looking at the painting feels that too.

People have been creating since the earliest times. There are cave paintings in Europe that go back around 65,000 years, and may have been painted by Neanderthals. They are said to show a sensibility as sophisticated as anything we have today. They were not 'primitive'.

Creativity is something we humans need to bring to our lives to experience meaning, because then we are bringing something of ourselves to the table. That can be scary, much scarier than being judged for anything else, for our very soul is on display. That is why it can be so painful for writers when they get critical reviews in the papers, there for the whole world to see. It is a fire of self-doubt that maybe all of us have to go through at one time or another. That ordeal is an initiation in itself, and it makes us stronger and surer of who we are. For more on thinking as a creative act, go to the Original Thought section in Chapter 5, the North.

The Sacred and the Everyday

There is a long chapter in *The Circle of Life* by James David Audlin, a book about the Native American ways, where the author talks about the difference between the sacred and the everyday. In a way it is simple: the sacred is that which is not everyday, anything that is unusual or that takes us out of the everyday with its predictability and safety. The wilderness, poisonous plants, dangerous animals, and lightning are examples. Or we create spaces and rituals that are not everyday. So, a Sweatlodge will be built, to be used on particular occasions (not because it is 'Sunday' as we do, but because it is needed, someone or the whole community needs help.) The Sweatlodge will be in an out-of-the way, not very well-known place. Eventually, that out-of-the-way place becomes familiar, so the Sweatlodge is moved to a new place to keep that element of freshness and the sense of the sacred that comes with that.

When something is unusual, we see it with fresh eyes, we are brought right into the present, we are not in the past (the South) where we respond automatically, using old memories and expectations. This brings out an important feature of the West: it is about the present, it is about being really here, really incarnated, if you like. That is when we are truly living. Rupert Sheldrake, the famous scientist turned mystic (whose TED talk on morphic resonance was eventually taken down for not being sufficiently 'scientific') talks about all heightened experience as that which brings us into the present. This is one of the purposes of the 'extreme' heat in the Sweatlodge: it takes us out of our heads, which are usually anywhere but in the present, and into our bodies and into hearts, brings us into what we are feeling and experiencing, now. A Vision Quest, out on the hillside with nothing to distract us except the natural world (which is never a distraction, but through its beauty and abundance and reflection of ourselves, an aid to being present), also has this effect. Sheldrake brings in some other interesting ways: extreme sports bring us into the present, as do pets, and this is part of their appeal. Dance, taking is into the body and into feeling, also has this effect. The list could go on.

The Everyday is also the Sacred

Part of the function of ceremony is to bring us into the present. It's not as though 'the sacred' is some special, faraway dimension. It is simply what we experience when we are fully present and connected to that which has most value for us. In Shamanic Journeying, we talk about 'this world' and 'the otherworld' as though they are separate places. That is a useful fiction for our everyday, distracted selves, for it is indeed very hard to be present in this way when we are busy. In *Spears of Twilight,* Philippe D'Escola refers to some of the Achuar in the Amazon (with whom he lived for two years) as continually praying about whatever activity it is they are doing. They are, in other words, in their hearts, and actively bringing good intentions to whatever they are doing, intentions that connect them to the sacred. There is no reason this should not be possible if life is relatively simple (which does not mean not sometimes strenuous also). In a busy city it would no doubt be harder. But the principle remains, of being continually mindful of the sacred, of that which has most value.

Ceremony is just a particular instance of something we want to be doing anyway, but generally don't manage to do. Audlin points out that traditionally (as mentioned earlier in this Chapter), children and old people are seen as having an ongoing experience of Spirit, and that ceremony is primarily for the adults, the busyness of whose lives inclines them towards a forgetting of Spirit. 'Special' occasions are created that are out of the ordinary to invoke Spirit. And 'special' objects too that are sacred, that are only brought out on ceremonial occasions, such as the Pipe. Over time, these ceremonies and objects really do acquire a power of their own, through repetition. They are not just artifices. So, if you like, we project the sacred out onto objects and ceremonies, which do gain a real power of their own as a result; but that sense of the sacred needs to gradually become internalised, claimed as an ongoing sense and power within, like the guys in the Amazon whose lives are a continual prayer. And also experienced as an attribute of the entire natural world. The connection with Spirit is where any real power in our lives comes from, not from position or wealth or force of personality.

My Medicine Wheel stones (see Chapter 1) are for me carriers of Spirit, and that has grown over time; the power is there in those stones, and other people can feel it. But at the same time, it causes that power to grow in me too. These objects are not just symbols, artifices, as the language of projection suggests. My East stone *is* the East, it doesn't just 'stand for' it.

The Woman Who Went to the Moon

There is a very good documentary film on CG Jung called *Matter of Heart*. In it his pupil Marie-Louise von Franz talks about her first encounter with Jung, who was recounting the story of a patient's dream in which, said Jung, she went to the Moon. You mean she dreamed she went to the Moon? replied von Franz, and Jung said no, she went to the Moon. Von Franz thought Jung must be crazy, but then later realised that Jung treats the psyche as an objective reality, and that what happens in dreams is no less real than waking experience. This is a strange way of looking at the world for us modern people. But if you can get that, you will get how my East Medicine Stone *is* the East, and how the Pipe is a sacred being in its own right and needs to be treated as such. And how, if you are an astrologer, the planets really do cause events in our lives (as opposed to the mealy-mouthed explanation that the planets 'reflect' events in our lives, a concession to rationalism by modern astrologers that neuters our great art.)

Creating our own Ceremonies

Community plays a central part in most ceremonies, which we shall look at in the North. As we saw in the section in Chapter 1, Origins of the Wheel and Making it Your Own, we do not have traditional ceremonies in the modern world. So we have to invent them. We draw on tradition for inspiration with the Sweatlodge or the Pipe Ceremony, for example. We need to ignore the fundamentalist voices that say any use of such ceremonies is cultural appropriation.

The Qualification to Hold Ceremonies

And we probably need to ignore anyone who says you have to train for ten years before you can run a Sweatlodge, because they may well be missing the point. *The real qualification to hold such ceremonies is your relationship with yourself and with Spirit*. Have you allowed your conventional, collective personality to loosen to such a degree that Spirit is calling the shots? It often takes the sort of crises we have been looking at, along with a decent trip to the Underworld and an encounter with the Shadow, to create that sort of relationship with ourself. From that place, we have some wisdom of our own. That is what 'authenticity' really means, it means we are the 'author', rather than the outer knowledge of a prescribed way of doing something.

When someone talks about the need for a ten-year training in running Sweatlodges, I think the real purpose behind this is not technical competence (which can be learnt very quickly): it is about forming the right relationship, a deep relationship, with Spirit. For then Spirit will be in the lodge, and people can be helped and healed. And it will usually take at least ten years to create this sort of relationship with ourselves and with Spirit.

But there are other ways it can happen. Life will do it for us, if we remain open and keep rising to the occasion, which usually means being prepared to stay with what is happening. Only you can 'authenticate' yourself in this regard, though some encouragement from others does not go amiss.

I'd say it has taken me 40 years to reach the point where I don't feel reservations about leading ceremonies. That may sound extreme, but it doesn't feel like it. Sure, along the way I have done plenty of work individually with people, and have danced in and out of leading collective events/groups. But I always felt there were still things to sort, balances to be found. Of course, there always will be. What I mean in particular is that recently I have come to feel sufficient balance of 'masculine' and 'feminine' within myself, and that I have a strong enough relationship with my shadow elements, to have the presence necessary for Spirit to be able to work effectively and consistently through me in that sort of situation.

Life as Ceremony

Ceremony is essentially about bringing the sacred into our lives, often with a specific intention. Maybe the best preparation for holding ceremonies is not ceremonies themselves, but an ongoing attitude of holding our highest intention, our deepest intention in our heart. It is always good to do a bit of prayer and ceremony, especially with others. But they are not an end in themselves: that is when you have religion. They are a reminder of how to live the rest of the time. If you hold your intentions fulsomely and impeccably in your heart, you will find that your prayers – another word for intention – are answered by the universe, as always in its own way, without the need for formal ceremonies.

Shamanic Journeying

I started out putting Shamanic Journeying in the East of the Wheel, because I thought it's about making direct contact with Spirit. But then I realised that that is also what ceremony is about, and journeying is ceremony, because it is generally done in specific, ritual ways. And its purpose is to bring Spirit reality, the East, into physical reality, the West.

Spirit Vision is what we are aiming to encounter, to be nourished by, when we undertake what gets called Shamanic Journeying. The usual practice has become to lie down blindfolded to the sound of rhythmic drumming, either live or recorded. Our consciousness shifts, and we are able to sense, and be inspired and nourished by, Spirit. It is sometimes called the Otherworld, and it is sometimes divided into three – the Lower, Middle and Upper Worlds. These are useful categories. This is not the place for a fuller description of these practices.

Making your own Otherworld Connections

But one point needs to be made, around the perennial human tendency to confuse forms with realities, and to make those forms the 'correct' ones. Many people think that they cannot do shamanic journeying because they may not have a clear perception of travelling to another world, or having a 'spirit guide' talk to them. And sometimes they struggle for years with this. In reality, we all have our own ways of being nourished by the Otherworld. It is a matter of discerning and trusting those ways. It may be that you feel the living presence of trees. Or that ideas and insights sometimes come to you out of nowhere, as it seems. Or, like me, when you dance, something takes you over, but you may not know what it is, and it doesn't have to have a name either. Or you have significant dreams. Or you just feel a bit of a nudge to do something, and it feels right, so you do it.

As ever, it is about finding whatever is already there in you, what comes naturally, and trusting it. But our education system and early life often teaches us to trust the ideas and perceptions of others, rather than our own. So, when it comes to shamanic journeying, we trust the ideas of others – usually, in this case, the three worlds – and try to fit our experience around that. For some, that may work. But it is putting the cart before the horse. As with the Medicine Wheel, we need to keep coming back to our own perceptions and connections, and trusting them and running with them.

Spirit and the Body

Shamanic Journeying is usually taught as a method where we lie down with a blindfold over our eyes, and let ourselves be taken on a journey to the sound of rhythmic drumming. That is all well and good. It works, and it can effect profound changes and healings. It is often billed as 'core shamanism', which gives an impression of a method that is traditional and tens of thousands of years old. Which, in a way, it is. Except that traditional shamans would often move and dance as they drummed for themselves (as opposed to being drummed for while lying down.)

Chosen by the Spirits

In her book *Chosen by the Spirits,* Sarangerel describes this way, calling it 'Ongod Orood'. Sarangerel was half-European, half-Buryat and had a traditional Buryat training. She says that if you feel attracted towards Shamanism, then you have indeed been 'chosen by the spirits' yourself. This is a wonderfully empowering thing to say, coming from a traditionally trained person, and takes much of the preciousness out of the subject. Sometimes the fiercest defenders of 'authenticity' are Westerners with little experience of indigenous traditions. And some indigenous people can be like this too, while others (like Sarangerel) can be generous and encouraging of us to find our own ways, and not to doubt that we are the 'real thing'. Which has my wholehearted approval! I had these opposite experiences in Sweatlodges I attended. One native guy, trained on the reservation, knew his stuff and there was much beauty in the lodges he ran. But the message also was that none of us could even think of running one ourselves. And then a woman from another reservation turned up and led a lodge, as I mentioned earlier in Chapter 1. She was clearly genuine and of some standing. It was also clear that she hadn't been formally trained in leading a lodge – she said she'd brought a Spirit with her in her handbag – but she didn't care. She just did whatever, and encouraged us all to go out and lead lodges for the benefit of other people. And I had a feeling there was an element in her of defying the men and their strict protocols! So, two very different approaches: one according to tradition, and one more from the heart. 'Male' and 'female'. And there is room for both. In her novel *Ceremony,* Leslie Marmon Silko addresses the need to update traditional ceremonies in keeping with the times and with the experiences people have been through.

Ongod Orood

Sarangerel writes:

> *"The state is called Ongod Orood, meaning the state of having the Ongon spirits inside the body. While you are Ongod Orood, you retain awareness of your surroundings, but your senses are heightened through your merging with the spirits. You will be able to see spiritual beings and forces, something that you will need for your shamanic work. You may have the sensation that you are working in two realities at once: the physical reality of your body and the ritual space and the ecstatic reality of spirit.*
>
> *While you are embodying the spirits, you are in perfect safety; the spirits will not allow any harm to come to your body while they are in it. You may find yourself singing songs you have never heard, doing ritual actions you have never learned, dancing dances you have never seen. This is because your udha (spirit helper) is working directly through you and teaching you the techniques that have passed down through the Sunsnii mur, the stream of shamanic experiences and techniques from the lives of all the shamans your udha has partnered with before. Just relax, release all expectation, observe, and learn."*

(The 'Ongon' Spirits are those helpers for which one has Ongons, ritual objects which are those Spirits.)

Trance Dance as Journeying

This is broadly the way I work myself. It took me some years to find it, and I had to work it out myself because it is not (as far as I am aware) taught within modern Shamanism. Rather, it is mainly the method of lying down to journey that is taught. Journeying had a big effect on me quite quickly when I took it up in 1997. But I also became aware that it did not come entirely naturally to me. I struggled, thinking there must be something lacking in me that I needed to 'work on'. But then I began to do 'Trance

Dance', where you move spontaneously, and with a blindfold, to the rhythmic sound of drums or electronic music. For my first few 'dances', not much happened. But then, at one point, I found myself taken over by something, who-knows-what, that was powerful and ecstatic. It felt like an ancient dinosaur that had not experienced embodiment for millions of years, and was looking around curiously. Since then, it has become my main way of journeying. I can 'see' a journey going on, and am usually part of it myself, while at the same time feeling this presence that has taken over my body and is working spontaneously through it, and maybe speaking also, in an unknown language whose main meaning, for me, lies in the intent that I feel behind the words: there can feel like an urgency in what is said, some change it wants to effect if I am doing work with someone else. I do not necessarily have much rational understanding of what is happening, and I do not need to.

Trust Where it Doesn't Work for You

I struggled for years with the ways in which my experience didn't match what I had been told 'should' happen. I had been taught that when doing Soul Retrieval, we need to also bring back a story of when and why the soul part went missing, and I didn't necessarily have that. It has been precisely these discrepancies between what I was taught and my experience, and the self-doubt that I have as a result been through along the way, that have taught me that we need to find our own ways. If you are not getting a 'story' from the Spirits, trust that, don't think you are somehow lacking. We learn as much from teachers through acknowledging and trusting our differences with them, as we do from the teachings that actually work as they are 'meant' to. I was also taught that you cannot do your own Soul Retrievals, someone else has to do them for you. And the guy who told me that had been taught that himself. Yet that was exactly what started happening for me early on, spontaneously. These things get passed on as gospel, as how things are, and they are not necessarily so. And we can find our power, learn to trust the Spirit within, from these discrepancies.

Trance Dance, for me, led into this new way of journeying, that turned out to be closer to the traditional ways of working than what I had been taught.

Trance Dance is Really Spirit Movement

I have come to think of 'Trance Dance' as a bit of a misnomer. It is neither Trance nor Dance, though I accept that the term has caught on. It is not Trance in the sense of the popular connotation of the word, which suggests loss of consciousness. And it places the emphasis on the type of consciousness, when that is a by-product, ecstatic as it often is: the emphasis should be on the sense of Spirit working through us, and that is indeed the emphasis too in the phrase 'Ongod Orood'.

It is not Dance because that suggests performance and choreography. In 'Trance Dance' we let go and allow the Spirits to move us. I led a Trance Dance once, in which one of the participants, an experienced leader of Trance Dance himself, spent much of the Dance lying flat on his back, with his legs vertically up against the wall, wiggling his toes! Or you might find yourself curled up in a ball, absolutely still, or making micro movements with your fingers. Or, indeed, you might find yourself moving vigorously and with abandon to the fast rhythm of the music. So 'Spirit Movement' is overall a more accurate term for this ceremony.

And the central point of it is that we are allowing the spirits to take over, to incarnate in, the body. Which is really what the West of the Wheel is about. And it is an area in which, culturally, we have a lot of baggage.

Dancing in the Streets

In her book *Dancing in the Streets: A History of Collective Joy*, the

American scholar Barbara Ehrenreich recounts the situation in the early Middle Ages, whereby there were no pews in the churches, and the congregation used to dance, alongside the priest. As we have seen from Trance Dance/Spirit Movement, when we dance in this way, we experience Spirit working directly through us, which is why it is joyful. This sounds like a wonderful thing that used to happen in the churches, doesn't it? And that was exactly the problem from the point of view of the ecclesiastical hierarchy: people were experiencing their own connection to Spirit/God, and when they do that, you cannot control them, and the Church starts to lose its authority. So dancing was banned in churches, and only the priest was allowed to have a hotline to God. A certain amount was allowed at carnivals, at certain specific times of the year, but that was that.

Several hundred years later, when the early European explorers started to visit far-off parts of the world, what they frequently encountered were the native people dancing to drums around fires, half-naked and wearing body paint. The response of these explorers was one of disgust, such had been the effectiveness of the church in demonising the body, and in-so-doing disempowering a large part of people's natural connection to Spirit. What followed was a vigorous suppression of these native practices, and an imposition of our own European neuroses, as we began to colonise those countries.

The Body is, perhaps, our strongest route through to Spirit. And yet we have a religious background that sets them in opposition to each other. Barbara Ehrenreich's book concludes with an account of how that connection is being made again in these more liberal times, through, for example, Rock'n'roll, Raves, Pentecostal churches and sporting events. And, in the context of our modern Shamanic world, Trance Dance.

Because of our 'baggage', Trance Dance is often tentative for people when they start. It is part of the reason everyone wears blindfolds: so that we feel nobody is watching, and we don't have to worry about our 'performance'. The blindfold also allows us to focus more on the inner world of Spirit, and that is indeed a help, but I think only up to a point. I now dance without a blindfold when I can, because my movements can be free and more vigorous, which is often what Spirit wants of me. And ultimately, there is no difference between 'inner' and 'outer'. We find this in the Dzogchen tradition within Tibetan Buddhism. They meditate with their eyes open for the same reason. This world is also the Otherworld.

For myself, I need neither music nor drumming nor blindfold when called to work in this way. I can slip straight into it; it is never very far away. It is said that Trance Dance is an opportunity for the spirits to experience embodiment. We do it for them, not for ourselves. And if I have not 'danced' for a while, I can feel a strong call to do so, not for any particular reason other than the spirits wanting to. And sometimes it goes very deep, and it takes me a while to come back, and I may head off to bed to 'sleep it off' for a couple of hours. I feel blessed and I feel changed by such immersions in the Spirit World.

As Sarangerel says, the shaman/dancer remains aware and self-possessed while at the same time abandoning herself to the spirits. This abandon requires trust, and it is a very good exercise from that point of view. I was once in the presence of someone drumming and dancing in this way, and because of the context the loud drumming was inappropriate and complaints were made. I heard people excusing the drummers on the grounds that they were deeply in a shamanic trance, and more than that had been traditionally trained, so were, of course, beyond reproach. And I thought no it doesn't work that way, awareness is maintained.

Spirit Possession

That said, there does seem to be a level in which self-awareness is lost, when we come to the voodoo dances of Africa and the

Caribbean. I have seen films of these dances and the resulting spirit possessions. Many villagers dance to the drums (without blindfolds) and eventually a dancer will be taken over completely by the spirits and will collapse onto the floor. They are carried off, and it is a sacred event, for Spirit has entered the village. This is not generally the intent of the modern Trance Dances, though there is no reason it should not be. Possession requires a level of surrender to Spirit that maybe most of us are not capable of, even without the cultural baggage around the body. I have, though, heard of one or two instances of people spontaneously reaching this state during Trance Dance.

Most of the dancers who become possessed are women, and I find this congruent with my observation that women, on average, take more naturally to Shamanic Journeying. Men seem to have a self that is more geared to this world and being controlled within that. I don't want to make any judgements here, because it can be a loaded area in a time when it often seems that neither gender seems to know what it is any more. But I think it is, nevertheless, an interesting observation about the different ways that men and women are (often but not always) wired.

'Core' Shamanism and the Body

I also find it interesting that Shamanic Journeying has come to us via 'core shamanism' that, by its terminology, suggests something ancient and traditional, yet by its very method excludes the body as a vehicle for Spirit. Core Shamanism was created by a Western academic, Michael Harner. He has given us something of tremendous value, and I do not want to take away from that. But it is at the same time 'safe', it is less likely that something that is truly powerful, or that cannot be controlled, is going to occur if the body is left out. Nobody is going to sue you!

The 'Call-Back' Signal

This concern for safety and maybe even respectability is also suggested by the 'call-back' signal. At the end of the Shamanic Journey, the rhythm of the drumming is changed to a very fast beat, in order to break up the non-ordinary state of consciousness that the previous drumbeat has engendered, and to bring people back to 'this world'. When I was taught this method, the call-back signal was spoken about alongside warnings that it is possible to get stuck in the Otherworld, and how important it was when you hear the call-back signal to come straight back.

I think this is over-cautious, and only necessary if you have the kind of mental health issues that mean you find it difficult to stay grounded in everyday reality, in which case you probably shouldn't be journeying in the first place. I was led to a different way of thinking about it through Jan van Ysslestyne's book *Spirits from the Edge of the World,* an account of the cosmology and practices of the Ulchi Shamans of Eastern Siberia (with whom the author spent much time over many years.) When she had them over in the US, they were horrified by the call-back signal, which they found barbaric, so much so that they were intent on walking out of the conference they were at, until Jan pointed out they were under contract and couldn't. That incident made me acknowledge to myself that I have always found the call-back jarring, but hadn't questioned it. As at the end of a trance dance, so at the end of a journey we are often in a very sensitive place, we have been somewhere else that is profound, and we need time and quiet to absorb it and come back fully. Which is why I may go to bed after a strong trance dance. The call-back signal is indeed a crude interruption of this sensitive process, and from this point of view I understand why the Ulchis thought it barbaric.

Balancing Spirit and Matter

In our journey around the West of the Wheel, we are on the one hand incarnating: coming fully into this reality, doing something with our gifts and abilities, finding our place in the world, learning to care of ourselves independently on the physical level; learning, too, to be responsible for our dependents. But none of this can take place in a balanced way without being informed by the East, by Spirit. Astrologically, it is the balance between Saturn (incarnating) and Neptune (Spirit). The Saturn side, the West side, can come to be all-consuming, it can seem to be all there is, which is the viewpoint of modern materialism. Saturn tries to dominate Neptune and to explain – or explain away – spirituality within his own limited purview. Ceremony, in whatever way, and it can be very informal, is a corrective to this perennial tendency. And some of these ceremonies can lead to a deep immersion in Spirit that will change our lives.

Shamanism is not 'Safe'

They are not necessarily 'safe': you might be out on a hillside for four days, naked apart from a blanket, with no food or water; or struggling to bear the heat in a Sweatlodge as you sit there, near-naked in small dark space, with a bunch of strangers; or you might find yourself carried away as you dance to the drumbeat, called by ancestral memory to some primeval place, in which abandon yourself, lose yourself.

Shamanic practices are not 'tame' or 'safe'. They are not an add-on to a respectable urban life, where you become a 'shamanic practitioner' alongside being a well-boundaried therapist and member of the parish council. No, they take you somewhere raw, primal, beyond the normal controlling ego.

This is on the one hand threatening, and most people will not want to go there. But it has a delicious, ambrosial, irresistible call too, for it is what we are here to do: to transform, and to transform deeply, and unless we can relish that call from the Otherworld, and abandon ourselves to it over many years, that deep transformation cannot occur.

It takes courage, and it takes persistence. You may not have much obviously to show for it, and we have to learn to live with that, because that is not what it is about. We may appear to be some kind of 'loser' on the world's terms. But really that does not matter. It is about who you are, and continually being with that on a deep level, together with its occasional periods of crisis – with or without any formal shamanic practices, which are just means to an end.

The Best Kind of Teaching

Other people will pick up on what you are, they will sense that there is something about you that is deeply alluring, but they may not quite know what it is. They will recognise, however, that you are being yourself, in an ordinary way that is also profound: you have had the courage and persistence to claim that freedom, and this is what they want too, though they may not fully know it, and that is what they find appealing. By virtue of who you are, you give others the implicit permission that it is OK for them also to be who they are. This is the best kind of teaching, and it is unspoken.

Chapter 5

The North – Perspective

Colour: White
Element: Air
Season: Winter
Time: The Future
Stage of Life: Old Age
Animal: Bison
Some key words for the North: Elder, Perspective, The Mind, Service, Community, Generosity, Knowing, Wisdom.

The Directions are Cumulative

You've probably noticed that the chapters have been getting longer as we go round the Wheel. On the one hand, each direction is a place, a power in itself, that has balancing relationships with the other directions. But on the other hand, the Wheel is a journey through life from birth to old age, and in that sense the directions are cumulative, they incorporate the ones that come before, and synergise with them. So, there is more to say. We find ourselves returning to the same themes, but in a new way. When we arrive in the North, we are arriving at old age: a synergy of all four elements, and a perspective on a life that has, to a great extent, been lived.

Elders and the Saturn Cycle

It is the place of the Elder, who is in service to the community; they have done the living of their personal life. Using the model of the Saturn cycle of incarnation, they have done their 29 or so years post-first Saturn Return aged 29, they have engaged with the practicalities and responsibilities of adult life and now, after the second Saturn Return aged 58, that starts to ease off a bit, they have fully arrived on the planet, and Spirit now has an adequate vehicle through which to function.

Another way of putting it is that we have lived the crises of the South and West that the East demands of us, its constant impetus for life to move forwards. Through those crises we have found something that is truly our own to live by. The very meaning of the crisis is the claiming of that new element within us: unless we do that, life can no longer move forward, and we remain in the Underworld.

Old Ageism

In our culture, not only do we have a system where people who have some real wisdom are rarely in positions of political influence (which is more of an ambitious youngish person's game), we also tend to write off the very age group that is most likely to have the wisdom. We live in a youth culture. Yes, youth can bring in something fresh that comes from somewhere quite deep, and that needs to be listened to. But age is, or should be, the place that has the experience to make good decisions and heal conflicts.

In the run-up to turning 60 in 2018, I was almost counting the days of not yet being 60. Rationally, I knew it was a nonsense. But there was a brainwashing in me that said once you are in your sixties, it is downhill from there on in. And maybe that is because it was indeed the case for a long time. In recent centuries, people had hard physical lives, with not necessarily the best diet, and did not live nearly as long as we do now. Note I am only saying recent centuries: I am not including, say, hunter gatherers who were reckoned to have 'worked' between 15 and 20 hours a week, and lived about as long as we do now.

That fact of relatively early physical decline in the recent past perhaps explains part of the attitude. And then there is death, which we looked at in the West. If death is something to be put off, because we are either going to hell or we are going to be extinguished, then old age is precisely the time when we move closer to that unwelcome outcome to all our strivings. Old age becomes something to resist, to deny, because death is something to deny.

How to Be in Old Age

Whatever the reason for our ageism, there is a brainwashing to be overcome. One of my favourite pieces of film is a 1959 BBC interview with CG Jung, when he was in his 80s and, it turned out, did not have long to live. He is serene and lively and deeply at ease with himself. And questioned about old people, and the best attitude to life for them to have, he says that the dreams of his elderly patients do not point to an extinction but to life going on. He says the best way to live as you get older is therefore as if life is going to go on forever. Jung says he does not know what happens after we die, and those dreams are not telling us either: nevertheless, he says that the correct way to live is according to nature, and nature behaves as though life continues.

The point about living according to nature is a very important one. Jung is saying that the correct way to live is not, ultimately, to be decided by our ideas about life, or by reason, but according to what nature – our bodies, our dreams, Spirit, they are all the same thing – are telling us. This is fully in accord with a Shamanic way of seeing the world. Jung was very open in his approach to life, he was not bound by limiting concepts (unlike say Freud who, ground-breaking though he was, tried to reduce too much to the sex drive, and to limit the nature of the Unconscious.) Which is why I am happy, as noted in the first Chapter, to use his typology of Thinking, Feeling, Intuition and Sensation as a way into the Medicine Wheel.

So, there I was dreading becoming 60 and the fated decline that was soon to present itself. But what happened 18 months later was the deepest renewal I have ever known. I'd been having dreams for some years about a woman I had forgotten about, and there was a longing and an urgency associated with that. Eventually, in June 2019, after two Sweatlodges in one weekend, which had thoroughly melted me, she descended, and has been an inspirational force ever since. She is a slender middle-aged woman, who has a wooden staff that connects her to the Earth, because that is where her power and wisdom come from. And I feel myself to be at the beginning of what will probably be the most fruitful period of my life.

My own experience tells me in no uncertain terms that we can remain fresh – indeed, become even younger – as we age. I have a friend who is 90. He has had two hip replacements, yet still regularly goes for walks, and generally keeps himself very busy. There is a spring in his step, a glint in his eye, and he attracts a lot of interest from women.

We are talking about the child, from the opposite point of the South, that can come out to play in her fullness as we age. Personally, I feel younger than I have ever felt. The prospect of death can, for some, gradually shut them down. And I think if you shut yourself down – and it is a choice – then you will probably die much sooner. The prospect of death can have the opposite effect: we have learnt in the West to live with ourselves, to trust in the next stage of life, and therefore we trust death. As the Indian poet Tagore said:

"And because I love this life, I know I shall love death as well."

Death is the great unknown, the greatest adventure of all – as well as a return home – so why would old age not be a time of excitement, a time when life opens out even more, rather than shuts down?

The child-like quality of old age, though, does not have the fragility of childhood, that trauma so often compromises. It is robust, it is based on a knowing that even though life is frequently difficult, and there can be much to bear, it can also be fundamentally trusted. And that is what makes our eyes shine, and which can be such an inspiration to younger people.

It is not just ageing people who need to overcome the brainwashing about getting older. Younger people, too, often have that brainwashing, that doesn't take older people seriously. It is not just brainwashing, however: power is in the hands of people older than them, and they are not taking care of the Earth. They need calling to account in this and other respects.

Embrace Your Invisibility

It is normal, however, for women to start experiencing themselves as invisible as they reach middle age, rather than being noticed with respect, as people who might have some wisdom to offer. The warrior approach to this 'invisibility' is to embrace it. Yes, there may be comments needing to be made to the wider culture. But like anything, do not take it personally, or you will not learn: observe it, understand it, and use it as a teaching to find that valuing of yourself that only Spirit can give. Be thankful for it. There is something profound here. Treat it as Pluto's Helmet of Invisibility: an initiation into his Underworld and the source of true power.

When Do You Become an Elder?

We have begun (hopefully) to find that nugget, that gold within us, which is essentially our inner guide, something within we can trust to take us through life and to make good decisions. Or a profound connection to a Spirit Guide from without, it is the same thing, essentially. Often it is by not trusting that inner guide, and by coming painfully unstuck – getting bitten sufficiently hard, and for long enough – that we come to trust it. In a way, it is simple. But it can take many years. And as we yield to that life-changing and pivotal process, as we find the courage to live from it, then we start to have some serious wisdom of our own. And we begin to have completed the journey round to the West, and into the place of the Elder. I say 'begin' to, because it is not cut and dried, nothing ever is. But the crucial quality is that source of independent wisdom within, that does not identify with received opinion but always comes out with something fresh – and not always popular.

My friend Ron the Chippewa-Cree teacher, who was probably in his late sixties at the time (he didn't know his exact age) said to me that he wouldn't be considered an elder back home with his people. It was the guys in their 80s and 90s who were considered to have the real wisdom. So that is why I say we can 'begin' to move into the North when we are 58 (a number which, of course, is very schematic and not to be taken too literally.)

This perspective takes the pressure off. There is plenty of time to get some serious wisdom, we have our whole lives ahead of us to do so. Of course, some people may have that sort of wisdom when considerably younger, and my advice is to make the assumption that that does not include you. I certainly didn't myself. I had something going on, but it has taken 40 years of living it, with and a couple of major dismemberments along the way, to start to feel I know enough within my own experience to write a book.

Fake Elders and Building an Identity

The Shamanic world has plenty of people claiming, or inferring, that they are Elders. I'm sure "twas always thus". It is human nature to puff ourselves up, to compensate for not feeling that sure of ourselves, not feeling that substantial within, by an outward show. It is how the world works. It has a lot to do with why some people are motivated to become very wealthy, for example. The search for that sense of solidity, of substance, consumes them, and it is aimed outwardly, towards something impermanent that can never give them what they are looking for. Which is why they always need more. I should know, my father was one. I am not damning them – we love to damn rich people nowadays, because we are envious, we have what they are in us too – I'm just trying to see what is going on, disinterestedly. And you notice that with the wealth comes a sense of being better than the neighbour, and probably needing a car to prove it, to show who you are. Eventually, who knows, a knighthood. It is not evil, just emotionally simple-minded and naïve (though such people are often intellectually pretty sharp, they need to be.) In recent centuries we have managed to twist Christianity, with its Protestant Work Ethic, so that rich people become the ones who will be saved. You can see why comedy is often the best approach to this situation. It is exhausting to have to damn people, but when we laugh it is invigorating and enlightening, it gives perspective.

But also, to laugh at ourselves, because what rich people do in building an identity for themselves in the world, is something we all do. Rich people are often rich because they can, they have the ability, and it is something many of us would also do if we felt we could. And the same with being a celebrity. Or being known for being exceptional at something: let us forgive such people their faults, and not use them to knock them down out of envy. The world is a richer place because of people who are gifted. That said, gifted people often also use those gifts to hide from themselves, to conceal a felt lack. Maybe it is a blessing not to be too successful, because then we cannot so easily hide from ourselves. I will say from my own experience that it is a relief and a joy to be able to appreciate and rejoice in people who are better at certain things than I am. And we can do that if we are living from that timeless place within ourselves, that centre of the Wheel, where we do not feel diminished by others' success. Indeed, we do not think in terms of comparison. Or, as Kipling put it,

"If you can meet with Triumph and Disaster
And treat those two impostors just the same."

Ambition is Normal

I am saying all this by way of understanding fake Elders, because it is the same thing. There is a story that the Indians tell, about a regular Indian who leaves the reservation and visits the capital city of the state, where he lets himself be known as a local leader. By the time he gets to Washington, he is a Chief, and then he goes to Europe, where he is a Medicine Man. Hungry for Elders and meaning, we lap it all up.

This has probably always happened to a degree, but I think our culture exacerbates it. Our emphasis on success, on being a winner, with little acknowledged place for the mystic, the hermit, the person of wisdom, means that sense of vocation also encounters the pressure to have something to show for itself outwardly.

Religion works like this too: it has its hierarchies, and you get more credibility the further up the hierarchy you have climbed. This is why the Church of England has its saying "Nolo Episcopari", which the bishop recites on his appointment. It means "I do not want to be a bishop", and that they are just doing it for the Glory of God. But of course, they usually want to be a bishop (they feel "honoured"), though they may conceal the extent of that desire even from themselves. In a sense there is nothing wrong with this personal element, it is human nature to have this mixture of idealism and ambition. (Though we love to damn politicians at the first sign of it.) In a worldly sense, would anything get done without ambition? It is, however, best just to be straightforwardly honest about it with ourselves, for then we will know why we are doing what we are doing.

If you look through the advertisements for healers and teachers, you see people claiming to come from a line of seers, they maybe also 'big up' their Celtic heritage, they certainly had second-sight themselves in childhood, and had transformative experiences when very young. They may have acquired authenticity and power by visiting teachers in a foreign culture, who may have recognised their gifts. In all these ways they become 'special'. If it is Tibetan Buddhism you are attracted to, it can be quite extraordinary the degree to which they make their lamas 'special'. (The Dalai Lama is a notable exception to this crazy tradition.)

People are then likely to come along already having put that teacher on a pedestal, and that is just the wrong place to start. What we need to be doing on these paths is to find a way of stopping projecting our power and our East outwards onto celebrities and gurus and dark shadowy authorities. People can think you are being cynical or maybe envious if you are critical of such teachers. But we are often naïve, we buy these claims that are made – I certainly have done so myself – and it can be hard to see clearly when everyone around you thinks that such-and-such a teacher is the bee's knees; it becomes a collective pressure to see in a particular way, an unconscious collusion. Ironically, seeing such claims for what they are can be an important part of our learning. And what makes it tricky is that often these teachers DO have something of value to offer. Take the teachings and run, I say.

Now I am not claiming the opposite for myself, that I have nothing to offer, but I've never been able to boast in this way, for that is what it amounts to. If I was offering a skill such as accountancy, sure I would not hesitate to list my accomplishments, it is something you need to do. But it is not *yourself* that you are making claims about. You are not saying "I am a brilliant, special person", you are just saying you are good at accountancy. However, as any sort of spiritual teacher or healer, if you advertise in this kind of way, you are saying what kind of an advanced soul you are, which is the opposite of the egolessness that is the aim of such a life.

It is far better to be matter of fact: what sort of teaching you do, and what sort of trainings you have had, with no claims or implications of specialness about yourself or about those who have taught you. And leave the rest to Spirit. You will attract more straightforward people, who want something genuine, rather than someone to worship. I hope I have been sufficiently open in this book about my own challenges and shortcomings not to be put in the 'special' category by my readers!

Shamanism is not a Profession (Again)

But even without that urge to be 'special', there is the cultural push to turn Shamanism into a profession, with certificates to back us up. It is standard to do, say, five or six weekends training as a shamanic healer, and you get your certificate (no-one ever seems to fail to get it) and off you go, you are now a 'Shamanic Practitioner'. I am not saying there isn't some good in all this. But what I am arguing for is a shift of perspective within which these courses and trainings occur. You can train for a profession in a few short years and be perfectly competent at it. It is not the same with Shamanism at all, and do not mistake your certificates for this deeper quality: it is about you as a human being, not about your skill set. But I think if we are genuine, if we have humility, we come to see all this. It is no judgement on us if people are not coming to see us for healing, and I have known people who, having done the courses, feel they have to put it all to bed for a while, an instinct that I think is sound.

Key to healing work is the relationship you build with the 'client'. Any psychotherapist can tell you that, even though their relationships can be a bit one-sided. The work with the spirits may or may not happen directly. We need to spend time getting to know the client. And maybe their family members as well, this is traditional, for that will tell you much about the client. In fact, what is also traditional is that the family and maybe the community as well is involved with and backing the healing of the sick family member. We do not have that context. It is a far cry from the way I was taught shamanic healing, and the ways I have seen others practise, where someone you do not know comes to see you, you have a short talk, then you go and ask the spirits what to do, you do it, and within an hour they are out of the door, with maybe a return visit needed some weeks down the line. I am not saying this doesn't work, but it is superficial, and symptomatic of our culture. We do not understand relationship, and that is because our understanding of the self is autonomous rather than relational.

The real qualification, as I have argued earlier, is the placing of that Spirit calling at the centre of our lives, not just as an aspiration, or as an identity, but as something that has been worked through over time, and through which we have made some serious inroads into our shadow side. I know plenty of people who have spent decades with the Buddhist path at the centre of their lives, and that is genuine, but they have never properly made that descent into their own darkness, out of which comes the light of their own wisdom. This is not a criticism, because things take the time they take with people. But they are not Elders. Out of this deeper approach to ourselves comes a deeper approach to healing work. The idea that there can be any kind of quick fix – which courses on shamanic healing can suggest – becomes absurd, because any healing that happens needs to be seen in the context of someone's whole life, and the gradualness of overall change.

A Slow-Burn Path

This path is slow-burn. It is like an oak tree, that takes centuries to reach maturity, but when it does, has substantial roots and a solid trunk and mighty limbs reaching towards the Sun. It is not like a birch tree, which grows very quickly and dies young. There is a place for birch trees. But it is the oak that is the Elder. This perspective can require a sacrifice of ego, it requires humility. How many times was I, in my 40s and 50s, feeling inadequate because all these other people seemed able to create 'names' for themselves, to write books and teach courses, while something in me never felt right about doing that myself. I felt OK about writing, and working individually with people, and that went very well. But that bigger stage was closed to me, and I experienced that as humiliating. In certain cases – by no means all – it was obvious to me that there was self-importance going on in those other teachers, but that didn't stop me feeling inadequate myself. However, all this was a good process for me, it forced me to change my perspective, if only for my own peace of mind. How else do we effectively address that propensity towards self-importance, as a compensation for an inner lack, other than by having it frustrated, and being honest about the sense of humiliation that comes with that? It is easy to deflect from: we can retreat into envy, and pulling others down. Or we can retreat into acting on that lack in public, becoming 'special' and important, with certain types of people worshipping us, and for some that is gratifying. But not if you have integrity: it leaves a bad taste. You just have to live honestly with yourself, and what else is there to do?

I would say, though, that there is a guarantee in here: if you live honestly with yourself, and don't shy away either from having the courage to act and take risks, you will change, you will move closer to that centre in yourself – the centre of the Wheel – and you will have something of substance to offer others as time goes on.

Service

The desire to be of service, doing the work of the spirits, unfolds naturally from that journey around who we are. And this is the work of the North, the Elder, which we gradually move into after the purifying tribulations of the Adult in the West. It is best seen as something that comes towards us, rather than something we seek out. We trust whoever does, and does not, come our way. We learn maybe as much from them as they do from us. We are observing and learning all the time. The North is a whole path in itself. Our biggest and deepest learning comes when we are older and have managed to establish Spirit at the centre of our lives – well, much of the time, anyway. None of us is perfect.

The Elder has done her living for herself, she has maybe established a home and raised her children and perhaps had a career. The sense of fulfilment and meaning now comes from being of service to the community. That sense of service doesn't just suddenly start at a certain age, it begins whenever we begin responding to the call of something bigger than ourselves – the call of the spirits. And it grows over time. We become capable of more and more as we sort our own 'stuff' so that it doesn't get in the way. But there are usually many years of working with the shadow, as well as the natural processes of unfoldment, before we are ready to be an Elder in its fuller sense. A key here is not to try to get too much of a sense of identity from doing 'good works'. It is difficult for that not to happen to some degree if you are earning a living from it. The main thing is to stay out of the way so that Spirit can send the people your way who need to be sent your way. And if no-one is coming your way, trust that and enjoy doing something else.

This is how Lewis Mehl-Madrona puts the matter in *Coyote Medicine* (p122):

> *"If you ask someone if he or she is a shaman, the closest you'll get to a positive response is "People say I am."*
>
> *Native American culture discourages bragging about having spiritual power. True Medicine men and women know only that the Creator and the spirits, or the patient, can really take credit for a healing. Besides, if we do not remain humble and respectful before the spirits, those who would otherwise help us in the work of healing are likely to desert us."*

So let us claim our own inner Elder, let us become her. But hold her lightly, do not make an identity of her, do not speak of her.

Becoming Our Own Teacher

Once we have found that inner guide, and maybe learnt to trust it through the painful consequences of not trusting it, we no longer need look for Elders, teachers, outside of ourselves. Of course, there will always still be people we can learn from. It will seem like they are pushed in our direction, because we are living from Spirit. Our whole life can be like that when Spirit is at the centre: Spirit will take care of everything.

Workshop Junkies

You see some people continuing to go to different teachers almost indefinitely: they become 'workshop junkies', because they do not yet trust their own inner guide sufficiently. What they often need to do is to stop going to so many workshops and to the latest teachings and methods, and work everything out for themselves. It doesn't matter if you make 'mistakes', or things mess up: the important thing is that they are your 'mistakes', and to learn from them. How else do we learn? Mistakes that we pay attention to are our greatest teachers, not workshop leaders. The more the better, in a way.

There are no New Teachings

There is nothing new under the Sun. The real wisdom, which comes simply from being honest with ourselves and learning from that, is timeless. And it is a process that is lifelong and slow. That is all you need to know. It is not confined to Shamanism, it is at the heart of all mystical traditions the world over (as opposed to religions, which have a large element of group control as an essential part of their make-up.) The latest teacher, the latest method that offers 'quick' results, will not offer you much from this larger perspective.

Elders are not Perfect

Let us not turn 'Elder' into too much of a fixed, reverential category. Like anything, it is a process. Some languages do not have nouns in the way we do, they have verbs, because they do not have 'things', only processes, and I think this is closer to reality.

I think being an Elder is a combination of a wider sense of Spirit working through you, along with the thoughtfulness and perspective than can come with the years. It is both this world and Otherworld. You may be reliable in this sense, or it may just be on a good day. There will be areas you can give good advice in, and others you can't, and you need to have the humility to know the difference. If you are a real Elder, you will have that humility. You won't be a know-all, ideally. But Elders have their faults like anyone. They may be a know-all, but also able to give sound advice. And you have to work around that.

I know someone, and we perhaps all know people like this, who can be profoundly helpful one moment, and blinded by her subjectivity the next moment. And she doesn't seem to be able to tell the difference. I expect we will all have those moments. Someone who is a 'proper' Elder will still have those kinds of moments, but will be able to acknowledge them, at least to themselves, and not be ultimately ruled by them.

Sorting the Pipework

It is not enough just to have a gift for communicating what the spirits have passed on to you. We all have gifts for that in our own way, and we may not experience it as spirits talking to us. More important is getting our own pipework, so to speak, sorted, through which the spirits speak. And that can take 10, 20, 30 years. That can never be the emphasis on a 'Become a Shamanic Healer' course, because they only last a year or a few years at most. There is no hurry. It may be something you are called to do, but it is not your identity. You can probably do far more good overall in your life by seeing just a few people, and doing some deep work with them, having waited 20 years for

Spirit to start sending those people your way.

It is said of some Medicine people that if you come to them for some help, they will go away and sit with it for a few days before coming back to you. I think there is a lot in this. It gives time for the spirits/the unconscious to do its work with what you have already picked up, probably on many levels, about the person, and what you then do with them will have some real depth and prove very effective. Contrast that with the modern approach one often finds, where someone comes to see you, you do a journey for them, and then do or say whatever the spirits advise. Of course, this can be effective, but it just doesn't have the same power to it.

And when I say getting the 'pipework' sorted, it is not just a matter of keeping our own subjectivity out of the way, being a 'hollow bone' as it is known. It is also about having plenty to offer from our own human experience, and this brings us back to the necessity of the encounter with the shadow. And once you are up and running in that kind of way, so to speak, and probably after many years, there is not really so much of a difference between what the spirits have to say and what comes out of consulting your own experience. It is one rich and deep mixture; this world and the Otherworld are, after all, not separate places. You come to have a particular kind of 'knowing' about you, which is not the relatively superficial kind that mediums often have (that can have its value), but which involves your whole being. In this way, 'Perspective' can be a keyword for the North, which is so much more than the one-sided, 'rational' mind.

The One-Sided Mind

The Mind can be very tricksy, and the Coyote of the South is a kindred spirit. It is precisely the tendency of the mind to divide everything into two, good and bad, right and wrong, and identify with one side or the other, that is the cause of much of our blindness and suffering. It is something that people seem to find very difficult not to do; they can find it very hard to grasp that they are doing it even when you point it out. This is perhaps one reason that we find the Mind in the North, the final position on the Wheel: because this one-sidedness is so difficult to see (yet very simple once you have). Age is no guarantee, for there are plenty of older people who bang on in a one-sided way, but at least the years will hopefully have given us a chance to see that things are rarely as black and white as the mind likes to think.

The great strength of the Mind is the ability to stand back and weigh things up. And its weakness lies in it thinking it is the master that knows, when all it is doing is mistaking ideas for realities.

I talked about this one-sidedness from an emotional point of view in Chapter 3, Beyond Good and Evil, focussing on the sense of identity and stability we get from our positions. In this chapter I will be focussing on that same phenomenon from a cognitive point of view. They are two sides of the same coin, South and North, emotion and reason, with our thoughts being like the froth on the ocean of emotion, thrown up by feeling. Where do thoughts come from? We don't know really, they seem to appear, we find ourselves wanting to dwell on and think about something, and then a few minutes later it may be something else.

Meditation

Our minds wander, and one of the first things you learn if you take up meditation is that you can't control your mind. When I was 22, I was naïve and wilful enough to think that I could control my mind, and I would sit there dutifully meditating every day, trying to force my mind to concentrate. All I did was to make myself feel out of sorts, like I had a hit a brick wall, and it would take some hours to recover from. It was the same sort of attitude that, ten years later, would give me chronic fatigue: my whole system going no, we are not going to let you treat yourself like this anymore.

What I was doing was the opposite of listening to Spirit, and I am fortunate enough that Spirit makes life so painful when I do that, that I cannot continue. Many people are not so fortunate. But it has still taken many years for me to start to learn to listen properly.

Meditation in the sense of observing the mind, and not trying to control it, is a North practice, and an excellent thing to do, because it inculcates an attitude that can spread to the rest of our life. Meditation can also be taught as a means of changing and purifying the mind, and I am not saying this does not work, up to a point; but as soon as you have methods or practices that are aimed at changing you in one way or another, I think you probably also have religion, control. I was originally taught some traditional methods for dealing with what were called the 'hindrances' to meditation that arise in the mind, for example, ill-will, or wandering thoughts, or sensory desire, or torpor. And the basis of this kind of approach is 'top down': the mind decides what are and are not desirable states to be in, it judges them, and attempts to change that which is not desirable.

Dzogchen Meditation

Years later I learnt the Dzogchen approach to meditation, that seems much more in line with Spirit: all you are doing is staying with whatever is happening, you are not trying to change it, you are not trying to become a 'good' meditator. One friend who has been doing this practice for decades was leading a meditation in this way, occasionally putting in a few quiet words, and at one point she said, "Now drop the meditation", which I thought nailed it. Stop 'trying' to do anything, stop even 'trying' to meditate. This is why Dzogchen practitioners meditate with their eyes open: there is nothing 'special' about what you are doing, it is no different to everyday life. This attitude to meditation can be hard to grasp: if you are not trying to 'do' anything, then what is the point?

First of all, you have to get out of the 'good' vs 'bad' mindset, which is at the foundation of religion, and of the mind which likes these kinds of opposition, and into the non-judging, observing state which we looked at extensively in the South. The most effective way to change is to just be with whatever is happening, rather than trying to change. Who are we to know what we need to change into? Does the tree know what shape it is going to become, or does it just reach for the Sun? It is the self-important, know-all quality of the mind, that logic-chopping froth on the surface of the ocean of feeling, that thinks it knows, indeed that it 'ought' to be in control if it is going to be a responsible human being. This is why surrendering to Spirit in more and more subtle ways can be so hard to grasp, because it goes against so many of the instincts of the human ego. And why the Coyote is such an apt symbol for the Mind, because it will always find a new way in, a new way to appropriate and attempt to control whatever is going on.

When Mountains are Mountains Again

There is a famous quote by Zen Master, Dogen:

> *"Before one studies Zen, mountains are mountains and waters are waters; after a first glimpse into the truth of Zen, mountains are no longer mountains and waters are no longer waters; after enlightenment, mountains are once again mountains and waters once again waters."*

This is often how it is. We begin with the naïve and natural assumption that the material reality around us and the collective values we have imbibed are what is most real, we take it all literally. Then we encounter indigenous ways, and we realise that it is all part of a bigger dream, it is contingent, that behind everything is the 'Spirit World', and maybe we become quite earnest about being guided by that world and all the various helpers we have there. And then one day we realise that all this striving and cultivation misses the point: this world is the Spirit world, and there was never anywhere to go. All there is, is what presents itself, there is no hidden reality. It was the ego that was striving to become more 'enlightened'. Maybe the main difference is that we no longer take the world so literally.

Stop Trying to be Good

This Zen quote can also be said to concern the shift from religion to spirituality. It is quite natural to start out with religion, in the sense of trying to better ourselves, to let 'Spirit' become the foundation of our lives. And it probably, in our own minds, makes us 'better' than, more profound than, the average person in the street. Be honest here: does your Shamanism make you feel like you are in some way superior to many other people? There is nothing 'wrong' with that feeling, it is natural, albeit limited. And then one day, perhaps in middle age, you get fed up with all the struggle to be a 'better' person, and all the judgement of yourself and others that comes with that, all the self-doubt that you are perpetually tied to as a consequence, and you yield. Like the lead character in the film *American Beauty*, who stops striving to succeed on the terms of the American Dream, and starts to just trust and follow his own impulses. And at that point, the mountains and waters become just the mountains and waters again, the world is no longer divided into good and bad. You have arrived, because you have realised that there was never anywhere to go.

Humanising Political Figures

The mind wanders, and the best approach to that is to just stay with it, be conscious, because its wanderings come from a deeper source within us, that cannot be controlled. And the mind also tends to polarise, to think in black and white and take one side or the other, and there *is* something we can do about that. And if you can do it with political figures and ideas, then you can do it anywhere. Which is why I am going to start there.

It can be extraordinary to watch people when political issues come up. It's like they turn into somebody else. So many of us talk about individual politicians, who we have little or no knowledge of, in highly judgemental and simplistic terms, in ways that we would never do about friends or neighbours or indeed probably anyone else. Apart from, maybe, CEOs of major corporations. The rules change there too, and many people feel they can talk in the same way about them.

The way to go beyond this is to humanise these distant figures. And the way to do that, as ever, is to try to look at things from their point of view, and to make a conscious choice to stop making unjustified assumptions about them, that simply suit what it is you want to believe in the first place. We believe what we want to believe, and there is little point discussing something with someone who is doing that: they become immune to reason and facts. They don't even know they are doing this, and university degrees are no protection from it. In fact, by their suggestion that we are cleverer than average, such degrees can make us more prone to this kind of blindness. I would go so far as to say that most people do this most of the time, and it is rare to find a discussion where people are interested in what is true, as opposed to defending their positions. Which means it's not really a discussion at all.

The Natures of Conservatives and Liberals

Someone who helped me step out of this common political rabbit-hole, this blind one-sidedness, was Jonathan Haidt, a moral psychologist from the USA. I highly recommend his TED Talk on *The Moral Roots of Liberals and Conservatives*: it can really change how you think. He begins by saying that when he first went to university, he identified as a Democrat, as did his friends, and he said they all genuinely assumed that anyone who voted Republican had something wrong with them, something bad had happened to them in their childhoods that made them like this. As you can see it is a deep hole, it is way beyond simply disagreeing with someone else's political viewpoint. It reminds me of a friend who is a Sunni Muslim, and he is urbane and gently spoken. And I asked him once what is the difference between the two main branches of Islam, Sunni and Shia? And he replied, in a friendly and matter of fact manner that the Shias aren't real Muslims. And I thought with friends like this, who needs enemies?

Projecting the Shadow onto Public Figures

It is very common to find ostensibly intelligent and well-meaning people talking and thinking in this sort of way. It is extremism, it is intolerant of difference to the point where those who disagree with you are damned. But it comes with a tolerant and open-minded persona. We project intolerance onto Muslims in the Middle East and onto American Christians in the Deep South, but it is hard for us to see that we are doing the same thing. During the Covid crisis in the UK, the Health Minister had been sweating blood for a year dealing with this unprecedented situation. When a vaccine eventually became available, he became quite emotional for a moment. And there was a whole stream of people on social media who believed his emotion was fake, simply because he is of a different political party to them. Many of these were otherwise intelligent (and usually liberal) people. But their own political one-sidedness blinded them, and caused them to dehumanise this very human government minister. In doing this, we ironically become separated from our own humanity, we lose the ability for fellow-feeling.

Escaping the Moral Matrix

Jonathan Haidt as a young man was in this rabbit-hole, or what he calls the Moral Matrix (as in the film *The Matrix*). If you want to live the North successfully, and become someone who has perspective and good advice to give, it is a rabbit-hole you need to get out of. Haidt, as a moral psychologist, began to do research on the values held by people who are conservative and people who are liberal. And it turns out to be a divide that occurs across the world, with similar sets of values on each political wing.

To put it simply, people who are politically liberal value taking care of people above all other values; people who are politically conservative hold a number of values about equally, but crucial among them is the "insight", as Haidt calls it, that order and stability are hard-won and easily lost. You can see from this that each grouping has something necessary to offer, and that without both you do not have balance. Yet instead, what tends to happen is that people judge each other across the political divide. Those on the right see those on the left as 'bleeding hearts' who are irresponsible with money, and those on the left see the right as cold-hearted and only interested in privilege and money. These caricatures are by and large not true if you get to know people on an individual level.

If you go away with anything from reading this section on the North, it will be the ability to appreciate the genuine values held by people on the other side of the political divide to you, assuming you are party-political, which most people are. I try not to be, because I find it divisive and blind, and I have put quite a lot of time and effort into appreciating both sides. Living in the UK, I centre that around trying to understand the leaders of both the Conservative and Labour parties, trying to get a sense of what their values and ideals are. They are not just self-serving idiots, rarely is a politician that. Even Donald Trump had certain things he wanted to do for the USA, but not many on the left are able to acknowledge that.

I don't expect too much from people who are not trying to be aware: I expect one-sidedness and dismissal and judgement across the political divide, that is just human nature, and if you don't expect too much of people, you will save yourself a lot of grief and you will understand them better. What I find more remarkable is encountering this one-sidedness, this blind judgement, in people who are to some extent trying to be self-aware and not judge. Like I said, it is like they are two different people, and they cannot see it. It seems so obvious to them, for example, that certain politicians are self-serving and heartless – less than human, in effect – that how could it be judgemental? For them, it is just reality. And it has a large element of group consciousness around it: one feels supported by others who make the same assumptions.

The Blue Pill or the Red Pill?

The choice is yours: do you want to take the blue pill or the red pill (from the film *The Matrix*)? The blue pill will preserve your current reality, where politicians on the other side of the political divide are bad lots, and their voters are misguided. Or you can take the red pill and step out of this matrix, and come to value both sides. It is not just about swapping one outlook for another, it is about a shift in consciousness, and it will change who you are.

If you do take the red pill, you will have to put up with being misunderstood and judged by people. Specifically, most people think in two categories, and if you are not in their category, you must be in the other one. Left wing people will think you are right wing, and vice-versa. They will not just be misunderstanding you; they will most likely also be making an unfair moral judgement about you. And this is where the Toltec practice of taking nothing personally comes into its own. It is an opportunity.

How Small, of all that Human Hearts Endure

Another factor at work here can be the projection of our East onto political figures and parties, in the same way as often happens with teachers and 'holy' books. Instead of saving ourselves, we want to save the world, and we have faith in a political creed or party to do that. Communism attracted a lot of this kind of faith in its day, from intellectuals as much as from anyone: education is no safeguard against this kind of naivety. And if you have faith in a political party, then you will find it hard to think well of the opposing parties. Your loyalties may be quasi-religious, or they may be tribal. Whatever they are, when considering political parties and governments (who we love to blame for just about everything), it is worth bearing in mind (again) Samuel Johnson's words:

> *"How small, of all that human hearts endure,*
> *That part which laws or kings can cause or cure."*

It is not just political parties that attract this East projection. The system itself, which for us in the West is democracy, attracts that kind of faith, so that to say someone is being 'undemocratic' is automatically a judgement against them. 'Liberal democracy' is today our great ideal. I am not saying that it does not have some things going for it, because I think it does. But what sort of way is it to run a country, that one of the most responsible jobs going can be filled by someone with little or no experience in government, on the promise of policies that they may or may not keep to, elected by people who have no experience of government or of the complexities of the issues involved? Would a brain surgeon be appointed in this sort of way? I am not suggesting an alternative, and as Churchill said (quoting someone else) democracy is the worst option, apart from all the others that have been tried from time to time.

I am bringing in this consideration of democracy not just

to elicit some independent thought about it as a system, but in-so-doing to loosen that East projection we unthinkingly and collectively make onto it, to the extent that we can feel justified in imposing it on other countries that have a different system 'for their own good'. As one relatively benign African dictator once complained, the Americans were imposing economic sanctions on his country to pressure it towards becoming a democracy. But, he continued, if his country became a democracy, the people would become divided along tribal and religious lines in ways that they currently were not. Democracy can be very divisive, promoting the very one-sidedness of mind that it is the purpose of the North to overcome.

We need to haul our projection of the East off not just politicians and parties and political systems, but from parents and bosses and partners and teachers and celebrities and royalty and indigenous people and whoever else we put it onto. It is in ourselves that we need to have faith, in our own ability to grow and to guide ourselves and make decisions.

Don't Judge your own Racism

I think these things always come back to how one treats oneself, one's own relationship to oneself. If we judge others (as opposed to being discerning, which is not self-serving) then we judge ourselves. It is that simple.

When we begin to stop judging ourselves – I say 'begin' because it is difficult – then we are sympathetic to whatever thoughts and feelings arise. And we need to do this particularly with the dark, less acceptable feelings. It is natural to humans of whatever skin colour to be racist to a degree, for example, especially under certain circumstances. I am not saying to act or speak from that, but to be honest about it, welcome the feeling in, find out what it is about. And then you can stop projecting racism onto working-class conservatives! That is always the way to start with these things: not by waving banners, but by owning it in ourselves.

We will keep judging, to a degree, probably for the rest of our lives. The human mind is 'righteous'. Jonathan Haidt has written a book called *The Righteous Mind*, and this is one of his main themes. It is something we do naturally. It has its uses, and there are probably evolutionary reasons, but it also has its limitations.

Asking for Forgiveness

Don Miguel Ruiz (who wrote *The Four Agreements*) talks about Forgiveness (see *The Gift of Forgiveness* by Olivier Clerc). But not in a way you might expect. What he says is that when you catch yourself making a judgement about someone, ask them (in your own mind) for forgiveness. The emphasis here is not on forgiving others, but on asking forgiveness for what we have done. When someone cuts you up on the road, and you feel anger, ask their forgiveness. When someone is taking forever at the check-out queue and you start to feel impatient with them, ask their forgiveness. When you read about the racist comments made by a politician on the right, and you damn them for it, ask their forgiveness.

This is a radical practice that comes from the Central American Toltec tradition. It is the Warrior training, of always holding yourself to account, of being impeccable. Paradoxically, this does not lead to a bland, naïve, undiscerning attitude to others. Rather, it leads to humility, in which you are not needing to be continually positioning your own ego in relation to others. And this humility leads to an unusual level of insight into others, because you are welcoming them in as humans instead of pushing them away and judging them. You see this quality in the Dalai Lama: an incredible lack of presumption about who he himself is, and treating others as equal, as people he can learn from. It is not a posture; it is for real. As a result, he has wisdom, he has a fresh and insightful point of view, and is justifiably held in high regard.

The Nature of Beliefs

One of Jonathan Haidt's other main themes, to be found in his book *The Righteous Mind*, is that the rational mind is like a rider on an elephant. Beliefs and decision-making are emotionally based in the first instance, and the reasons come afterwards. We can easily persuade ourselves that such reasons are why we hold particular beliefs, or make particular decisions, but that just shows our almost infinite capacity for self-deception, for rationalisation.

I am not going to tell you which way I voted in the referendum that was held in the UK in 2016 on our membership of the EU. What I was aware of, however, was that there was an instinct in me to vote a particular way, and I decided to follow that. I then created reasons for that, but I am aware that they were secondary. I think it was right for me to vote according to my instincts. I think it is generally right to do so, providing reason – which has its supporting place – does not suggest overall harmful consequences. And it is perfectly possible that others had instincts telling them to vote in the other direction, and I think it would have been right also for them to vote accordingly. It is not about 'right' and 'wrong' projected out into the world. It is about becoming true to who we are – the Centre of our Wheel – which can take quite some consideration. It is a very different thing, which can lead two people in opposite directions.

A belief is generally in the service of an emotion, which is why we can feel the need to be in the right. I sometimes joke that there is only one fear greater than the fear of death, and that is the fear of being wrong. There was a well-known scene in the 1970s American sitcom *Happy Days* in which a central character, 'The Fonze', who is just so cool, was wrong about something, so blatantly wrong that he had to admit it. And you seem him struggling to get the words out: I was wr-wr-wr-wr…

and he almost manages to say 'wrong', but can't quite get it out. Eventually he manages to say he was wrong.

What is this need to be 'right'? It is strange when you stand back and observe it. It also suggests that there is a thing called 'right' in the first place. The EU referendum was a good case in point. It was not enough for people to be disappointed that the vote had not gone the way they wanted. They had to add to that by making the people who voted the other way 'wrong', and in this way they could hang on to some of their previous sense of who they were. It was so divisive, and even now years later, I may be alienating some of my readers by talking about it. But the whole thing was, in a way, notional. It was based on two different ideas of who as a nation we are, and many people's sense of who they were was very tied up with their idea of who the nation was. Which is, in a way, crazy, but also very human. Whether the UK was in the EU or not was probably not going to be readily observable in day-to-day life several years down the line.

This is what the mind does – or rather, what emotions do to the mind, below the level of awareness: an abstraction is created that we then think of as who we are. And the reason we do that is that the real nature of things is too much for us:

> *"Humankind cannot bear very much reality",*

as TS Eliot said, as I have already quoted and may yet quote again.

The World has no Solid Foundation

In reality there is no solid foundation to the world or to ourselves. The dream of a solid material reality is a vast prop that we use to shield ourselves. This idea is basic to Buddhist thought, and it also provides the true point of balance at the centre of the Medicine Wheel. We seek permanence, a solid sense of self, and unalloyed happiness in something that does not have those attributes. Those attributes can indeed be found, but not in the way we think. The solidity and certainty and security we seek can be found not by building a wall against the stream, an island in the river, but by letting go and flowing with that current, bathing in it, delighting in it, returning home to it, to what we always were. That is the real point of balance at the centre, where we are in balance not just with ourselves, but with everything around us, because there is no separation between ourselves and the world around us. It is, however, a big ask: we cling on to everything we know, it is why we fear death, and it is generally a lifetime's work to let go of all these points of false security. It would be literally traumatic to lose too many of those reference points at once. That is why times of major change can be so difficult and why people can feel they are losing their sanity at such times.

This is not about becoming detached from life; it is the opposite of that. How can you truly enjoy something if you are hanging onto it for dear life? We need to "kiss the joy as it flies", as William Blake put it, and "live in eternity's Sunrise".

Shamanic Cognitive Behaviour Therapy

The mind gets used to create abstractions like 'national identity' for us to lean on. But the mind can also be used to identify those abstractions. This is the basis of Cognitive Behavioural Therapy, a North-oriented psychotherapy that uses the mind to analyse our emotionally-held beliefs to see if they square up to reality. The earliest form of this type of therapy, called Rational Emotive Behaviour Therapy (REBT), was founded by an American called Albert Ellis. As a 19 year-old, he was painfully shy around women. So, during a month of visits to the Bronx Botanical Garden, he sat on a bench and spoke to every woman he saw. His 130 attempts at conversation did not lead to true love, but that was beside the point. He had proved to himself that rejection, though unpleasant, was not unbearable: there was no need to "awfulise" it.

> *"Nobody vomited and ran away,"* he wrote. *"Nobody called the cops."*

The experience led directly to the "shame-attacking exercises" he later prescribed to his patients.

> *"Stop somebody on the street,"* he advised, *"and say 'I just got out of the loony bin. What month is it?' And learn not to feel ashamed when they look in horror at you, and think you're off your rocker, which they think you are. But you're really not. You're being very much saner than they are."*

He used to run Friday night workshops which became legendary.

> *"Let me tell you why people are always making you so angry,"* he informed a troubled young woman in 2005 (when aged 91), *"Because they're screwed up! They're out of their fucking minds! We're all out of our fucking minds!"*

This mantra, which he repeated regularly, was behind his REBT. Its starting point was that we have negative emotional reactions not to events themselves, but to our beliefs about them. He rejected Freud's focus on unpicking a patient's childhood experiences. Instead, he advocated identifying and modifying these "irrational beliefs", which usually take the form of a hidden demand that reality should be different than it is.

> *"There are three musts that hold us back,"* he wrote. *"I must do well. You must treat me well. And the world must be easy."*

We upset ourselves with the grandiose requirement that we

should perform perfectly, and that others should be nice to us. But in fact, we are imperfect: we fail, in love and work, all the time. And other people, often enough, "act like jerks."

Many of our behaviours are due to fears that exist largely in our minds. These fears have corresponding beliefs, which we can deconstruct, and in this way start to become free of them. Using the North to transform the South. These beliefs are often leftovers from childhood, that no longer serve us. A short while back, I found myself in a state of constant anxiety, that went on for about a year. It involved problems around letting out a property I owned. When I thought about it rationally, I could see that I would have enough to live on in the meantime, there was no reason it should not eventually sort, so what was I worrying for? Of course, I could explore my childhood and find reasons. That can be useful, don't get me wrong. But we will often never get to the bottom of these things. Meanwhile, holding that rational position that contradicts the fear is a powerful thing to do.

Think about it as spirits (which Albert Ellis, who was quite the rationalist, would never have done.) I have this spirit of anxiety visiting me. So, as we saw in the South and the work of Eduardo Duran, invite the anxiety in, make friends with it, get to know it, and do this ceremonially. And then invite in this other thought-form, a spirit, that is free of this anxiety because it can see there is no good reason for it. And just let those two spirits live alongside each other. Keep calling them to mind over the months. You will forget sometimes, and be consumed by the anxiety for a while. And you do not give the spirit of anxiety a hard time, you are sympathetic to it and not trying to force it to change. Just keep the two spirits living alongside each other, and you will gradually change. I certainly did: after a year of this anxiety, it had much less hold on me than it did at the start.

There is a mysterious way in which the universe sometimes seems to send these situations our way in order that we will learn and change. It can be almost like our life is moving from A to B, and we can see that is happening, but along the way Spirit/ Coyote chucks in an extra difficulty that gives an opportunity to learn in a way that is precisely where we need to learn: don't curse but trust the difficulties that are sent your way. The bigger the difficulty, the more it can change you. Sometimes it can seem like a tank in your front garden, taking aim at the house, and that is where we really do learn.

So maybe this is a shamanic twist on the cognitive therapies: they are using the North to address the South, and the reality-based reasoning we use is itself a thought-form, a spirit that can exist in friendly relationship with the tormenting spirit.

Don't Make Assumptions

In this cognitive approach, we do not just weigh the observable facts and consequences against our fears or whatever is tormenting us. We also need to discern assumptions, and stop making them. The assumptions are based in those fears, or in our desires for the world to be a particular way. This goes deep. We make assumptions all the time about how the world is and how people are. That is OK if we are conscious of it, because certain assumptions are necessary. But most assumptions are not conscious. They are rooted in the mind thinking it knows what is going on, which is in turn rooted in the emotions wanting certainty and safety.

I recommend the chapter subtitled *Don't Make Assumptions* in Don Miguel Ruiz's *The Four Agreements.* Instead of making assumptions, ask questions, acknowledge you don't know, appear naïve if necessary. Who cares what other people think, that is a cowardly way to live, that most of us are guilty of to some degree.

I know someone who likes to have life and other people in neat categories. And as this person was getting to know me, she realised that I did not always fit into her neat categories. In particular, I did not hold the political views that she thought I ought to hold. One evening, she gave me an extensive character analysis, describing all the shortcomings I allegedly have that would explain my 'perverse' views. There was nothing I could say in my defence, for it was clear she was not going to listen to me: she knew who I was, and I was the one who needed to listen. It was all assumption and fantasy about me, and I was working hard at Don Miguel Ruiz's second agreement, which is 'Don't take anything personally'. I still felt a bit sore the next day, I hadn't completely escaped the force of her barrage, but I hadn't done too badly by my own lights. I had done my best to sidestep and observe, and to be honest with myself if I thought anything she said was true, despite the way it was being said.

This is a good example of the opposite of what I am talking about. What this friend was articulating is often what goes on in our heads about other people, the views we form about them, the assumptions we make. The opposite to this is listening and asking questions. What I find when I do this is that the truth behind someone's actions is always different to what I thought. There are always factors that I could never have thought of. This does not mean that I won't occasionally have insights about other people that can be helpful for them to hear. But those insights need to be held lightly, for they will always need modifying when they come up against the complexity and subtlety of the other person's experience.

Dropping assumptions about other people, and not taking it personally when they don't conform to your expectations/assumptions, will transform you. It is a very different way of being. And because your mind is not filled up with assumptions about other people – and the little resentments and the sense of being let down that often come with that – it means your mind is empty and open and receptive to the reality of the other person. And this gives us the possibility of some wisdom. And not running into the practical messes that happen when we make assumptions about what others want and how they will behave. As Marion in the film *Priscilla, Queen of the Desert* says:

"Assumption, my dear Mitz, is the mother of all fuck-ups."

Watching how people talk about others is an object lesson in how the mind works. Say someone is always late. Many of your friends will probably have theories as to why this person is always late, quite possibly fuelled with some resentment at this person's lateness. And those theories justify the feelings of resentment. The theories are just fantasies, and the resentment is a result of having taken that person's lateness personally, as though it was something they deliberately set out to do to you. If you have read some psychology, and consider yourself knowledgeable in the subject, you may compound your fantasies by applying some theories as to what must have happened to that person in their childhood to make them always late.

And then there is gossip. This activity that we delight in is not about truth and not about goodwill either, because criticising others puts us in a better light by comparison, and so we feel better about ourselves. And you've probably noticed that it begins guardedly, one person saying something critical about the third party that maybe does need to be said, and the other person maybe acknowledging that guardedly. We are guarded partly for good reasons, but also because we are checking out the other person, seeing if they are willing to go there. And if they are, that is when you have to be careful, because before you know it the floodgates open and we are both delighting in speaking critically of that third person. It is an unholy alliance that bolsters, in an unwholesome way, how we like to think of ourselves.

From the point of view of that which is authentic in us, that longs to live truthfully, it is actually a relief to be able to let go of these fantasies and personalised feelings about other people and just to hold them in our minds and hearts sympathetically and without judgement, knowing that we don't really know who they are, and what they want, and why they do what they do. They may not even know these things very well themselves. And that means, when we talk to them, we can listen, and they will sense that we are not judging, and may therefore even want to talk about why they are, for example, always late and the way they judge themselves for it, and what it is that actually happens in their minds in the run-up to a meeting that has an agreed time. And I can guarantee it will be a complex thing. People become so much more interesting once we can let go of our views about them, and listen to their own versions of themselves.

Balancing North and South

Really, we need both the North and the South acting together. Ideally you need all aspects wherever you are on the Wheel, but you certainly need the opposite direction. The East without the West is just spiritual bypass, visions that do not grow corn; the West without the East is a life without meaning – it is Peter Bell from Wordsworth's eponymous poem, for whom

> *"a primrose by a river's brim, a yellow primrose was to him, and it was nothing more."*

The South without the North is immersion in subjective feeling, with no perspective; and the North without the South is the mind thinking it is in control, divorced from feeling.

The Red Road of North-South is the work of everyday life: being present to ourselves, and having perspective on that. The North gives us the crucial ability to stand back from what we are feeling: it is disinterested (but not dissociated), while the South enables us at the same time to be in that feeling.

The North quality of disinterestedness is very powerful.

Note I am not saying 'uninterested' or 'dissociated' from feeling. 'Disidentified' is another word for this: we are still 'in' the feeling, but we are not letting it determine who we are in that moment. Feeling is sometimes a good guide to what is going on around us, and sometimes it is a bad guide. We need to learn when to trust our feelings, and when to know not to, because for example it is Monday morning and we are feeling that the whole world is against us. The North guides us in this, it shows us how to be impeccable. Feelings are always telling us something, we always need to pay close attention, but that may be something about ourselves rather than the world around us.

Jordan Peterson Under Attack

There is a guy called Jordan Peterson who is well worth watching on **YouTube**. One of his notable qualities is to remain unruffled under fire: he takes nothing personally, and remains quick-witted and rational. (To see an exceptional example of this, watch his interview with Cathy Newman.) This is quite unusual. For myself, I quickly feel flustered under that sort of attack, and it takes me a while afterwards for my feelings to calm down: when feeling is aroused, we easily imagine a lot of things are being said that aren't being said. This is normal. Peterson was asked how he manages to stay cool and rational under fire, and he responded that it was due to his extensive experience as a psychologist, in that he was always having to stand outside his personal responses and stay objective. Some people mistake this quality of Peterson's for coldness and lack of compassion, but it is not, you can see the feeling in him. It is just that he has a very well-developed North, and that is not possible unless the South is brought in also, otherwise feeling will sooner or later take over and we won't be aware of it, we will think we are being reasonable, when everyone around can see that we are not.

The North working together with the South can bring

an unusual self-mastery. That is the goal of the Red Road of everyday life, and it is a lifetime's work.

Original Thought

The disinterested qualities of the North that we have been looking at – not being one-sided, not making assumptions, not taking things personally, not caring what others think, listening to people and to yourself, checking sources on 'well-known facts' – lend themselves to thinking originally. This is something that anyone can do, it is not some special quality that only 'creative' people have. Being original means coming from your origin, coming from who you are. And that can be looked at as a matter of clearing out of the way all those tendencies that stop us doing that. What can appear as original to other people – or maybe as 'contrary', if they want you to think like they do – to oneself can appear as straightforward. If you do not have an emotional investment in seeing something or someone a particular way, then how it actually is can appear to you. These things can be obvious. Like what I said about the characteristics of democracy: its divisiveness, its promotion of unqualified people, the way it is often used to appeal to people's prejudices (which doesn't mean it's not the best worst system.) All this is obvious if you do not 'believe' in it, but harder to see so clearly if you do 'believe' in it. This quality of originality has nothing to do with intellectual ability, which is much over-rated in our education system. Intellectual ability can stand in the way of straightforward seeing, it can be like the Emperor's new clothes, because it gets given such high status. But as with all attributes, it needs to be in balance with the other directions, or it will tend to exist in its shadow form.

What Zebras Teach Us

What originality maybe has most to do with is courage. The warrior quality of the North. If you look in a fresh and original way, and you speak it, you will sometimes lose friends, because you are no longer 'right-thinking'. But you will also have friends who value that quality. Humans are herd animals. We are wired to fit in and to conform, and there is nothing wrong with that, up to a point. Our survival would once have depended on it, and it helps us feel connected to others. There is a story that some naturalists were studying zebras in the wild, and because they are hard to tell apart, they fired some red paint at the ones they wanted to study. What happened very quickly is that those zebras were eaten by the lions, because the lion pack could now all home in on the same animal. Keeping your head down, looking the same as everyone else, is a deep survival instinct. It takes a lot to stick your head above the parapet, and very few people are capable of that.

To think originally, we also need to be willing to change. Our beliefs in many ways define who we are, which is why people defend their positions fiercely and get into arguments on social media. You may even take pride in some of your beliefs, because they make you one of the 'good guys'. One of the 'rational' people, maybe, unlike those superstitious religious people. Or someone on the political left who cares about people, unlike those right-wing capitalists. And so on. Original thinking requires dropping all these ways we define ourselves – because otherwise how can you think, if certain outcomes are predetermined? It requires a deep reckoning with ourselves, a very different way of being, that is also free. And you can see people refusing to think, because it would threaten their sense of who they are, maybe what they have built their lives on, and the good opinion of the people they know.

Being Both Trusting and Discerning of Feeling

If you are working as a healer or counsellor, your feeling response to the client is central. You can sometimes know what they are feeling better than they do. Or if you do not know the person, and you are doing some journeying work for them, the information you get may be partly in the form of feeling, and you need to be able to distinguish between what is your feeling, and what is coming disinterestedly from Spirit. My experience in the Shamanic world is that this quality of discrimination is not sufficiently taught: rather, people are often encouraged to trust, in a one-sided way, the information they are given. The development of this trust is, on the one hand, very important, as our early upbringing often teaches us not to trust ourselves, but to trust what others tell us. But within that, discrimination is needed. There have been many times that I have had people do journeys for me, or mediumship-type work, and the information turns out at the time, or subsequently, to be inaccurate. We are here talking about using the North to critique the East (Intuition) as well as the South (feeling.)

As the receiver of information from journeyers/channellers, I can usually tell the difference by the quality of the energy. Sometimes it is like a bolt of lightning, and I know the person is onto something important, though they may not have the words exactly right. Other times it feels a bit flat, or what they are saying seems a bit obvious, like what they imagine I want to hear: there isn't that twist of something I hadn't thought of, that Spirit usually seems to give.

Sometimes it is that the person has one big thing to say to me that I need to hear, which can be done in a minute or two. The rest of the session, as one psychic reader admitted to me, is filling out the time to justify the fee. Fair enough, in a way. With astrology readings I find there can be one big thing I need to say, and it may not concern why the person thought they had come, and very often it seems to be just when the reading is about to finish, after an hour or so, that the big thing suddenly emerges out of the chart. With shamanic journeying, I usually get my information very quickly, even before the journey has 'officially' begun, so that I spent years thinking I was a 'bad' journeyer, before I understood the way I work.

Rationality as the Shadow of the Counter-Culture

Both in our approach to ourselves, and in our work with others, the North asks us to bring in the quality of rationality. We tend to use the word in quite a narrow way, to denote an abstract logical process. But if you think about it, the word comes from ratio, which means seeing things in proportion, which is far closer to the quality of perspective than is mere abstract logic. I think of the rationality of the North in this fuller sense.

I think that rationality can be part of the shadow side of the shamanic world. I think the reason for that is that modern shamanism arose in the context of the 'counter-culture' of the 1960s and its aftermath. The counter-culture itself arose as a reaction to the excessive materialism and rationality of the time (West and North respectively), which still continues. As a reaction, the counter-culture stands for the opposite qualities of imagination and feeling (East and South).

This is why, for example, there can be so much spiritual bypass in the counter-culture, where 'spirituality' is set up in opposition to ordinary, embodied existence, and becomes an escape from, instead of a deeper encounter with, ourselves. And why so many people readily believe, for example, conspiracy theories that have no grounding in fact and reason.

During the Covid lockdowns, it was striking how many people in the shamanic world believed, for example, that the pandemic had been planned in advance by governments, or that the vaccine had secret agendas behind it to, for example, manipulate your DNA. None of this had any basis in fact, but there was clearly a strong need to believe fuelling these ideas, along with a strong need to have others believing the same as they did. It was a perplexing and fascinating phenomenon, that revealed much about how human beings work. If you down-value rationality, then it ends up in the service of unexamined feeling.

Shamanic Tall-Tales

It has also resulted in the extraordinary phenomenon of people publishing exaggerated or falsified memoirs, as though the factual truth does not matter. Carlos Castaneda started this dishonourable tradition, and a number of other authors have followed suit. As a qualifier, this does not mean that Castaneda has not been a genuine inspiration to many, and brought qualities of imagination and story into Shamanism, as Andrei Znamenski points out in his book *The Beauty of the Primitive,* which is a history of Shamanism in the West. It was the same with Marlo Morgan's *Mutant Message Down Under*. It was a great story about the author's experience with aboriginal people in Australia. But eventually, confronted by Aboriginal Elders, she admitted making it up. Similarly, Simon Buxton's memoir *The Shamanic Way of the Bee* was described as a 'fairy tale' by Timothy White, editor of the major periodical magazine Shaman's Drum (*The Beauty of the Primitive* p219.)

My most generous interpretation is that these authors are concerned to present an imaginative, visionary truth, and it may be OK in certain cultures to present such truth as literal truth. But in our culture, we distinguish between imaginative and literal truth, and it amounts to a falsehood to present the former as the latter.

In all these ways: spiritual bypass, conspiracy thinking, invented memoirs and lack of critical awareness in journeying work, we see this need for more emphasis on the North and on rationality in the Shamanic world. It is perhaps interesting that the founder of 'core shamanism', probably the leading model in the way Shamanism is taught, was an academic, Michael Harner. The emphasis in the academic world is, of course, rationality, often one-sidedly so, I would suggest. And the 'core-shamanism' that he founded tends to have its emphasis in the opposite direction. That further suggests to me the phenomenon of one extreme throwing up its opposite, which is not balance, but (hopefully) the first step on the path to balance. In the same way the 1960s counter culture (and the 19th century Romantics before) was a necessary assertion of the same psychic opposite, that may eventually, but not necessarily, lead to a new synthesis, a new balance.

The Knowing Place

The North is the place of knowing. And it is where we come to realise that we know in different ways. Our feelings tell us things. You get a 'feeling' about somebody or something: pay attention to it. Do not absolutise it: the feeling may be superficial, or you may be in a fearful mood, so check these things. It is telling you something, though sometimes it may be about yourself and not, as you think, about someone or something else. But sometimes such feelings are unmistakable: get out, do not pass go, do not dally, just go before something bad happens. What is a feeling and what is an intuition can be hard to separate, and maybe the problem is partly linguistic. But sometimes we just know that something is right for us, or wrong for us, or we get a sense of a bigger picture that pulls us in a particular direction, even though we don't know the outcome. And when do we ever know outcomes anyway? One thing astrology has, ironically, taught me is just how unpredictable the future is. You can get a sense of the shape of the future sometimes. Before Covid, for example, many astrologers could see that something big was on its way in early 2020. But I don't know of anyone who got the specifics – i.e. a pandemic – right.

Non-rational means of knowing are often disempowered in our culture. Which is why you can get the swing to the opposite extreme in the counter-culture. And it puts you at a disadvantage if you are not quick with words. More than once I have encountered women wanting desperately to leave their marriages, but not knowing how to put it to their husbands, who they feared would easily out-argue them: in one case, the woman's husband was a lawyer, so she was right. Sometimes you just don't have the words, maybe because words aren't your thing, or maybe because you know what you have to do, but it may be several years before you know why, because life has to unfold. When I do astrology readings, and I see a significant element of Scorpio in the chart, I home in on this non-rational means of knowing, which exists in opposition to the Shadow of the North, the rational mind that thinks that only its way of knowing is valid.

What I say to Scorpios is that the education system tends to teach us that knowledge is only valid if supported by theory and evidence (North and West), and that instinct/intuition is downgraded to the merely subjective. It is seen as 'unreliable' and is, I think, part of our historical suppression of the feminine principle. I continue that, with this pronounced Scorpio, you need to learn to trust that instinct, and one of the ways we do that is by the consequences of not listening to and acting on it: we get bitten hard. We betray ourselves, and then life betrays us. And then, hopefully, we learn. I think that kind of knowing is always there, and it is a matter of choice as to whether we listen to it.

In the case of the person leaving the marriage, this can be about trusting that voice that is telling you what to do, to the extent that you actually leave, as we said in the section on Relationship Crises in the West. That voice is you, you in a way that you have never fully been before – it is also Spirit – and you are learning to be that. And then having the right words does not matter. The shadow of the North with its weaselly words no longer has power over us. And nor do all those other voices telling you that you must be a bad person for making this marriage fail. And how could you do this to the children etc. Sometimes we just know what the right thing to do is, and reason may have its reservations, but sometimes that just has to be ignored, because we are answering the call of the Spirit. We also covered this in the West, from the point of view of crises and claiming some new element in yourself around which your life needs to be re-arranged.

Knowing who to Trust and who not to Trust

This knowing also extents to knowing who to trust and who not to trust. The South is the natural trust in life that the child has, which we often have to re-learn later on. If the child is cared for properly, they will grow up with good starting models of what men and women are like, and that will help them later on in knowing who to trust and who not to trust. You often see in relationships where one person is having a terrible time, because they have got involved with someone they have given too much trust to, and this can sometimes be traced back to childhood and the lack of the sort of parenting that would have helped them know who to be around intimately, and who not to be around. It can happen too where too much trust has been given to 'spiritual' teachers who mistreat their followers in one way or another.

The classic case involves teachers using them for casual sex, dressed up as being for the student's own good. The more common, lower-level mistreatment, however, is the mind-control, the requirement that the followers should think and behave as they say. It is good when these teachers are eventually held to account, but the followers who feel betrayed can learn from this: why did I give this person so much trust? It is a tough lesson, but those sorts of lessons are the ones we often learn the most from. It usually goes back to parental issues. We learn better who to trust and who not to trust, and that turns us into an adult who is able to steer their own path without continually falling over. With relationships, you see people making the same mistakes over and over: sometimes it takes a long time.

Knowing We Know Nothing

Socrates claimed to be the wisest man in Athens because he was the only one who knew that he knew nothing. Ignorance could be defined not as lack of knowledge, but as thinking you know. Etymologically, it comes from the word 'ignore', which suggests it is also about not listening, in the deeper way that we have been discussing: listening to the Spirit within, rather than to the clamour of received opinions around us, or to the defences of our South. Ultimately, everything is the Great Mystery.

The venerable Bede tells the story of the missionary bishop Paulinus who, in converting King Edwin of Northumberland, likened life to that of a sparrow which flies in through the door of the banqueting hall they were in, stays a short time, and flies out another door: we do not know where the sparrow has come from, or where it is going. Just so with our own lives: we do not know where we have come from, or where we will go. Any knowing we have in this life is in the context of this greater not-knowing, this mystery that surrounds our life and even the fact that we exist. Anything we think we know has to be provisional. And yet we seek the security of false certainties. We do not feel entirely sure of those certainties, or we would not need to defend them so fiercely.

A traditional way of looking at this is that we humans each have a tiny slice of consciousness, and the cosmos is a vast consciousness. How can we ever know more than a very tiny slice of what is going on? But that is not how people work: we have a strong desire to think we know more than we do, because of the sense of certainty it gives us. The humility to admit we don't know – not in theory, which anyone can, and probably will, say, but specifically – can be experienced as very threatening.

Decision-Making

The North is the place in which we learn how to make decisions, using the mind to gather information from the three other directions. That is why the North is also the place of the Elder, because they know how to make wise decisions. There is a Native American saying to wait four days before making an important decision. That is also why we sometimes need to 'sleep on it'. Spirit, Emotion and the Body all need time to make their input. I can personally find the process of waiting quite uncomfortable, even at my advanced age. There is still a headstrong youth in me that wants to decide and to act immediately. And I have to use Cognitive Behaviour Therapy on myself sometimes: Is there any rush, I ask myself? Usually there isn't. And up to a point, that works. But it can remain uncomfortable. However, what I invariably find is that, having waited, my perspective on the situation changes in ways that I could not have foreseen. It was the mind, that thought it knew, and driven by child-like emotion in the South, that wanted to act. Whereas what is needed, as always, is that deeper knowing of the North, that arises out of the other three directions. And that has as its context the awareness that really, we know nothing. I forgive myself somewhat, however, because I know my impatience is usually also a result of being quite passionate about whatever it is that I want to do.

Festina Lente

And if you can't make a decision, trust that. The deeper things, the important things, take time, they unfold over years. There is no hurry, and patterns which we cannot perceive with our tiny minds need time to fall into place. Whose idea is it that you need to make a decision now? Or that you need this thing called 'clarity'?

The Future

As we go around the Wheel, we move from the timeless East to the past of the Child in the South, to the present time of the Adult in the West, and then to the future in the North. The adult in the West is very tied up with his or her day-to-day responsibilities. Their future orientation is largely limited to practical planning, rather than the deep perspective of the North, that has the space and experience to ponder not just the immediate future, but for generations ahead. This is exactly what has not been happening in our collective stewardship of the planet. We are guided far more by short-term material interest than by what the Earth will be like for our grandchildren, and all the animals and plants too.

The future orientation of the North is a combination of long experience and visionary ability, that have grown in the decades it has taken to traverse the East, South and West. It is about far more than mere planning. Planning takes us out of the present, which is all we actually have, into an imagined future, which is fantasy. "Life is what happens to you while you're busy making other plans."

The future orientation of the North does not contradict the ability to be present that has been learned, maybe painfully, in the West, through learning to live with, rather than avoiding, ourselves. Rather, it grows out of it. It is, in a way, starting to move towards something timeless, in which past, present and future are one, all parts of one vast pattern.

To make the move from West to North, we need to stop planning – or at least, stop being identified with, living for, our plans, our 'bucket list' maybe, and allow life to unfold. It is often best just to muddle along, approaching each new thing as it presents itself, leaving Spirit to take care of the longer-term future. And you will then start to get a sense of that bigger future, because there is space for it, because you have let go of that shadow aspect of the North that tries to get everything pinned down and 'clear'. There are times to be clear, and times not to be clear, and it can take the wisdom of the North to know the difference. But even when we are clear about what to do, the action we take still needs to be surrounded by Spirit rather than by too many plans, so that it can go the way it needs to, which will invariably be different to what we may have imagined.

In writing this book, I have been trying not to let my mind concern itself with whether or not I will find a publisher, or what its reception will be. There will be a time for that, and how to do that will present itself. For now, there is an impulse in me to do this writing: that impulse, and all the help I get from Spirit along the way, cannot have full rein if my mind is taken over by 'planning', which itself can be just a mask for a desire for certainty and security. And part of the help I get from Spirit is based on Egregore, the Medicine Wheel that exists in the Spirit World, that has been gathering power from the millions of people over the millennia who have become more balanced through exposure to it. Live with the uncertainty of not-knowing, so that the future can present itself in a visionary way.

Stories

Stories were the traditional means by which wisdom was passed on. The Elder was often also the story-teller. I used to have a traditionally-trained story teller staying with me. And the way he worked was quite different to how it is done nowadays, where story tellers turn up with a particular story to tell. He would begin by asking people to ask him questions about issues that were on their minds, and as they did so, a story in response would eventually present itself to him, and he would tell it. You can see how teaching in this context is a spontaneous thing, based on where people are right this minute, and what it is they need to hear. There is, of course, a place for pre-set teachings, but if you don't have a fixed idea of what it is that you are going to teach, and people have not come with a pre-set expectation, then the Spirit can speak. Spirit knows what people need to hear, so as the teacher you just need to be an open and adequate conduit for that. It is not Spirit alone, for it has to come through the medium of your own experience: it is not enough just to be a 'channel', though that is certainly part of it. If you are in the teaching position, and you are working in this spontaneous way, you learn to trust what you end up talking about, and where it leads. A friend told me that the workshops he has led that have gone the worst, were those he had planned in advance.

A traditional story-teller will really know his stories in detail, and he will know many of them: that requires a feat of trained memory that we don't have any more. I have a theory that indigenous people carried a lot more in their memories than we do now. They were bearers of their culture in ways that we no longer are. They had to be more creative and sharper in their everyday living, with a wider range of skills, because they did not have so many things done for them as we do nowadays. In other words, they were more cultured, creative and smart. I certainly don't want to idealise them, which many people do nowadays, just as they idealise Tibetan Lamas and Hindu gurus, because of the meaning-lack at the heart of our culture. But it interesting to think of ourselves as perhaps a step down, instead of the step up which talk of 'primitive' people suggests. We do not have a large brain for no reason, yet we get told that we only use some of it: the logical corollary would seem to be that early people had greater mental powers then us.

In his book *The Wayfinders*, Canadian anthropologist Wade Davis describes his encounters with a number of indigenous cultures that still have a living link to their traditional ways. It is notable how deeply immersed and knowledgeable these people are about the natural world that they live in, with a way of relating to it and understanding it that is frequently incomprehensible to us moderns – far more subtle and alive, I would say, compared to the crude, literal world we now live in. Davis also describes the incredible sea-faring exploits of the Polynesians in canoes over an area of 25 million square km

– 1/5 of the surface of the planet. The navigator would spend much of the long journeys in a trance, as he remembered all the movements of the boat, and was sensitive to something like five different levels of current in the water. And that is to say nothing of their fine awareness of the sky and its clouds and beyond that the constellations. These 'primitive' peoples were skilled in ways we can only dream about.

The traditional stories that I have heard centre around a character called Wisahitsa, who is a trickster figure in the Chippewa Cree tradition. He is characterised by self-importance and by thinking he is smarter than everyone else; he is also very self-centred. And because of this, he always comes unstuck, and it is comical. So really the stories, this wisdom tradition, are about the human ego and its propensity to become full of itself – and deluded, accordingly. What I noticed was how sophisticated and subtle is the psychology and philosophy of this tradition, at least equal to our own, and not constrained by the materialism and literalism that bedevil our modern attempts to understand people and the universe.

It is also worth exploring Lewis Mehl-Madrona's books *Coyote Medicine, Coyote Healing* and *Coyote Wisdom,* where he recounts his own work using traditional Native American stories to help people in their healing journeys. Their suffering may begin with a physical illness, but there is always a story behind it, which Lewis uncovers from the patient. He then sometimes ties in their story with a traditional story, and the journeys of transformation some of the characters undergo. And the starting point is always the East: do you want to get well, and why do you want to get well? What is it, in other words, that gives meaning to your life?

Creation Mythologies

We have a patronising approach to the Creation Myths of other cultures. We are, of course, 'open-minded' about them, and treat them with the 'respect' that liberal, post-modern culture demands. But really, they are 'just' stories, aren't they, whereas science tells us what 'really' happened? Traditional cultures often have a number of stories about how the world came to be. We have just one, the scientific narrative: and if it finds itself with two stories – or 'theories' – then they have to slug it out until one of them wins.

Science as Story and as Belief System

To appreciate the mythologies of other cultures, we need to understand first that our story is a story, and not this other category called 'fact' that transcends story. This is not an easy thing to do. I have spent years addressing this brainwashing in myself. The story of the sparrow flying through the hall says it all, really. We don't know where we came from, or where we are going, or indeed why anything exists. And a cursory consideration of brain science shows that what we call reality is a construct of the brain, that enables us to live our lives. It is a model that works. But even its categories of space and time and a separate self are just that, categories for orienting ourselves, nothing more. And then if you bring in the findings of quantum physics, where events can precede causes, where there are no certainties, only probabilities, and where events and observers are inextricable linked; if you consider all that, it becomes obvious that this world, experienced as so tangible and certain and external to ourselves, and where one event leads to another, is all just a convenient illusion. When you really think about it, there is nothing we can know, everything is baffling at the deepest possible level!

The pre-condition to this realisation is reflection on the existential situation, and allowing that to percolate through your being over time. And that doesn't interest a lot of people: life with its everyday demands and 'obvious' reality is enough for them. So, when people sometimes say ah, but science is catching up with this more subtle, less materialistic view of the universe, after all look at quantum physics, I say no, quantum physics has been around for over 100 years and yet, by and large, science still thinks about reality in this naïve way; as though the world is this solid, objective, material thing, with consciousness as an epiphenomenon, instead of at the foundation, as primary, as the double slit experiment showed over 100 years ago.

And why hasn't the mainstream understanding of reality caught up with quantum physics, after all this time? The answer is straightforward: it is because quantum physics is subtle, it does not give the simple certainties that are the perennial demand of humanity. In this respect, it is the same situation as we find between religion (for the majority) and mysticism (for the minority), and why wouldn't it be, because science is nothing other than our modern-day belief system?

Think about it. Who has seen an atom, or the ozone layer, or even the Earth go round the Sun? The answer is, none of us. We therefore have beliefs, not knowledge about these things. That science is essentially a belief system about a series of models of the universe is important to understand. It helps to remove the curse of facticity, of these ultimate realities called 'facts' that you can't argue with, and which deny any other ways of looking at the universe, reducing them to 'just' stories.

Now I am not saying that scientific beliefs are unreasonable beliefs. They seem to me to be eminently reasonable and practical in many ways. I am not bashing science, because I don't like bashing people's stories about the universe. They are all lenses on reality. We need beliefs in order to live. We can't drive a car unless we believe that the road is going to continue in front of us, and not suddenly disappear. Belief here becomes intertwined with a basic trust in life.

What we need to do is to become aware of the status of our beliefs and what we think we know. We need to be aware that it is all provisional and that there are other ways of looking at the universe that are also valid, and which can enlarge our perspective by giving us a point of comparison.

As I say, most people do not want to do this. We generally believe what we want to believe, and we can get very emotive about it because it is at the base of who we think they are, and we do not want to seriously examine those beliefs. If you can accept that about people, and not expect too much, you will save yourself a lot of grief. I still find myself rising when I see political prejudice, in either direction, but I am slowly teaching myself to ignore it and not expect otherwise.

The Modern Fundamentalism

One of the biggest modern superstitions is that we left superstition behind in the Middle Ages, and that we now live in an age of reason, and know how things 'really' are, unlike the 'primitive' people who came before.

In the Middle Ages, there was only one reality, and that was the Christian reality, with its simple certainties of good and bad and heaven and hell. You knew where you stood. Is it essentially any different now? We have inherited the medieval fundamentalist attitude, fundamentalism being the idea that there is only one reality. That one reality is scientific, and it admits no competitors. Rival theories fight it out until only one survives, and older disciplines such as herbalism or astrology, which do not use its methods, are denied mainstream acceptance or respectability. Within that one scientific reality are some simple certainties: the universe began with the big bang, life arose through evolution, and when we die, we are extinguished. I think it is more important for our sense of existential security to know where we stand, than for that place to necessarily be very palatable. And we believe these things by and large because we are told them. So, what is the difference, in that sense, to the medieval world? Not a lot, as far as I can see.

I said that I do not want to bash science or indeed any other stories about the world. It can be tempting to do so when you are rigid in your beliefs in the stories you subscribe to. Maybe it is even natural to do so. But if you are attempting to find the awareness and balance that the Medicine Wheel points us towards, then it becomes more difficult to privilege one way of seeing the universe over another, or to want to attack those who have different stories.

Liberal Hypocrisy

There can be a great deal of hypocrisy in the rational, liberal position that is often adopted in the West. Stephen Fry, who came up in the Chapter on the South for his exclusively 'chemical' approach to his bi-polar syndrome, is well known for his support of free speech and reason and generally wanting people to be nice to each other. That is all laudable. But when it comes to subjects like astrology or religion, he becomes quite vehemently oppositional, and speaks in very condemnatory, intolerant language. As he says:

> *"All astrology is absolutely and without reservation the bullest of bullsh*t that ever there was. It is a senseless delusion that does not even have the benefit of being harmless fun. It is a harmful bore. Harmful to the human spirit, harmful to the dignity and wonder of the real universe and the real power of the mind to think for itself. I hate astrology with a fervour that is almost frightening."*

What is interesting to me here is not whether or not Fry thinks astrology has any validity. That is because the stories we subscribe to are personal, and in a way it does not matter. What I think matters is the openness, or lack of it, with which we hold those stories. If we use our stories to condemn other stories, as Fry is doing here, then we are, ironically, back in the medieval mindset, but with a god who has changed his name from Jehovah to Reason. And Fry feels entitled not to tolerate anything that offends this god.

Whose idea was it that the universe is founded on reason? It is an assumption that does not stand much examination. It is, ironically, a superstition. You see what I mean about us moderns being no less superstitious than medieval people. What is interesting about Stephen Fry, however, is that while on the one hand he promotes the god of reason like a religious zealot, he is on the other hand prone to manic-depression and the occasional suicide attempt, which he speaks openly about, to his credit. I do not want to sound callous about this, but the man has a deeply non-rational side – like we all do, we are the elephant, not the rider – but it is as though Fry is afraid of this, and clings on to reason. It does not, of course, work, because when we deny something, it is likely to come back at us in an unpleasant and disruptive way. Don't get me wrong, there is much I appreciate about Stephen Fry. But I think he illustrates very well the shortcomings of a one-sided worship of reason, and the hypocrisy that can lead to. And that there can be psychological reasons, woundings we are trying to protect, in our espousal of reason. Just as there can be in the way some people cling to religion. It is spiritual bypass, transposed to the rational-scientific framework. It illustrates very well the shadow of the North that characterises our modern culture.

Two-Eyed Seeing

Two-Eyed seeing is a term created in 2004 by Mi'kmaw Elder Albert Marshall.

> *"It refers to learning to see from one eye with the strengths of Indigenous knowledges and ways of knowing, and from the other eye with the strengths of Western knowledges and ways of knowing ... and learning to use both these eyes together, for the benefit of all."* http://www.integrativescience.ca/Principles/TwoEyedSeeing/

In the Philosophy of Science, it comes under the heading 'Explanatory Pluralism'.

It is an essentially pragmatic philosophy. As modern Westerners, our instinct is often to burrow away at different theories, until we have proved one of them right, and the other wrong. All that really matters, however, is that the practice which comes out of the theory works, that it gets good results. Like I quoted at the start of the book "If it works, it's real." Astrology works, I have no doubt about that. And homeopathy. And acupuncture. But they are not very amenable to being proved scientifically. Science says that something is only true if it can be proved to be so on its own very particular terms, using repeatability, statistics and theory. This is not unreasonable within certain parameters, but the world got along very well without these parameters for millennia.

Two-Eyed Seeing is partly a corrective to this tendency of science towards fundamentalism, towards wanting everything to be true and valid purely on its own terms. And how can that ever be? Theories are only descriptions of reality, they are not reality itself, which is unknowable. More than that, Two-Eyed Seeing is asking that conventional and alternative medicines leave each other alone and stop criticising each other; rather, they need to respect and appreciate each other. This intolerance goes both ways. We have probably all seen how conventional medicine can be so dismissive and antagonistic towards disciplines such as homeopathy. But people on the 'alternative' side can be just as dismissive and disrespectful of conventional medicine. Vaccination, for example, is one of the better things that conventional medicine does. It is using a small amount of like-for-like to catalyse the body into marshalling its own defences against disease. The science is pretty solid. And yet it gets attacked, using pseudo-science that makes very little sense. Such attacks make their proponents look ignorant and prejudiced. Now there is nothing wrong with having an alternative to vaccine, using, for example, homeopathy. That is laudable. But it is not either/or. If your alternative approach has to be 'right' and conventional medicine 'wrong', then you are participating in the rigid, fundamentalist mindset that caused the problems in the first place.

It is liberating to be able to hold two different ways of seeing the world at once. It changes the way we see the whole of life. It grounds us more in experience and less in ideas. And it shows us the real nature of the mind in the North. It is not there to create rigid theories to explain and justify our life (though it can certainly be used like that.) The mind used rightly is a servant that holds a number of different and useful explanations of reality, but all they are is explanations, and their multiplicity reveals the abundance and variety of life itself, if we allow ourselves into its flow. Achieving this, however, is more than a mental exercise: we tend to be one-sided about everything, for emotional reasons. So, the work of the South is also needed here.

The Righteous Mind

One friend had a strong dislike for the Tory Party. They were always wrong, whatever the issue. He was prepared, however, to concede that his views were emotionally based. This went back to how he had been brought up, it was a tribal hatred, and he was not prepared to let go of that. Even this level of honesty is unusual: many people cannot see the emotional basis to their views, meaning that they will always find the other Party wrong, whatever the issue, and think that position to be rational. Eventually this friend was able to separate his viewpoints from his emotional bias against the political right, and the bias itself also eventually evaporated. But without the emotional awareness, it is very hard to change the one-sided views, because they seem to be so obviously reflecting what seems to you to be reality. The one-sided views tend to be judgemental, because they exist in opposition to some other view. But as Jonathan Haidt points out, it is in the nature of the mind to be 'righteous'. It is normal to be judgemental, it is unusual not to be. If you think about it, any view is just that, it is a 'view': it is a description of something, it is not the thing itself, so how can it ever be anything other than partial?

Buddhist Emptiness

This is a central insight of Buddhist contemplative practice. Buddhism has the concept 'Sunyata', which means 'emptiness': one version of what this means is that all words, all ideas, are just that, words and ideas. They are not realities. In a way, it is obvious, why am I labouring such an obvious point? Because emotionally, we hang on to words and ideas, sometimes for dear life, and they give us a sense of being 'right'. This is why a contemplative meditation is needed: so that what we understand on a mind level can percolate down onto the emotional level and change how we are, soften and open us. Don't take any of your ideas too seriously, and don't take them literally. The reality they describe is unknowable, and beyond words. Sunyata, or Emptiness, can seem quite a remote, and even bleak, profundity. But it is quite practical: it could be said to simply mean don't take anything literally. So simple, and yet so difficult!

Never be For or Against

The Chinese Chan Master Sengcan addressed this perennial human one-sidedness when he said:

> *"If you want the truth to stand clear before you, never be for or against. The struggle between for or against is the mind's worst disease."*

This nicely sums up the central task of the North.

The Modern Creation Myths

We began looking at Creation Mythologies a few sections back, and then did a big loop around the nature of ideas and science as story rather than fact, so that we could have a suitable and open basis for exploring these deeper stories, and not be too tied in to literal truth and 'facts'.

All cultures have stories about how the world began, and ours is no exception. 1000 years ago, we believed that God created the Earth and all the life on it. Today we have a different Creation story because we 'know better': the Universe began with the Big Bang, and life arose through a process of Evolution, in which the fittest survive. This is what 'actually' happened. Yet the medieval mind was no less certain that their creation story was what 'actually' happened. But I hope I have made my point sufficiently that ultimately, we do not know.

The Big Bang and Evolution

I accept the Big Bang and Evolution as useful stories, but that does not mean they cannot be tweaked. My principal reservation to these stories is that they do not ascribe magical or miraculous origins to the universe or to life. These are maybe the first such myths in human history not to do so. From the scientific point of view, this is because we see ourselves as grounded in 'fact', we know better, and we have gone beyond superstition.

The Need for Magic

But the psyche needs magic and miracles. That is part of the function of the astrology readings I do: using the chart (and my own connection to whatever it is that is out there), I am able to say things about the person that they recognise to be true, often things that I would have no way of knowing. I always begin a reading by asking the person not to tell me anything about themselves just yet, so that I can do this magic. The bigger purpose of the reading is to help the person understand themselves, but that initial enchantment is important: it says that the universe knows you, you are connected in ways you can hardly even guess at.

The Age of Reason (so-called 'reason': there is nothing reasonable about enthroning this servant of the psyche) has resulted in a disenchanted universe, hence the nature of our creation stories. Magic, however, has a way of creeping back in, because it is part of the human psyche, which is no different to the universe itself. What else is 'counter-intuitive' quantum physics than a form of magical reality? And what else is the Big Bang, in which everything arose out of nothing in an instant, but a miracle? We are supposed to believe that the Big Bang is scientific fact. But how could anything this implausible and unlikely be a 'fact'?

Tweaking the Big Bang

I have my own explanation of the Big Bang, using astrology and its ancient gods, in particular Uranus, Neptune and Pluto, the three outer planets of the solar system, that describe collective events. These three gods were present at the creation event. Uranus provided the creative spark, which is by definition something new that has never been thought of before. Uranus said "Hey guys, I've had this idea for a thing called a universe, let's do it!" And Pluto comes in with his tremendous power, which begins as a tiny seed, rather like the power in the tiny centre of an atom. A huge expansion begins. And as it does so, consciousness simultaneously imagines beauty through diverse forms and symmetries – stars, planets, elements, galaxies, black holes and so on – which gradually come into being over this thing called time, that has also been imagined along with space: all this is the result of the primordial imaginative power of the god Neptune.

So that is something of my own magical tweak, in which the universe arose out of timeless, spaceless archetypal powers that are always present: the power of consciousness, and its creativity and imagination. And these powers continue to inform our lives personally and collectively. They take us, willingly or unwillingly, on our transformative journey around the Medicine Wheel. Whatever your magical tweak, I think it important to recognise that the Big Bang is not primarily a scientific fact: it is hardly the case that some intrepid Victorian explorer was there to photograph it, and that the pictures lie gathering dust in the British Museum. No, it is a story about the unimaginably distant past that is beyond any direct human verification – whatever the specialists and their balancing equations of arcane symbols say – and I think that is how the Unconscious understands it. We do not understand things in just one way. There is the rational understanding, but there is the understanding of the elephant – the real boss – which sees things quite differently. And for the elephant, the Big Bang is a timeless magical event.

Tweaking Evolution

Having tweaked the Big Bang so that it can also speak to the magical part of the psyche, it is time to move on to Evolution. Let me begin by saying that it is a good story that explains a lot. But not everything. It has lots of holes in it if you start to look closely, and do not accept the modern dogmatism around it. Evolution has become a rallying point in our breaking away from the 'superstitious' past, to the point that any questioning of it can put you under suspicion. For people who can only think in two categories, questioning makes you a Creationist. Evolution has for many people become a dogma, but it does not appear to them as dogma: it appears as fact, and what could be more reasonable than to accept 'facts' and to criticise those who do not accept such 'facts'?

I am not saying that there is not good evidence for this story, just as there is evidence for the Big Bang. But that evidence just makes it a good story with, in this case, practical uses. Any thoughtful scientist could tell you this about the whole of science: it is just a series of models of reality. It is not reality itself.

Scientific Evidence is not the only Evidence

Science's reliance on 'evidence' is what some people like to hit you over the head with, as though that ends the argument against any alternative explanations. Because, of course, in their minds only one explanation can be 'right'. I was struck when reading about the Catholic Church canonising a particular Saint in recent years. What impressed me was how rigorously they went about it. People had to have prayed to this Saint for healing, and the healing had to have occurred. The evidence had to be thoroughly investigated and verified before it would be accepted, and there had to be a number of instances. And I thought well what is so wrong with this? Are they not using evidence just as a scientist would? Why is one seen as reasonable and rational, and the other as superstition, just because it doesn't have an equation to show how it happened? Saints and their miracles make good stories in my opinion. They have prayer and healing, they have miraculous intervention, and they have sworn testimonies. What is not to like?

The Confusion Between Ideas and Reality

Science deals with a certain type of reality, and that is fair enough. It is a valuable thing to do. The problem with it comes from the mind's perennial tendency to confuse ideas about reality with reality itself. The undoing of this confusion is one of the central concerns of the North.

I take the view that consciousness, spirit, is not separate from matter; that indeed matter is the dream of spirit. This view seems fully traditional from an indigenous point of view. It is how people always thought, whatever part of the world they came from, until the last few millennia. That does not make it 'true'. But as Jung said in our discussion on ageing, the correct way to live is always according to nature. And that gives me faith in the indigenous attitude, which is fundamentally the same the world over: it reflects how people are when they feel they are part of the natural world, and it is therefore the best and most balanced attitude to have.

Evolution: Competition or Co-operation?

The theory of Evolution says that life forms change over time, driven by a self-centred drive to survive: whichever individuals in a population leave the most offspring are the 'fittest', and their particular characteristics will be passed on and contribute to the 'evolution' of that species. That life forms have changed over millions of years is hard to dispute, for we have the fossil record. That the mechanism for such change should be brutal competition between individuals is an assumption. Out of this assumption came Richard Dawkins' famous – or notorious – book *The Selfish Gene* which was even more reductive, seeing life as a selfish struggle not between individual members of a species, but between the individual genes of which they are made.

What is remarkable to anyone who has studied the natural world is the degree to which different life forms live together in harmony, creating complex ecosystems that benefit all. A more natural and straightforward conclusion would seem to be that life progresses through co-operation as much as it may through competition.

And how does one explain the arising in humans of the ability to make music or write poetry? Would poets have generally left more offspring than other people? It seems ridiculous to think in these terms. And yet you see evolutionary biologists refusing to actually think about such phenomena and, in their banal and Procrustean way, trying to reduce everything to competitive advantage, because that is how it 'had' to have arisen. It is a modern dogma.

The Theory of Evolution arose in the 19th century, as Victorian capitalism was thriving, and what could be more natural than to suggest a mechanism for the whole of life that reflected and even justified the competitive capitalist ethos of the time, and which endures to this day? For an indigenous person, the natural world takes care of us, it is fundamentally benign, and the idea that life can be reduced to a ruthless competition would be abhorrent, and contrary to observation. I cannot prove scientifically that Evolution is about co-operation as much as it is about competition (if it is about that at all) but I don't feel obliged to, just as I don't feel obliged to prove astrology works scientifically. Science is a specialised form of truth, whose parameters only apply to a thin slice of life.

Evolution and the Great Chain of Being

Evolution thinks of itself as a scientific theory rather than as a mythology, but you only have to look at the medieval Great Chain of Being to see its predecessor. At the top is God, and then it goes down through angels, demons, men, women, animals, plants and minerals. Evolution is an inversion of this Chain of Being, in that it begins at the bottom, with minerals, and then works its way upwards until it reaches... you got it, humans! So, all we have really done with our 'scientific' theory of evolution is to invert the direction of the Great Chain of Being, and put ourselves, rather than God, at the top. And we have done this because the mind works primarily mythologically rather than rationally. Science lives within a pile of myths about the nature of the universe.

Humans are the 'New-Born' ones

This hubris, that sees mankind as more evolved than other species, also goes against indigenous attitudes. It is wrong if only because it is hubristic, a human tendency that indigenous peoples are very aware of. For the Chippewa Cree, humans are seen as the 'new-born' ones, recent arrivals, because we are the only species that does not know who it is. If you look at other species, they know how to live, what to do to survive and to reproduce, and how to behave in a way that is according to their natures, and in balance with the world around them. But we humans do not know how to live in a balanced way with the natural world, and it is usually a lifetime's task to know who we are. Far from putting down other species as 'mere' animals or plants, indigenous people look at them as conscious beings with a point of view – just as, indeed, they will see rocks and the Sun and lakes in this way too – and try to see from their point of view. This is how we learn: through observing the world with an attitude of humility, rather than by imposing ourselves with an attitude of superiority.

There is a thoughtful and radical book by Richard Milton called *Shattering the Myths of Darwinism*, that questions all the dogmas around Evolution. Authors such as Milton easily get written off as 'anti-science', but he is not, he is just thoughtful.

Life Dreams itself into Being

Note that I am not trying to write off Evolution. I want to tweak it, because it is our modern creation story, and we need one. I had a dream some years ago in which I saw a speckled butterfly, and it was perfectly adapted to its surroundings. And I was given to understand that the theory of Evolution only explains a very thin slice of how this situation came to be. Evolution is not wrong; it is just limited as an explanation. We tend to see causality as an external, objective material phenomenon. But how about the subjective dimension as cause? You could say that consciousness and matter are one, with consciousness being the subjective dimension, and matter the objective dimension. And life forms arise because they are dreamed into being. Life is stunningly beautiful (not that there is a scientific measurement for that), so why not say that the creation of new forms beauty, rather than brute competition, drives Evolution? Just as we humans experience a drive to create, that gives us our most meaningful experiences, so is life itself essentially creative, and we are one expression of that.

What About the End of the Universe?

We have the Big Bang and Evolution bringing the Universe and Life into being respectively. There is also an End Times to our modern Creation Mythology: instead of Armageddon, we have Heat Death. This idea arises out of the Second Law of Thermodynamics, which says that the amount of disorder (entropy) in a system always increases over time. This means that the Universe as a whole is gradually running down: it is gradually becoming more dispersed and less ordered. The eventual result of this, billions of years down the line, is that the universe will be so dispersed that there will be nothing, no energy, there at all. And this is called Heat Death.

Can we introduce magic into this grey nothingness? There is a way in which I view scientific theories, and the evidence for them, as the universe corresponding to the way we imagine it. If you have imagined the Higgs Boson, and you go looking for it, sooner or later there is a good chance you will find it. That does not make it 'imaginary'. It is real. But consciousness and matter inform each other. I think the idea of Heat Death reflects our modern demonisation of the universe: we have already decided the universe is essentially dead and indifferent to us (what a contrast to the indigenous idea that Mother Earth is alive and takes care of us), and Heat Death just seems to be a corollary of that. It is a denial of the reality of Spirit and the Imagination.

Is the Universe Gradually Running Down?

Maybe Heat Death is salvageable in the sense that we can tweak it to make it imaginatively satisfying. But what I want to do is to put in a counter-notion. Is your experience of the world that it is gradually running down? If we leave out the actions of modern humanity for a moment, surely our experience of the natural world is that it is continually renewing itself? That it does so is one of the wonders and beauties of life. Moreover, there are indigenous people who greet the Sun every day, with the idea that if they did not express gratitude to the Sun in this way, it would cease to rise. Putting this together, the continued renewal of the world and the life within it, is dependent upon our appreciation of it. That is why it is good to leave offerings to the natural world and to the various beings, seen and unseen, which inhabit her. If we do not relate to the natural world with an attitude of appreciation, but one of exploitation, then she will gradually die – she will suffer from 'entropy'. That is why it is said that the fairies are disappearing: because we forget to remember them nowadays (I try to leave them offerings myself at places where I feel they are present.) Science and an attitude of treating the world as a 'thing' to be exploited often go together (they don't have to), so the idea of entropy is a natural consequence. The way the psyche understands this theory is that everything is gradually getting worse. But it doesn't have to be like this. Make offerings to the natural world to avoid Heat Death! Modern science has its 'laws' of physics. But who says they do not change over time, that they have to remain the same? Personally, I take it quite literally that if we were all to feed and appreciate the natural world, then she would not be slowly running down as alleged.

I think there is another End Times myth that fuels us, that is much closer at hand, which is the end of life as we know it due to man-made climate change and environmental degradation. I that that many of us have been caught in an apocalyptic narrative around this issue, that weighs very heavily on us. It can be a difficult issue to discuss, because as usual it has become black-and-white, so that any attempt to qualify the issue can make you seem like a climate-change denier. I recommend *Ten Global Trends That Every Smart Person Needs to Know* by Marian Tupy. The media and politicians between them have added an apocalyptic flavour to what is a genuine and urgent issue, which is not conducive to clear thinking. Psychological studies have shown that humans give much more weight to bad possibilities than to good possibilities, and this makes evolutionary sense in a natural environment in which your survival may be at stake. But I think we need what optimism we can about the future, for our own well-being. Apocalyptic thinking is an old myth, and people do not realise how much it is fuelling them in their attitude to the environmental issue.

Treat the World as A Dream, and take Miracles Literally

I have argued against taking anything literally. To nuance it, I think it is important not to take the material world as literal, as objective and solid, in any kind of ultimate sense – it is a dream. As for magical events, I think it is good to take them literally in a world that tends not to believe in them. Yes, miracles really do happen. The right ceremony really can sometimes cure someone's incurable disease. There is no limit to what Spirit can do. If you like, treat the West as a dream, and the East as literal. But both need serious engagement in our lives.

Evolution 'vs' Creationism

Note (again) that I am not saying that the Big Bang, Evolution or Heat Death are wrong in their own terms. What I am saying is that they are not the only valid Creation Mythologies, and they can be tweaked, probably not in a scientifically valid way, but in imaginatively valid ones, that speak to the psyche in a more complete way.

I am in favour of the American approach of teaching both Evolution and Creationism (or Intelligent design, as they call it) in schools. This is because children are then exposed to two different ways of seeing the world. I think that is what matters: not that they grow up with the 'correct' views, but with a sense that there is more than one way of looking at something. This is also an argument in favour of parents not always getting on. The irony of this situation is that both Evolution and Creationism tend to be fundamentalisms – theirs is the only way of seeing the world – and in pitching them against each other, that tendency to fundamentalism is being undermined. I don't think it matters what Creation Mythologies we have. The main issue is to be flexible, to be able not to hang on to any of them as the 'correct' one. And to have the underlying appreciation that really, we don't know, and never will, that it is all the Great Mystery. This is where postmodernism, with its relativisation of all ideas and narratives, becomes a philosophy for those able to sit at the Centre of the Wheel and embrace the mystery. But it is an uncomfortable place for most of us.

If I had to choose between Evolution or Creationism, I would go for Creationism, because at least it gives miraculous origins to life. Of course, I do not take it literally, and I do not take God literally. But the miraculous origins speak to my psyche in a way that Evolution, as a purely scientific story, never can. And here is a point: it is not about feeding the psyche something that is not true just to keep it happy. As Jung pointed out (in the story of The Woman who went to the Moon in the West Chapter) the psyche, or Spirit, is an objective reality, it is *the* objective reality. And that makes Creationism objectively true in a particular way that an untweaked theory of Evolution cannot be.

There are no Hidden Realities

We are led to believe by science that there is a hidden reality behind our experience that is 'really' what is there. Audlin, in *The Circle of Life,* emphasises that for Native American people, reality is what presents itself. You trust your experience. What we call short-sightedness, for example, is just another way of seeing the world. You are always trying to see the world from the other's point of view, whether that is human or non-human, and not pre-judging it either as inferior (for example, animal) or wrong (short-sighted). I don't want to be absolute about this – I don't want to be absolute about anything – and on the principle of Two-Eyed Seeing we also need to acknowledge that it is helpful if the 'short-sighted' person gets some contact lenses so that he can see the world from the point of view of people who see in the more usual way. But this is purely pragmatic: it does not mean there is something 'wrong' with the short-sighted person, that nature made a mistake which we humans, with our greater knowledge, need to 'correct'. We need to trust who we are, and that includes our bodies and the way they are made, because they are an intrinsic part of who we are. From the conventional point of view, yes get some glasses. But from an indigenous viewpoint, we are led on a contemplation about what the short-sighted person sees and what that tells us about the world. What do they see that we don't, for example? It is such a different attitude, in which nature is to be trusted, rather than being seen as something to be 'corrected'.

We can take this further. Suppose you are looking at a tree, and on one of the branches you see an owl. You approach the tree, and as you do so, what you saw as an owl now appears to you as a pine cone. The western point of view here is that what you saw was a pine cone all along, but you mistook it for an owl. Your vision was 'wrong'. A traditional point of view – trusting the experience – would that be that what you saw first of all dressed itself up as an owl, and then as a pine cone. How interesting, what is that telling me? What do I need to pay attention to? As with the short-sightedness, the world becomes a much more interesting place once we stop trying to judge and correct it, and instead take it on its own terms.

In the western philosophical tradition, Idealism is the theory that perception is all there is. The owl and the pine cone are an example of that. Everything is dependent on the mind and how it constructs experience. All we have, ultimately, is subjectivity – or consciousness – the very quality that is discarded by science as a means of knowledge.

The natural world speaks to us, because we are not different to it. Lie down on the Earth (as I suggested in Chapter two) and feel your connection, your belonging to her, that you are nothing but her, you can feel her heart with your heart. So how could the natural world not be speaking to us all the time, because we are her? Our culture suffers from the shadow form of the North, in which the mind and its tendency to abstraction (which has its place) has taken over, and we have lost the sense of connection.

When you see something unusual in the natural world – a 'sign' – pay attention. She is saying something to you. And think symbolically, because that is the language of nature and of what we call the Unconscious (which Jung, who created the term in its larger sense, also simply called 'Life'.)

Hidden Realities Disempower

In its positing of a hidden reality that is more real than our experience, science can have a disempowering effect. We stop trusting our senses, and instead we trust the people who tell us how things are. Our experience, for example, tells us that the Sun goes around the Earth. We see it travel across the sky every day. We are told, however, that our experience is 'wrong', that in reality the Earth goes around the Sun. This might seem like a mind-game that I am playing, but I am not. I am in earnest. The problem here is not just that we have been taught to mistrust our senses, but also that only one version of reality can be right. So, either the Sun goes around the Earth, or the Earth goes around the Sun. This is the fundamentalism, the idea that there can only be one reality, that we inherited from the Middle Ages and which has been passed on down through science. So let us get back to experience (which is usually a good antidote to fundamentalism): if you were in a spacecraft millions of miles from Earth, your experience would be of the Earth going around the Sun. If you are on Earth, you have the opposite experience. How wonderful, how interesting. What you see changes according to where you are looking from. Why not just leave it at that? Why does one have to be 'right' and the other 'wrong'? It is just the unaware mind yet again in search of certainty, having to pin things down so that it knows where it stands – and the child within feels secure as a result. We maybe need that certainty when we are a child, and as adults we learn to leave it behind so that we can enter the flow of Spirit.

The Shadow Power and the Real Power of the Mind

The real power of the mind lies not in positing hidden, or abstract, realities and pinning our experience to them. That is its shadow power. Its real power lies in its ability to hold differing, even contradictory, perspectives at once, and using that as a point of contemplation. It is Keats' Negative Capability again, the ability to hold these different points of view "without any irritable reaching after fact and reason."

The scientific method is a specialised way of looking at the world which can only reveal certain truths. It leaves out feeling and intuition – perhaps our most valuable ways of knowing – as 'subjective'. When my experience of the natural world contradicts the scientific mechanism, on principle I will give my experience at least equal weight. I refuse to downgrade it as 'subjective' (though I will not discount the scientific understanding either, I will hold both in my mind.) This is one way in which science disempowers people: it tells them their experience is wrong, and that true knowledge can only be had by specialists who understand arcane symbols. What is the difference between that, and the medieval Church, where the hotline to God was in the hands of the priests? This is not a conspiracy by a shadowy authority to control, however, (the reflex assumption of many people), rather it is humanity collectively wanting to feel the security that there are people who know the 'real' truth. It is a deal, you give away your own authority, in return for which you receive belonging and some simple certainties.

Other Mythologies

I think it is good to have more than one Creation Mythology that appeals to you. One of the purposes in deconstructing the 'facticity' of the scientific story was to create room for other stories to co-exist alongside it, without one being judged as more real than the other. I think the main criterion needs to be imaginative appeal. We are, hopefully, too sophisticated to believe any of them, including the scientific mythology, in a literal sense.

Imagination is Reality

The poet William Blake said that

> *"Imagination is the real and eternal world of which this vegetable universe is but a faint shadow."*

Asked,

> *"When the Sun rises, do you not see a round disc of Fire somewhat like a guinea?"*

he replied,

> *"O no, no, I see an innumerable company of the heavenly host crying Holy, Holy, Holy is the Lord God Almighty."*

Blake speaks of reality from the point of view of the East. Science at its most rigid speaks of reality from the point of view of the

West (data) and North (theory) alone. But the East is the starting point of the Wheel, it is the source: without its perspective, which is fundamental, there is disconnect and imbalance. This is why I say the criterion for a Creation Mythology needs to be imaginative appeal (and why we need magical origins in the Big Bang and Evolution stories.) Not in the sense of fancy, but something deeper and more enduring. Let stories and mythologies claim you, rather than the other way round. Then your connection will be visceral. Something doesn't have to be literally true to be real.

Shamanism is Universal

Nowadays we are inheritors of the culture of the whole world, from all ages. Our Shamanism is no longer locally rooted, though it probably needs to start there, in terms of connection to the natural world. Shamanism has become universal, there is a melting pot of traditions. The Medicine Wheel is no longer just a local Native American phenomenon. The principles behind it are universal. And it is the same with stories and mythologies.

Living in the UK, I'm not a great fan of trying to reclaim the Celtic tradition, as though that is what is truly mine and authentic. It belonged to this land, sure, so there is a connection there. But it is long gone, the Celts are only a small part of my genetic make-up, and they spoke another language. They are, to all intents and purposes, a foreign people, lost in the mists of time. That is not to say that their stories will not speak to me. Of course, they do. The story of Merlin, for example, is well worth reading or, if you get the chance, listening to. We can draw on these things, while creating something entirely new that takes its inspirations from all over the world.

Don't Identify with an Imaginary Past

I was once on a weekend that led up to a ceremony where the participants were enacting an old Irish story, that was big on the battle between good and evil, which seemed to me more like crude Christian psychology than subtle indigenous psychology. And afterwards I was left scratching my head, wondering what it had all been about. It had the flavour of trying to find our own indigeneity by reaching back and attempting to reclaim an imaginary past. It was an attempt to impose something on our current experience. And people are often all too willing to do that, especially when there is a group dynamic: it is called religion.

I am not saying that some people might not want to specialise in investigating Celtic culture and drawing inspiration from that. But we are not ancient Celts, we have become something else, and that is what we ultimately need to be true to. It is the same with any foreign way. You see people identify with, for example, Tibetan Buddhism, visualising exotic figures while chanting in another language. There can be value in this, it can be a stage along the way. It is the same with people dressing up in 'witchy' gear. But finally, and it may take many years, we have to come back to ourselves in an ordinary and real way, beyond any kind of tradition, identification with which, we may have imagined, made us more 'spiritual'.

The Medicine Wheel as Creation Mythology

If you are reading this book, and the Medicine Wheel draws you in, then it has become a mythology for you. We are not drawn in just on the basis of an intellectual appeal, and the Medicine Wheel for you is not just four directions and elements with a list of meanings. It has meaning on other levels, and the meditations I described in the first Chapter are one way – along with, for example, ceremony and building a Wheel – of speaking to those levels. A Creation Mythology is only such if it speaks to us in that way, so that somewhere, deep in our being, we know, "This is where I come from."

There isn't a Creation Mythology in the sense of a story

behind the Wheel, but in itself it shows us what the world is made of: Sun, Rain, Soil and Wind – Fire, Water, Earth and Air. It could hardly be more tangible. That is the beauty of the Wheel, that is why it has such appeal to me, because it is a concrete, rather than an abstract, philosophy. It tells us all about life and the universe and what gives it meaning in terms that we can experience through the senses.

Contrast that with the modern scientific explanation of what the world is made of. It is wonderful in its own way – a sub-microscopic world of strange particles that break all the rules of rational behaviour. It is almost as though that world was thrown up by whatever keeps dreaming the universe into existence, as a counterpoint to the extreme rationality of the scientific ways of knowledge, like there is a trickster at work. The same with dark energy: suddenly most of the universe is missing and undetectable, just as we were getting it nicely pinned down. What a cosmic joke!

Be that as it may, the quantum mythology (how can such a world be anything other than a mythology?) is beyond anybody's immediate experience, discernible only by inference, and comprehensible only by means of elaborate and complex ideas that only a few specialists can understand. That in itself seems another cosmic joke.

But why, at the same time, should we allow ourselves to be disempowered in this way? Why not have a mythology that we can be part of, that we can think about and even contribute to? Once you have persuaded yourself that scientific reality is not the only reality, that it is a human birth-right, if you like, to be able to know the universe, and not just the province of a few specialists (like the priests before them in the Middle Ages), then something essential can fall into place. We experience Sun, Rain, Soil and Wind all the time, we are embedded in them, we are nothing apart from that experience. We can know what the universe is, and by the same token we know what we are, not just in our minds, but through our senses. There is no hidden reality. The Medicine Wheel as a Creation Mythology brings us into the present, brings us closer to our immediate experience, rather than to a place of mental abstraction, and isn't that what we are here to do? If it works, it's real.

Community

Community is another aspect of the North. In the same way that we may bemoan the lack of initiation ceremonies in the modern world (missing the fact that life initiates us, if we are open to it), we may also bemoan the lack of community and the atomised lives within which, it is said, we live.

If you are reading this book, the chances are that you want community in the sense of others who are also attempting to step outside the stream of collective values and find their own orientation to the world (that is why the Medicine Wheel has directions: they help us to orient ourselves.) But that is only ever going to be a minority interest. Most people have always been happy to live by the collective values as they are presented to them, there is nothing wrong with that, and some societies are healthier in this respect than others. Modern society, for example, is probably the first ever to deny the existence of Spirit, which is implicit in its scientific mythology, though that doesn't mean everyone goes along with that denial. However, my purpose here isn't to list off what is wrong with our society compared with what we imagine indigenous societies to be like.

Small Communities can be Suffocating

I don't think community is a problem if you are living from the received values of the collective. What I want to emphasise, though, is just how suffocating a 'close-knit' village, which is easy to romanticise, can be if you are being called to something else. The people in that village will all naturally think they are autonomous, that they are not living by received opinions and values, and they will find it offensive if you say otherwise. This is slightly dangerous territory, because this perspective on people can sound arrogant, and it can actually be arrogant. But I think it is important to quietly acknowledge this difference for the sake of understanding who we are, and so that we do not get brought down by family or collective judgement, that wants us to be like they are. That opposition and judgement from the community for being different is painful, but it is a great spur to growth, you have to find who you are, and value who you are, in order to find meaning. And you may be arrogant when young and fighting your way out of it – I certainly was – but that was a necessary stage for me. I had to rebel and oppose for my own psychological survival.

A friend was telling me that in the Italian village she grew up in, she was known by the family nickname. It was a nickname for the whole family, and other families also had nicknames they were known by. She was never very taken by this arrangement, and left as soon as she could. But you can see the sense of belonging and connection and familiarity, the warmth and security of it, implied in this arrangement. Who you are is the group you belong to. For many people, this is necessary, and it would destroy them psychologically to take that away. For others, it could destroy them if there was no way out. Some communities can be fiercely judgemental of anyone who is different, and that can be an incredibly difficult situation to be in. It is human nature to judge in this way, and the health of a community needs to be weighed, I think, not according to whether that judgement happens, because I think it is inevitable, but by the degree to which it doesn't happen. So going back to the two Spirits, there was considerable room for that kind of difference in the Native American communities. Yet you also hear of some of the young men who are warrior types being disdainful of the Two-Spirits for not being real men. It is the nature of the warrior temperament to divide up the world in this sort of arrogant way. So, it is more a matter of managing that, maybe putting the warriors in Sweatlodges and melting them into their hearts from time to time. But not deriding the warrior energy itself, for it is an important part of life, whatever modern gender politics may say to the contrary. As for the modern Indian reservation, the novelist Sherman Alexei said he had to leave his in order to become a writer: anyone who stood out, who had talent, would get pulled down in that particular community.

I'm sure this does not reflect how things generally once were. My main point, however, is to emphasise just how intolerant and suffocating 'community' can be, and not to romanticise it.

This submersion in collective values – which is, and always has been, the norm for humanity – easily leads to the mob consciousness of which we have become rightly wary. A collective that is threatened or insecure in some way is prepared to believe anything that a leader tells them. No evidence is required. In the 2020 US election, millions of people were prepared to believe that the election had been stolen, and there was never any evidence presented to substantiate that.

Sobornost

But there is another kind of collective consciousness, and there is a word for it that comes from the Russian Orthodox Church: Sobornost. It is community at its best, and you find it in Ceremony. It is the kind of collective consciousness that occurs when those present have shared individual values, and in which the sense of collectivity heightens, rather than diminishes, the sense of individuality. There is a synergy between self and other. A Sweatlodge might be a good example. You may not personally know the people you are sweating with. But in a Sweatlodge, we are brought back to essentials, all the 'add-ons' by which we usually identify ourselves are gone: we are in the dark, wearing nothing or very little, close to the Elements, and focussing our minds on that which is of most value to us.

There can be a sense of deep connection on a Spirit level with the other people in the lodge, which heightens that sense of connection to Spirit that we are, on an individual level, focussed on. That is Sobornost. It is a beautiful thing. It may occur in a 'sharing circle', where people are attempting to be true to their experience, and not fearing that others present will judge them. Or in a prayer ceremony, where people take turns in having a conversation with the natural world, and talk in a heartfelt way about their lives.

Sobornost can happen on a one-to-one level also, where two people are being authentic, maybe even having quite a 'difficult' conversation as a result, but that honesty comes from a shared sense of being true to the Spirit. If you are on this kind of path, then if you have just one or two people in your life that you can talk to in this kind of way, count your blessings. It is not that there is some phenomenon called 'community' which we are missing in modern life. Finding that kind of connection, with its deeper honesty, has always been difficult, because most people are not interested in that: it threatens them. Modern social media, and the freedom of speech we have in our democracies (for all their faults and their tendencies to rule by mob-consciousness) give us ample opportunities to make connection with people of like mind. We have it good.

Even then, people usually only want honesty up to a point. They are sticking their heads out of the collective mindset, but it is tentative, and we are liable to recreate collective mindsets around, for example, shamanic communities. It is inevitable to a degree, and it has to be danced around. It is where the trickster has her role: pushing these kinds of collectives by breaking the rules, by speaking for the elephant under the carpet that everybody is pretending is not there. And you will not be thanked by some people. As I mentioned earlier, I got blocked from two of the biggest Facebook shamanic groups for saying we shouldn't put indigenous people on pedestals: but not before a considerable number of people had expressed their appreciation to me for saying it. For others, it was like I had insulted the Pope.

Our shamanic communities tend to be half-way houses: there is a certain respect for the deeper honesty I am talking about, and that is inspiring when it happens. But also, an adherence to a new set of collective values, that are quite rebellious, that contain the exaggerated mistrust of authority that I wrote about earlier, and which permeates the wider counter-culture. It is understandable as a point from which to break away from collective pressures, but we eventually need to make our peace with the wider society if we are to make peace with ourselves.

Our role in these communities, if we are trying to be some kind of Elder, is to push at those rebellious boundaries, but in a skilful way. And maybe the best way of doing that is by creating contexts such as Sweatlodges and other ceremonies where people do feel free to be honest about themselves, and so incrementally reducing the need to define themselves by their opposition to the conventional establishment. This is important also for the sake of the wider community: what use are we to it if we are forever critical and in opposition to it, fearful of its 'authorities', and not able to feel part of it? That does not mean adopting an uncritical attitude towards it, but it does mean not expecting too much of it, not expecting it to be fundamentally other than it is, even though it will always need serious tweaking.

Guiding Principles of Community

In the modern world, we cherish our rights and freedoms. They are fundamental to the way we see our societies. And those rights and freedoms may have been hard won. However, such a perspective does not represent an absolute value in the way we may assume it does. Emphasising rights and freedoms is a natural outcome of seeing the individual as autonomous. If the self is seen as fundamentally relational, then responsibilities and relatedness to others come to the fore. In his book *Drawing Out Law*, Professor John Borrows, a Canadian Law professor from the Anishinabek people, gives the example of abortion. He has a lot of respect for the modern perspective that emphasises the rights of a woman over her body. However, he says that amongst his people, if a woman falls pregnant and that is problematic for her, the father is held to his responsibilities, and the community becomes involved in the raising of the child (something that happens more in those societies anyway.) As a result, says Borrows, the incidence of abortion is much lower. Borrows is not setting one approach against the other. His approach is an example of Two-Eyed Seeing. But it is an interesting instance of how the two different ways of seeing the self can work out in practice, and its implications for the community and how it governs itself.

Activism

If you are temperamentally an activist, then perhaps your main contribution lies is in guiding people away from the 'us and them' mentality that tends to define protest. It needs to be 'us and us', otherwise you are blaming someone for the cause you are espousing, whether it be CEOs, rich people, men, offshore banks, fossil fuel corporations, big pharma, right wing politicians, or governments (the usual suspects.) "Never be for or against." As we have seen, people can't help but be one-sided about practically everything, because it helps them define, to themselves, who they are. This is very difficult to see beyond, especially when the cause seems to be self-evidently justified. But you will create a very different atmosphere, and have greater chances of long-term success, if 'the opposition' feel you are on their side, instead of against them. We would ourselves act in the same way if opposed, while any truth makes a hurried exit. Not many people have done the personal shadow work that is necessary to leave the 'for and against' matrix. The great leaders like Martin Luther King and Nelson Mandela did not lead so much by opposing as by including, and that is why they were successful. The Dalai Lama is the same. But it is a rare quality.

Marshall Rosenberg's book *Non-Violent Communication*, is well-worth reading in this respect. The main idea behind it is simple, but requires a lot of self-awareness to put into practice. Do not judge what people are saying, show you have understood their point of view by reflecting it back to them, and take it from there. This is not the same as agreeing with them. It is about people feeling listened to, which goes deeper than mere agreement or disagreement. And once people feel listened to, remarkable things can happen.

Prayer as Activism

Prayer is also a way to change the world. I was told once, on the subject of activism, that all some Elders do is pray. Prayer is maybe the most effective activism there is, because if done in a heartfelt way, you know it's going to do some good, even though you will probably never know in what way – not definitively, anyway. If you are directing good feeling towards the world, and we are an intimate part of that world, how can it not have an effect? As ever with prayer, it's usually best to pray in a fairly general way, rather than for outcomes that are too specific, unless you really know what you are doing. This is because you never know what the bigger picture is, and something that may appear undesirable to us may have an important role to play in some bigger design. Like Gandalf said about Gollum, who just appeared to be a hindrance, in *The Lord of the Rings*: he had a sense that Gollum still had a part to play, and indeed he did. Without Gollum's obsession for the ring, it would not have been consumed in the fires of Mount Doom.

The Warrior

I am placing the Warrior in the North because he divides the world into good and bad, and fights for what he sees as good. And it is the Mind that makes these divisions. I want to say something about the warrior because he needs redeeming. It is indeed the one-sided warrior energy of the North, divorced from the feminine energy of the South, that is the cause of many of the world's difficulties. And in the resurgence of respect for the feminine that has come about through feminism, the masculine has sometimes been put down unfairly.

A woman therapist friend told me that it had been difficult raising her sons in the 90s, because men were being taught to feel bad about themselves, because masculinity was seen as essentially toxic. This is how collective changes work: they tend to swing from one extreme to another before, hopefully, eventually finding balance.

I think it is important that men feel pride in that warrior aspect of themselves, but in a way that listens to the Earth and to feeling. And we probably need regular Sweatlodges to keep us listening to our hearts – instead of fantasies of right and wrong that are in our heads. It is warrior energy that got us to the Moon, and it is something women also have, though it is more usually associated with men. It is warrior energy that does all the physically dangerous jobs that keep us safe, and it is nearly always men that do them. It is warrior energy that invents, that brings new ideas into the world (which both men and women do).

And, maybe most important of all, it is warrior energy that keeps us at the coal-face with ourselves, that demands that we be impeccable, that we act with integrity and speak the truth, even when that is uncomfortable. The warrior, acting in balance, is to be hugely admired, for without him we would get nowhere on the difficult path of transformation. He needs to be the servant of the king and of the feminine, even though he tends to head off on his own, and that is a perennial issue. At our personal coal-face, he is in the service of the East – the Great Spirit; the West, the responsible authority, the king; and the South, the feminine. He wins battles, but not on behalf of himself.

Animals of the North

In the Wheel we are using, the animal of the North is the Bison. The Bison is what the people live off, all parts of him are used. In that sense he gives all of himself, just as the Elder does, her life belongs to the Community. The Elder has also learnt to bear suffering, and has the endurance of the bison, who lives through the extreme cold and blizzards of the plains' winters. In the UK, we do not have wild bison. That does not mean we cannot connect: I have a bison hide on the floor of the room I use for my shamanic journeying. Horses also have that quality of endurance. I live on Dartmoor, a wilderness area in Devon, UK, where the weather is often extreme in winter. The Dartmoor ponies live wild on the moor, and the weather doesn't seem to be a problem for them. Horses have also given of themselves to people in many ways over the millennia, and continue to do so.

Don't Think of Yourself as an Elder

Don't try to become an 'Elder' and don't think of yourself like that. Don't think of yourself as anything. You see some people who you know have thought of themselves as 'Elders' from quite a young age. Leave them to it, and keep a cautious distance. Unless you are at least in your 70s, you are spared that responsibility, and only then if you have put in the work and gained the perspective. Nolo Episcopari!

Chapter 6

The Non-Cardinal Directions

Adding Complexity

With the non-Cardinal, or intermediate directions we introduce complexity into the Wheel. From a mind point of view, it is not complex, it is quite easy to grasp; but from a symbolic point of view, there is no longer that elemental simplicity. When you think East, for example, you also see yellow and the Sun, the language of image and the senses, which is also the language of the Unconscious; there are deeper resonances and connections that are invoked. This is why the Medicine Wheel as just the four directions and four elements makes a good meditation: by sitting with those powers, you imbibe them, they form an inspirational structure in your being.

This is not to say it cannot be done using eight directions. It can. They also have their resonances: think, for example, the Ancestors in the SouthEast. That word carries a lot of weight, and is good to meditate on. But there is a lot more to remember at once, and each non-cardinal direction (as they are called) doesn't have a single colour or element associated with them. We are making a move towards the mind. But they still work. They add a lot to our understanding of ourselves, and help turn the Wheel into a transformative tool. The Cardinal Directions are like primal powers in the universe, whereas the non-Cardinals are more concrete, they give us something specific to grapple with.

For myself, I have a Wheel of nine stones (including the Centre) and I have painted the non-Cardinal directions each in two colours: half the colour of the direction to one side, and half the colour of the direction on the other. It has taken me a good while to be able see that level of complexity in my mind's eye, but even so the sense of it – this inspirational multicoloured circle – is there in my mind's eye.

The Journey Through the Eight Directions

The eight directions are all powers in themselves, but also work as a progression through life, just as the four directions do. And that is maybe the way to remember them.

We start in the East with the spark of new life, coming in from outside time and space. And we find ourselves with a body, inherited from all who came before: the Ancestors/the SouthEast. Then we are a child, and as we grow into a teenager, we begin to have dreams about what we will do when are an adult: this is the SouthWest/the Dream. Then we find ourselves physically an Adult in the West; to move onwards from there towards the Elder, we have to encounter our 'stuff', all those patterns of behaviour inherited from the ancestors (the opposite point) and from our own pre-this life past, whatever that might be. This is the NorthWest. Out of this comes the self-knowledge of the North, the Elder. And out of that we become able to make real choices with our life, that come from our whole being: this is the NorthEast/Choice or Choreography. It is opposite the dream of our life, which can easily be partial and limited and unconscious.

That is the sequential pattern of the eight directions. We will consider the four non-cardinal directions both as part of the sequence of eight, and as powers in themselves. But primarily we will be viewing them as two pairs of directions, because those opposite directions are functionally connected to each other.

The Ancestors

This is the SouthEast of the Wheel, with Fire on the right, and Water on the left. The ancestors comprise all those influences that have contributed to making us who we are. As such, they naturally have our appreciation and gratitude. Most immediately, there are our parents. But then there are our four grandparents, eight great-grandparents and so on, lines that go way back: we are the end product of all these people, both physically and in terms of many of our personality traits. Then there are the cultural influences from the past, the great figures that have shaped our culture and all the people in it. Nowadays, that can be worldwide: we live in times of incredible cultural breadth, if we choose to take up on that. In the evolutionary story, all the other animals came before us, for we are very recent. We grew out of them. The animals, too, are our ancestors. And behind it all, the Great Mother, the natural world, made us, she is the greatest ancestor of all.

If you have a thought, it is not 'yours': it is the product of your whole body, which is animal, vegetable and mineral. Without those elements, there would be no thought, there would not even be a 'you'. If you take away all the 'not you' elements, there is no 'you' left. There is a brilliant 7-minute YouTube conversation called *Nonduality and the Consciousness of 'Things',* in which the Vietnamese Buddhist teacher Thich Nhat Hanh demolishes the argument of a physics professor, who is making fun of the consciousness of animals, saying that, of course, humans are superior. Thich Nhat Hanh does not address this directly, but rather talks about the problem being the discriminating mind that even thinks in such categories as superior, inferior and equal. How can we think of ourselves as superior, he asks, when we are the product of all these factors that are not us, as I outlined above?

Acknowledgement and appreciation of the ancestors is a natural thing to do, that keeps us aware of who we really are, that we are a product of all these factors. It stops us getting above ourselves, a perennial human propensity, which the traditional trickster tales are there to teach us about. It is also why the traditional self is relational rather than autonomous.

The human ego frequently thinks and acts as though it is autonomous, and contemplation of the ancestors reminds us that we are relational. And fills us with love and appreciation for all that has come before and gone towards giving us our lives. In enshrining the autonomy of the individual, as we have done in the modern West, we are giving license to the human ego and its delusions of omnipotence. It is a trickster tale in itself.

Of course, people need to be treated as individuals – and we all come bearing particular gifts – but it needs to be in the context of a more fundamental relatedness. As ever, it is not one or the other, that is the shadow, or discriminating, mind, the source of all our troubles, but balance that is needed. And balance is dynamic, it is something that has to be continually found through awareness and ceremony.

In all indigenous societies, awareness of the ancestors and ceremonial remembrance of them is central. When something is universal like this, I have faith that it is a natural part of being human. There is at least one society in which they build little houses for their parents after they have passed on, and they leave food out for them, feeding the spirits. This means that their parents are actively remembered and remain part of their lives. But the houses are outside the main house, they are separate, because life is also for the living, you need also to let your parents go on whatever spirit journey they are on, and to get on with your own life, separate to them.

Parents Give the Power to Live

It can be difficult to feel good about the ancestors – and therefore appreciative of what has gone into making you – when the relationship with the parents is difficult. The parents are the most immediate and powerful ancestors, and they don't always do a good job of taking care of us as children. They may be absent, or damaging in others ways, landing what are their own difficulties onto the children, often quite unconsciously.

In a trance-dance once, I found myself on a shamanic journey, as sometimes happens, in which I was setting off onto the open sea in a Viking boat. It was the adventure of life. And in the rear of the boat, behind me, were my parents, my father on one side, my mother on the other. And I thought that is odd, what are they doing there? And then I realised that, however difficult I found them, and however much I had had to keep my distance for my own psychological well-being, they had still given me the power to live, quite literally.

This is the dance with our ancestor-parents that we sometimes need to do: on the one hand, to have a discerning perspective, and to process whatever it is that we need to; but on the other hand, to acknowledge that, however inadequate they may have been, they gave us the power to live, and that it is healthy for us to experience an ongoing gratitude for that.

In the section on Death, I recounted an LSD experience (during the early months of the 2020 Covid lockdown) in which I was at the gates of life and death, and they were the same place, there was no barrier, and both places were joyful and abundant. And having been opened in this way, I afterwards began to experience the presence of my father, who died in 2015. I felt connected to him in a way that I never had when he was alive, because he was always very judging of me – and me of him, until a few years before the end. And this is nothing that I can prove, because I don't know what happens after death, but it felt like he was present in the spirit world, and less rigid and judging than he had been when embodied, and that I was therefore more able to move close to him.

On the one hand, we need to let go of close relatives who have died, for our own sakes and for their sakes. But on the other, they can be felt as a living presence and we can create our own ceremonies of acknowledgement of that. Ceremonies in which we give thanks to all the ancestors who have gone into our making and into giving us the power to live. It is good for us, and good for them. Intention and connection continue into the Spirit world, outside of time and space.

Karma

This is the NorthWest of the Wheel, with Earth on the right and Air on the left, and opposite the Ancestors. Our karma is something we can experience immediately in our habitual ways of being. That is what karma is. And those habitual ways do not always serve us. They can be patterns that were created in childhood, in response to the conditions and people around us; they can be inherited down the family line, genetically or 'energetically'; they may have been created or magnified by ourselves as adults; and we may have uniquely brought them in ourselves, wherever it is we may have come from, something we shall probably never know.

Past Lives

People sometimes go on shamanic journeys or the equivalent to find what happened in past lives, that has contributed to the type of person they now are. If asked about past lives, I say I believe in them on Tuesdays, Thursdays and Saturdays. I think it is best to hold these things lightly, because they are usually beliefs rather than direct experiences, and like any belief, if you hold on to it too rigidly, it shuts you down, it closes you off from the openness that Spirit needs to shape and guide us. And similarly with the content of the journeying into past lives: you may have a strong experience, and if so, then that is telling you something important. But however strong it is, that does not mean we should take the way it presents itself literally. Maybe we can do so, but even then, it is still best held lightly, and certainly best kept separate from your life now, rather than made into part of your identity: our purpose here is to let go of all identities, rather than build new ones.

Witch-Burnings

A common experience that people, particularly women, have is memories of having been executed or tortured as witches in a past life. This is where I will try not to put my foot in it! I attended a course with Sharon Blackie, who is a story-teller and scholar, and she says that from the records in Europe, between 40 and 60,000 people, a quarter of them men, were executed as witches over about 400 years. This figure has been inflated by some to a holocaust of up to nine million, so clearly it has become politicised, even though there is a genuine issue of the scapegoating of the feminine, as well as of simply anyone who was a bit different (the women doing the actual healing work with herbs, and the midwifery, were valued members of the community, so tended not to be persecuted in this way.) I don't mean this comically, because it is a serious issue, but I rarely meet women who do not have past-life memories of being persecuted as witches, and I know others who have been encouraged to find such memories. And the way journeying works, if you go looking for a past life as a witch, you will probably find one. There are simply not enough historical witches to go round! My point here is not to devalue this particular issue, because there is a lot in it about the persecution of the feminine by the one-sided masculine, that has become an ancestral wound that needs addressing. Rather, my point is that we need to be wary of taking recovered memories from past lives too literally as part of our karma. They are certainly telling us something, if there is power and energy in the journey. I think journeys are usually best read symbolically, like dreams. They are sometimes literal, but usually they need interpreting: it is like looking at a painting, and describing it. No two people will do so in the same way. Both may capture its beauty in their own way, but there is no objective truth.

The Brown Road

The axis from the SouthEast to the NorthWest, Ancestors to Karma, has humorously been referred to as the Brown Road (in the same way that East-West is the Blue Road, and North-South the Red Road.) This is because it is the road where we process our 'shit'. Coming from the past of the SouthEast and Ancestors, we find ourselves in the present/future of the NorthWest, living out those ancestral patterns and, hopefully, finding ways of tolerating the experience of them and so giving them the space to transform. This is how one therapist friend put her work to me: helping people to tolerate themselves.

We are back at the coalface of the South and the West. In a way, it doesn't matter where these patterns come from. It may be from childhood, it may be from a past life, it may be cultural or is may be that the spirit of, for example, anger has chosen to visit us for no reason we know of. What matters is that we come into relationship with that spirit, find a way to live with it without being taken over by it. Then transformation is possible. It is the ongoing task of life. If we take care of the 'Brown Road', then everything else will take care of itself.

De-Colonising the Mind

The word 'colonised' is sometimes used with indigenous people to describe the cultural imposition, over the generations, of white people's ways of thinking as the 'correct' ones, and the concomitant devaluation and loss of the traditional perspectives on life, so that people end up losing their roots and their sense of who they are, with all the addictions and other dysfunctional behaviours that come with that. So, an important part of the therapeutic process becomes recovering the traditional roots, which are still recognised, like an ancestral memory, by the 'patient', and making conscious the colonisation process, so that it can be transformed. This process is described by Eduardo Duran in his book *Healing the Soul Wound.*

Colonisation doesn't just happen to indigenous people. It happens wherever there is a cultural attempt to discredit a natural way of being and replace it with an agenda that serves the power-agenda of the culture. Brainwashing is another word for it. The English boarding school system is a good example, particularly at the early years stage. Children as young as seven are sent away from their parents, in a way that prematurely disrupts the bond with the mother, so that they can mix with the 'right' people and, eventually, rise high in the world.

These children are encouraged to over-identify with their academic achievement as a statement of who they are, and to follow the security and certainty of a regulated life, as a substitute for the natural love and spontaneity of the family situation. Having been sent away aged eight, I know this colonisation well, and it has taken many decades to recognise and then recover from it. I recommend Joy Schaverien's book *Boarding School Syndrome*, which covers the Jungian analysis and healing of several adults. Nick Duffell's book *The Making of Them* is also worth reading (Duffell was the first to highlight this issue), though his book can be quite theoretical. Schaverien has created the ABCD of Boarding Schools: Abduction, Bereavement, Captivity and Dissociation. There are parallels with the Indian boarding school system in the USA, which was a more extreme attempt at colonisation of the children's minds, that has caused lasting inter-generational damage.

Gifts from the Ancestors

It is probably unfair to call the SouthEast-NorthWest axis the Brown Road, even though it makes a good point, because we also inherit gifts from the ancestors that come out as 'good' karma – or maybe as somewhat mixed, and needing to be unpicked. This appreciation of the good karma that has been passed down is an important part of remembrance of the ancestors as a living part of our lives.

I find myself with this mixed appreciation of what came down from my father, and his grandfather before him: the confidence and ability and drive to build a substantial business. On the one hand, I was encouraged to feel that that was who I had to be myself, and that left no room for the kind of soulfulness that was always in me. So, I felt crushed by that that one-sided karmic pattern that said you need to achieve as a businessman to have value, and nothing else has that central value. On the other hand, it has meant that I have marched in quite confidently when I wanted to do things, and have usually succeeded. This is the gift aspect that has come down to me.

And let us not forget boarding school. Let us be balanced about it. People can be quite one-sided about the harmful aspects of their childhood. Yes, it can do a lot of damage, and it did so to me. But it also gives a lot of people the confidence to step out and lead, in a way that is expressive of their actual abilities, their competence. It is not just about power and entitlement, which people often try (for reasons of envy, or of not having come to terms with their own past) to reduce it to. And, along with my family background, it has given me a measure of that confidence, along with a lack of confidence in other ways. These things are complex, and when looking at the elements in our background that have damaged us, it is easy, with the one-sided, discriminating mind, to see them as all bad. But it is never like that. To see like that keeps us in a state of opposition to, rather than balanced understanding and perspective on, our past. It can turn us into permanent victims of the past. Personally, I think it best to see the difficulties in our backgrounds as 'worthy opponents', because we really do achieve something, we gain in substance and stature, when we are no longer subject to them.

Otherworldly Inheritances

There was also the ancestral inheritance from my mother. This one is more elusive, less obvious than through my father. My mother was from the west of Ireland, and as a young girl she used to wander off into the woods on her own. And, as she told me, she would hang out with the 'Little People', which you find under different names in all parts of the world. (For a very good exposition of this theme, and a contemplation of what we mean by 'reality', see *Daimonic Reality* by Patrick Harpur.) She once gave me a detailed account of these encounters. I asked her about it again a few months later, and her response was 'Did I say that?' This was partly because you never quite knew if she meant what she said; but is it also characteristic of Daimonic Reality that it cannot be pinned down. It will go tricksy on you if you try to pin it down. Much like astrology or homeopathy, which certainly work, but if you try to pin them down with scientific testing, they appear to fall apart. The refusal of these realities to co-operate with the criteria of the mind shows that we live in a much more layered universe than science might like to admit.

Be that as it may, before I was born my father decided I would be called 'Barry'. He was English and straight and certainly did not believe in fairies. So 'Barry' I was, because my father generally got his way. When in later years I looked up the origin of the name, I saw that under one interpretation that it comes from Fionnbharr, who was the King of the Fairies at Knockmaa, a fairy mound about an hour's drive from where my mother grew up in Ireland. The fairies, in their tricksy way, had given me my mother's lineage through leading my father by the nose to call me 'Barry'. Naming something or someone is powerful. My father, without knowing it, blessed that fairy lineage in me. Not only that, but when my son was born 42 years later, I called him Finn, which is the other half of Fionnbharr, without my having yet made the connection with Knockmaa. So, the fairies came in through me too, and continued the lineage in my son. Now all this is a story I have created; I am not really claiming a special otherworldly lineage for myself to put on my 'Shamanic

CV' (though there are plenty of people who are not shy of making such claims for themselves). But it is an interesting way of thinking about the ancestors and inheritance. It is worth holding, but lightly. If you insist on it, it will probably evaporate. Among Shamanic people in the Far East, the spirits, and the call to them, can be inherited within a family line. There can be such a thing as an Otherworldly inheritance.

And here is a strange tale for you. We talked above about ancestral inheritance, using the specific example of the 'colonising' of minds that gets passed down the generations. Here, it seems, is another route, recounted by Caitlin Matthews, who works within a neo-Celtic tradition, in her introduction to Dora van Gelder's *The Real World of Fairies:*

> *"In Ireland it is still a great breach of courtesy to tamper with the traditional haunts of fairy folk, and most country people are very careful to avoid such places. It is still considered a terrible thing to take wood from, let alone cut down, a fairy thorn tree.*
>
> *A recent case revealed this to me in a shocking way. My client Michael asked for soul healing for himself concerning the death of his younger sister some years before. As I began to journey in spirit towards my spirit allies, my way was suddenly blocked by a fairy man in a great rage. He told me that Michael's family had injured his family, that unless Michael was prepared to plant a thorn tree as reparation, I could not go any further and get help for him. My own allies urged me to accept this agreement on Michael's behalf. They further told me that the fairies had been taking the souls of children from Michael's family in recompense for a terrible insult.*
>
> *When I told Michael about the fairy man's anger and his demand for a thorn tree to be planted, Michael's face went white. He stopped me suddenly and told me about his grandfather, who had unaccountably cut down an ancient fairy thorn tree. Michael told me that in every branch of his family since that day a young child had died. Michael promised solemnly that he would not*

only plant a thorn tree on his land and dedicate it to the fairies in recompense, he would also ensure that no-one ever touched the tree, not even prune it! It is a promise I am sure he will keep."

Healing the Ancestral Inheritance

Not only can there be these esoteric, Otherworldly ways of looking at issues running through families, there is also the strange phenomenon, that if one person heals the ancestral inheritance, it can do so for everyone in the ensuing generations. If you are the person in the family who is open to these sorts of things, it may well be you. And probably being a bit different, you may also be a scapegoat for the family's problems, you may be seen as the one with the 'problems' – unless you keep a good distance.

The Jungian Analyst and Astrologer, Liz Greene says in *The Astrology of Fate* (p 95):

"The sins of father and mother are in truth visited upon the children, not through overt action, but through what has never emerged from primordial darkness. This is the child's Moira [Fate], his allotment. The unconscious conflicts that have remained unresolved come home to roost in the child, in the form of psychic inheritance. In later life, that secret bond between the unconscious of the child now grown to adulthood and the unconscious inheritance of the parents remains as potent as ever..... it is the experience of many psychotherapists, including myself, that work on these family issues affects, in a strange and inexplicable way, the other members of the family. It is as though the real unity of the family psyche is revealed by one individual taking on the responsibility of working with the family complexes. The unity of substance in the family does not die with the physical death of the parents either, for they are not only actual people but images within the psyche of the child. 'The ancestors' thus remain a living inheritance, just as the genetic inheritance remains alive within the body and continues to

be passed on to future generations."

Dreams and Choices

This is the SouthWest of the Wheel, situated between Water on the right and Earth on the left. As we move from the child of the South towards the Adult of the West, so do we begin to have dreams about who we would like to be and what we would like to do. That is why there are initiation rites at this age, which catalyse and guide this process, and make it part of the community, the gifts you have to bring.

Dreams are something we have at night. The Dream also refers to this apparently solid material reality we live in: it is being dreamed, in an ongoing way. The dream is also what we imagine we might do with our lives. It could be quite specific. Or it might just be a sense of something, that there is some dream carrying us forward, but we leave it to Spirit.

The purpose of this direction is to make the dream conscious, so that we can, in the opposite direction, make real choices, instead of just being 'in a dream', following, without realizing it, the dreams that others have put in our heads, or the dreams that come out of our unexamined selves.

When CG Jung was in Africa in the 1920s, he asked an African about their dreams, and he said they no longer dreamed, because the white man did the dreaming for them. What an indictment, what a colonisation of people's minds!

What dreams did you have as a young adult about your life? And, looking back, how much were they your own dreams, and how much were they inherited from your family and from society? Just because they were inherited from others does not make them 'wrong': the point is that they need to become our own dreams, just as the Medicine Wheel needs to become our own if we are going to engage with it creatively rather than mechanically.

Unlived Parental Dreams

The dream I was given by my father was of the self-made rich man, the 'big' man who had a better car than everyone else, who was naturally looked up to. He was a capable guy, sharper than most (in a narrow way), and if you are like this and not reflective, you are likely to start seeing yourself as 'better' than other people. I tried to adopt this dream in my early teens, because he was after all my father, but even then, I was kidding myself, because at the same time I felt that my life had been stolen from me, that I was not left with my own choices, and I couldn't understand how that had happened. I spent years fighting off this dream, and to do that I had to find my own dream. Would I have found it if I had not had to struggle like that, would there have been the necessary psychic pressure to forge the gold within? This 'worthy opponent' idea can cast a different perspective on what we can see as our 'difficulties'. Jung said,

> *"Nothing has a stronger influence psychologically on their children than the unlived life of the parent."*

I don't know how true this statement is, but it provides food for thought, and that is the main thing. It makes me realise that my father didn't just want me to be like him, he wanted me to exceed him, to be a super-rich man, at a very young age. It was what he hadn't lived. For me, this felt like an impossible burden. And if I had achieved that, I am sure he would have felt both proud and envious at the same time. It is worth looking at some of your dreams in this way too: are they the unlived dreams of your parents? And has that served you or hindered you, or both? But as an astrologer, I see an aspect to my father's chart that suggests an unlived capacity for non-ordinary states of consciousness. And it is this unconscious unlived life to which Jung is probably referring primarily, and it gives one explanation for the course of my own life.

Enacting the Dream

I'm not really one for 'bucket lists' of things I want to do before I die. Writing this book is the enactment of a dream. I have felt for years that I could write a book – I have written a number of books' worth of content in my astrological and shamanic blogs since 2006. And then after teaching a couple of long courses on the Medicine Wheel, I realised I had quite a lot to say. So, I started thinking about it. And then one morning I just thought dammit, start writing. It was a sudden decision. And out it all came, quite quickly, because it has years of pondering and writing already behind it. So that was where I moved into Choice, the opposite point in the NorthEast, made up of Air and Fire: a visionary combination of elements.

The Dream is made up of Earth and Water, the two static, holding, nurturing elements. It is the fertile soil in which a dream can germinate. But then it takes wing, we choose to live it, we seize it with both hands. Well, maybe, depending on your temperament.

A Good Dream is Congruent with Spirit

A good Dream is something that slowly grows in us, it is congruent with who we are – or rather, it is congruent with the bigger dream of Spirit, because who we are is unlimited. So, when we pray, we are dreaming. We are dreaming in the future, and it can be when we talk like this about how our lives can move forward, that we find out what is real, and what isn't, what is in accord with the bigger dream of Spirit, and what is just our tiny human desire.

The dream can just be a sense that there is a bigger design at work, and we don't know what it is, and we don't need to know what it is. Just sensing it, and sensing that what we are doing now is in accord with that, is enough. I have that sense with my Medicine Wheel stones: as long as I have them laid out somewhere, and I pay attention to them, then they carry the dream of my live forward. And I am happy not to know where that is going.

I think this is really what the Dream is about: working our way towards aligning with the bigger dream of Spirit, and then making choices on that basis.

'Big' Dreams

Night-time dreams can be part of this process, particularly 'big' dreams, the ones that shake us and stay with us. I talked in the opening Chapter about the dream of an Eagle soaring that I had in my 20s, that was pointing me towards the long task of finding the confidence to do that. I also had a dream around then in which I was told that my name was 'he who has the ghost mind', because I was neither male nor female. The ensuing 40 years have been a demanding process of finding that male and female within me. I generally get dreams that help me forward at pivotal times. In 2015, at a time when I was floundering, I met a wise woman in a dream who told me I was undergoing my second Psychosynthesis. This is a process where a new element of the Self comes in, and the whole personality has to come apart and reform around this new element. And it helped me trust that it was OK to flounder. Sometimes we need to flounder, we need to not know what is going on. The human mind does not like this, and reaches after certainties and stabilities, it thinks something must be wrong. But times when we don't know who we are and can plan nothing are often, in retrospect, some of the most creative times in our lives.

Writing in 2021, that floundering in me continues in certain deep ways: these processes of deeper change are often very slow. But the dream has helped me keep faith with the process, to trust that it is OK to feel at sea. But also, what appears like floundering, relative to our usual certainties, can also be an initiation into a long-term way of being, where we are never again so sure about what we are doing with our lives or who we are, because we are learning to surrender, moment by moment, to the dream of Spirit.

Make Choices with the Whole of You

Then when we do make the choices that are the NorthEast, it is not 'us' that is making the choice, it is something working through us. Shortly before I led a Medicine Wheel group that would include the NorthEast, I had a dream that told me that when it comes to starting a relationship, it needs to be with my whole being, it needs to be a total decision. And I realised that this is what the North is getting at more broadly: the need to make choices with the whole of ourselves, so that we don't have reservations. Many people seem to be like this with relationships, ten years or so down the road: they say they had a reservation at the start, but chose to overlook it. Trust your reservations, trust your 'indecisiveness', as we sometimes unfairly judge it. If something doesn't feel completely right, don't do it until it does, if it ever does. Then we act with the whole of ourselves, with impeccability. It may take years to get to that point, but when we choose in that sort of way, the world moves too. And if you can make that choice, if the central part of you knows what to do, begin it now. Life is short, and you will not regret it.

In a sense, the choice of the North is not really a choice: it involves being so aligned with ourselves, so aligned with Spirit, that what to do becomes straightforward. It is the aim of the prayers we may make in the Pipe Ceremony or in the Sweatlodge: what we are doing, in a way, is having a conversation with ourselves and with Spirit until what is in our heart becomes clear and expresses itself. That is the sort of choice that works. It is how magic works, not by trying to impose our will on events, but by flowing with them in a way that is congruent with who we are. There is nothing to be done, no choices to be made, just a life to be lived in alignment with Spirit.

Chapter 7

Using The Wheel

I 'use' my Wheel in a general sense, in that it is there and it carries my life forward – just as it has carried me forward in writing this book, and for that I want to express my thanks. But I have also used it specifically in a way that began spontaneously. I was doing a Pipe Ceremony on my own, chewing over some issues that needing chewing over and praying about. I was sitting at the edge of the Wheel talking, and I realised I wanted to move, so I did. And I talked from the Direction I had moved to. And I kept moving as the focus of what I was talking about changed, but it was still the same underlying me with the same issues to talk about, but with different powers being brought in.

That is a way you can use it on your own. In Chapter 1 I talked about how to use it as a counselling tool, although counselling is a mild word for it – we are bringing in transformative powers from Spirit, and handing ourselves over to Spirit. There is little that we puny humans can do to change ourselves, we do not even know what it is that needs to change. But Spirit knows, and in bringing ourselves to the Wheel, we are bringing ourselves, in a sacred way, to the Universe and asking her for the help we need. The person doing the 'counselling' will be changed along with the 'client'. Strong powers, that humans have been engaging with for thousands of years, are being called in. It is white magic, and not to be approached lightly.

Suppose someone comes along and their life doesn't have meaning any more, it is not fulfilling them. Put them in the East, you sit in the West. Ask them, what is it that would give their life meaning? Do they want to have meaning, do they want to be here in this life? And they talk for as long as they need to, and you can respond as necessary from the West, the practical place that balances the East: open yourself up, say in response whatever might want to come through you, for you are being used by Spirit to help that person. Then the other person moves to the SouthEast, the Ancestors, and you move to the opposite direction and respond as before: what were you told gives life meaning? Then the South, the Child: what does the child in you want, does he/she get to play, for that is meaningful in itself? Then the Dream of the SouthWest: forget for a moment about what you imagine might be practical, what is it that would really 'do it' for you in an ideal world? And the West: how can that be made practical? The NorthWest: what patterns do you have that stand in the way of living that which gives you meaning? The North: what is your 'knowing' around this issue, not what your mind, with all its different ideas is telling you, nor what your depressed mood is telling you, but what comes to you when you stand back and weigh up with your whole being, and listen? The NorthEast: what choices are you now going to make, having 'cooked' this issue around the Wheel? And then back to the East: what is your vision now about what gives you meaning?

We are not looking for 'answers' in this ceremony, we are looking for understanding, perhaps for healing, for perspective, for knowing and for inspirations. It may not be as simple and schematic as I have laid it out. You may get a feeling that the person needs to revisit a direction, or they might have that feeling. Or they might move unsystematically and intuitively from direction to direction. It can be an idea not to tell them what the Direction means, at least to start with, and see what spontaneously happens.

With one person, we arrived in the NorthEast, choice, and it involved an issue around a difficult relationship she was in. And she realised that she was not ready to make a choice. And that is fine, there is no success and failure around this process. As it happened, this person went back and chewed it over from one or two other directions, and then suddenly she felt able to make a choice. You never know how it is going to go.

Another method is to have the person sitting in the centre of the Wheel, and they begin by talking about their issue. They then face each direction in turn, and somebody else speaks from Spirit back to them. It may be just you doing it, or you may have a group of people. If it is a group of people, you need to take the pressure off them: they do not 'have' to have anything to say, and again there are no good and bad marks for it. It is, if you like, an exercise in speaking intuitively, as much for them as for the person in the middle. This method is known as the 'Star Maiden's Circle', which Leo Rutherford talks about at more length in his book *The View Through the Medicine Wheel.* But this is the essence of it.

The Wheel can also be used ceremonially. If you can build one outside, so much the better, for a whole other quality comes in when it is embedded in the natural world. You feel you have the powers of nature behind you too, which are not separate to the powers of the Wheel. If it stays in the same place, that place too will acquire a sacred quality. The Wheel will grow in power over time as all that dreaming is done around it. You can invent ceremonies: well, you have to, because we do not have a tradition,

With Leo Rutherford I did a simple ceremony once, where we let go of our parents as parents, to become the adults ourselves. We stood in the East, and let go of our father, with gratitude for all he did, and allowed the Sun to be our true father. And then we did the same in the West, and allowed the Earth to be our true mother. It was about making an archetypal shift, and freeing ourselves.

Or you could simply call in and acknowledge the powers of each direction, with different people standing in different directions on the Wheel. Maybe you are about to enter a Sweatlodge, which is structured around the four Directions and their powers. So, you can go round the Wheel beforehand, praying for a good lodge that will help people in whatever ways are needed.

The Medicine Wheel too can be used in a divinatory way. You can play a game with it. Have four stones, one for each direction. Have four plastic animals, one for each direction. Ask a question, then close your eyes and pick a stone and an animal, or ask someone else to pick them for you. You then have two symbols to bring together. What does it mean that the Bear, who normally lives in the West, is now in the North? The Bear is the dreamer, so maybe you need to look at some of your dreams through the perspective of the North, the ability to stand back and weigh up? The Bear, who eats honey, also reminds us of the sweetness of life, so maybe you have got into an over-intellectual mind place, consumed by plans, and you need to stop and enjoy some simple pleasures? There are any number of ways of interpreting symbols: this does not make it vague, rather it means that Spirit has the freedom to range among many possibilities and if you listen to yourself while holding these symbols, a relevant and useful interpretation will probably come to you. Just as interesting is picking the symbols on behalf of someone else and seeing what words come to you then. This is the moment when you need to trust and not be afraid of looking foolish. It is surprising how well these things can work.

Chapter 8

Correlations – Jung's Typology, Archetypes, Astrology, the Mandorla

In the opening Chapter we looked briefly at the correlation between Jung's Psychological Typology and the Medicine Wheel. Broadly speaking, we can correlate Fire, Water, Earth and Air with Jung's Intuition, Feeling, Sensation and Thinking. These different systems never fit exactly when you compare them, but this one is pretty good. It is good that they don't exactly fit, because it reminds us that we are dealing with forms, and they can never do full justice to realities, they are just pointers. I think it is always helpful to look for cross-cultural equivalences: the perspective deepens our understanding, and lessens the drift towards narrowness and even fundamentalism, which easily occurs when engaging with particular traditions too exclusively.

Jung's Typology

Central to Jung's purpose in creating his typology was as an aid in understanding what type of person you are, and where you need to find balance, or wholeness. What he said was that we tend to have a leading faculty, and the one opposite that tends to be noticeably undeveloped. If your leading edge is thinking, then awareness of feeling will be difficult for you. Similarly, the other two faculties will also be unbalanced, but not to the same degree as the first two. You may, for example, be a Thinking-Intuitive type. In which case, your secondary strength is Intuition, and Sensation – the reality principle – tends to be a bit lacking, but less so than Feeling. You may well have noticed these imbalances in people. We are partial beings, which is why we have a Medicine Wheel, for example, in order to become more balanced. If you are good at one thing, there is probably a corresponding opposite which you find harder.

Finding Your Character Type

People who are good with people tend not to be so good at organising, and vice versa. Being good with people requires intuition and feeling. Being good at organising requires mind and sensation. So, Jung's typology is a pointer to what we need to develop. That may change throughout life, it is not a fixed thing, and ultimately it is just a system, as is the Medicine Wheel. And it may be that we always remain, for example, noticeably strong in Thinking, and our Feeling responses becomes more adequate and immediate over the course of our lives, and that is as far as it goes. It is to do with how we are built, what type of character we are. Becoming balanced does not mean having everything functioning equally, adequately is good enough.

Jung's colleague Toni Wolff was a good example of the Intuition-Sensation imbalance. She was a gifted therapist, and was able to help guide Jung during his descent into the Unconscious during the First World War. She was at a Jung family dinner once (she was also Jung's lover, and came to an accommodation with Jung's wife.) Jung asked Wolff if she could gather some chives from the garden for the meal, and a while later she returned with the plants in hand, having uprooted them. Jung could hardly believe that someone could be so disconnected from this reality to do something like that, even though he did not view himself as particularly well connected in that respect. But that was what came with Toni Wolff's gift as an inner guide: a lack of connection to this reality. And it is not necessarily something to be 'corrected': the Spirit will find ways of prompting us when more of a balance is required.

There is also Jung's typology of Extraversion and Introversion, which Eduardo Duran correlates with the Above and the Below respectively. Where do you look for what is real, is it outside of you or within you? Different people function differently in this respect, sometimes quite extremely. And, of course, reality is both, the distinction between within and without is ultimately an illusion, albeit one that is quite useful for functioning within time and space, as we have to.

We can bring Jung's understanding to the Medicine Wheel, and assess what type we think we may be. I would say I am North and East – Air and Fire, Thinking and Intuition – predominantly, though I am not sure which is stronger, and I have become more balanced during my life. My friends would no doubt have an opinion about which I am. It can be hard to see ourselves accurately. As for Above and Below, I am not extreme in either direction. I can be very social, which is an extraverted quality. But the base of it seems to be lots of time on my own. Without that, I do not have the resources or the desire to be social.

'Spiritual Bypass', which we looked at in Chapter is typically Fire (spiritual vision) and Air (Ideas) at the expense of groundedness (Earth) and honest feeling (Water). I tended in this direction when younger, it can be a necessary stage.

Senex and Puer

There are also the archetypal principles of the Senex and Puer Aeternus, which Jung's colleague Marie-Louise von Franz has written about. The Senex is the old man of the West, who is rooted in this Earthly reality, and able to negotiate it well, but who at an extreme denies the reality of the Spirit and the new life that is always trying to emerge. The Puer Aeternus is the 'Eternal Boy' of the East, who at an extreme is wholly identified with his spiritual vision and does not want to get his hands dirty with 'mundane' realities. The union of the two is the well-used expression "Don't tell me about your visions unless they grow corn." Peter Pan is the classic eternal boy who wants to never grow up. It is often the natural beginning of a 'spiritual' path, we need the eternal boy (or girl – puella aeternus) to propel us out of a life of fixed collective values, that are often a shield from existential realities. But eventually, maybe through a crisis, we need to get our hands dirty too, to engage with the world on its terms, as the Senex does. Sometimes it is the other way round: we begin as Senex, creating a life that is successful in conventional terms, and that can be a good launching pad. But eventually a crisis of meaning dawns, the Puer/Puella – the Magical Child of the East – comes calling, often at mid-life. The Senex can be female just as much as male, but there doesn't seem to be a convenient Latin word.

Amazon-Medial-Maternal-Hetaira

Toni Wolff (I recommend *Toni Wolff and CG Jung: A Collaboration* by Nan Savage Healy) was not entirely satisfied with Jung's typology of Thinking-Feeling-Intuition-Sensation. She felt that it leant towards masculine psychology, and came up with her own for women. Like many mandalas or circular representations of reality, which are found universally, Wolff created a set of four in her typology, arranged in two pairs of opposites. It was the only article she wrote, *Structural Forms of the Feminine Psyche,* which can readily be found on the internet.

The two pairs are: Amazon and Medial; Mother and Hetaira. The Amazon and Mother, in a way, speak for themselves. The Amazon is the woman warrior, the businesswoman who can succeed in the competitive world that is usually dominated by men. This is just one type of woman, and probably in the minority, because it is only one of four. I think it is a useful corrective to the way the pendulum has swung in these times, where women can feel inadequate if they do not have a successful career. 60 years ago, it was the man who felt inadequate if his wife did go out to work, for it suggested he could not provide. A woman may naturally be a maternal type, she may feel fulfilled looking after the home and the children, but today that is often undervalued. And that can mean that the children do not feel their mother is properly available to them as they need her to be. There is a positive value in the Mother in respect of children being properly cared for. It should not need saying, it is so obvious. But it is the way collective pendulums go: there has been a strong need to give women equal opportunities in the workplace, and any sane person would support that. But in-so-doing, it is easy to go to the other extreme.

Opposite the Mother type is the Hetaira, who is the woman who loves the Other for the sake of his or her growth. What we call 'love' is often restrictive or conditional in nature, and it goes both ways: we need the other person to be something particular for us, and when they step outside of that, there is trouble. It is rare to love someone without the self-interest that is the normal and natural state of affairs, because we are partial beings looking for completion. Romantic love involves unconscious processes whereby we let the other carry large undeveloped parts of our psyche, and we do the same for them in return: that is often what is meant by 'soulmate'. The Hetaira does not have this self-interest. It is the opposite to the Mother love, which is unconditional, as it needs to be, but is about 'my' children and is something the child may eventually have to break away from, which we saw earlier in the story of Ceres and Proserpina. It would (according to this system) be a rare type of wife/mother who is also Hetaira (and vice-versa for husband), but that principle would be functioning well in a good therapist, for example, or any type of healer. You hold the other person in your heart, disinterestedly, and they can feel that, and that in itself promotes their unfoldment. And, according to Wolff's schema at any rate, women will tend towards one or the other.

Then there is the Medial type, which is quite mysterious. They are the guide to the Unconscious, as Toni Wolff was, and therefore often not totally in this reality, and unlikely to be Amazons. Jung had much of this quality too. My observation through journeying work is that it is generally easier for women than men to engage with this realm, there is often (by no means always) a natural quality to their journeying, whereas others of us may be left wondering if anything actually happened, and was it real? The Medial is another quality of a good therapist or healer. They may or may not be so good at loving the client. Some intuitive people can be a bit cold like that, even disconnected. Toni Wolff herself does not come across as very warm. But what they say, coming seemingly out of nowhere, can really hit the nail on the head. A good medial will prompt you to look at something in a way that you never have, they will bring the Spirit perspective that is so much bigger. Someone who can get good information from journeying will often be this Medial type. Two people with this ability in a marked way spring to mind, and neither of them are easy people on a personal level, both are quite disconnected in their own ways.

We can see elements of Toni Wolff's schema in the Medicine Wheel and in Jung's typology. Is there an exact match? These sorts of positionings are often arguable, which is a good thing. In Chapter 5, I put the warrior in the North, because he divides things into good and bad and fights on behalf of the good. You could equally argue that he is the one that get things done, so should be in the Earthy West.

I am going to put the Amazon in the North, because she is that warrior energy that goes into the world and fights for her place. Mother goes in the West, because she is grounded, the queen of her Earthly domain, the home and family. Medial goes in the intuitive East, the vision from Spirit. And the Hetaira, who loves, is in the Watery South. The only problem with this correlation is that I have paired the Amazon with the Hetaira, and the Medial with the Maternal, which is not Wolff's scheme. But for me, that is a point of interest. It keeps us looking at these things.

King, Warrior, Magician, Lover

There is another Mandala that we can consider, that is also divided into two pairs of opposites, and these are what are sometimes held to be the four archetypes of the masculine psyche: King, Warrior, Magician, Lover, which I first encountered in a book of the same name many years ago, written by Robert Moore and Douglas Gillette. This set fits well with the Medicine Wheel: King, the ruler of the Earthly realm, in the West; Warrior in the North; Magician, who can make anything happen though the intervention of Spirit, in the East; and the Lover in the Watery South.

A key insight of this scheme is that unless the Lover is working well, the other three tend to function in their shadow form. The Lover is the Musician, the Artist, the man whose feeling function is to the fore. Feeling is what men often find difficult. It tends to come at mid-life. There is more cultural allowance for it than there used to be, but men are still often wary of seeming feminine. It started to come to me much more in my mid 50s onwards. For men, I think it is like an initiation when it happens. It is not just about repressed wounding from childhood, that is stopping us feeling and that takes decades to come to consciousness. That may be part of the story, but there is also an archetypal process at work. In the late 90s I was at a weekend on which Robert Moore was presenting, and he talked about his own emotional awakening in middle age when he visited India and saw the need in which many people were living. We men can be not awake to feeling, and not realise it. Shamanism, with its emphasis on being part of the natural world, which is a feminine principle, is very good for us.

Using the Lover as the starting point in our journey towards balance corresponds well with, and illumines, the nature of the South of the Wheel. The South is where the serious work begins, as we move round from the initial inspiration of the East. It is saying that in coming into a deeper emotional awareness, and in forming a relationship with the shadow, all those things that torment us, what we are doing is learning to love. To love and cherish ourselves, warts and all. And to love also the whole of the natural world and her life forms. It is this love that empowers the ability to incarnate in the West, because it means we love life, we love showing up and being present. In the North it enables the development of a Mind that does not judge (rather, it loves) and from which is gained perspective and wisdom. In the East, the Lover stops us becoming the black magician, who manipulates the world for his own cold purposes, and instead we become the white magician who can dream and manifest for the benefit of all.

Astrology

Like the other symbolic representations considered above, astrology also uses a circle divided into four, both the circle and the number four being symbols of wholeness and balance. Astrology is divinatory. It tells you what the universe, in the form of the planets, was saying about you the moment you were born. These are the particular gifts you came bearing. We are not just herd animals to be moulded into a uniform configuration. Each chart is unique, because the universe was uniquely configured at the moment you were born. Everything is interconnected, as both The Web of Wyrd from ancient Europe and Indra's Net from the Buddhist tradition suggest. So, if you look back at the universe at the moment you were born, it will tell you who you are. A skilful diviner can read the patterns, just as a South American healer can reader the patterns in a guinea-pig's entrails. How wonderful, the universe already knows you!

In that sense, the Medicine Wheel is also a map of who you are, and can tell you who you are. If you ask a question, those powers can respond, they can help you ponder and clarify whatever it is you want to shed light on, or to move on. That is what is happening in the Star Maiden's Circle, when people respond to you from the different directions. Or when you pick a stone and animal combination: the Wheel is wanting to tell you something via the synergy of those two symbols. And remember, they are not just symbols, they actually *are* those things they 'represent'.

Astrology treats the planets in the solar system as different pieces of our soul, with each being shaped by the star constellation behind them. That gives them a 'sign'. But those 12 signs are divided into four elements, which are more fundamental than the signs. They are pretty much the same elements as we find in the Medicine Wheel. You can look at your elemental balance by totalling the number of planets in those elements. It can give another point of contemplation as to who you are, and it may be different to your own assessment, which is always interesting. My own planets have an Air and Fire predominance, which accords with how I experience myself. I do have some Earth, and I am reasonably grounded. Water is the one in short supply – it is there, but in a transpersonal way – so it has always taken me a while to know what I am feeling, what my responses are, in a given situation. It may take me a day or two to catch up. I will probably always be like that, because it is to do with how I am structured, and it is difficult to be everything. That said, it is considerably better than it used to be, though it has taken a long time.

You can also see from charts that some people are very particular types of characters, while others are more spread out among the possibilities. And this gives us insight into what 'balance' in the Medicine Wheel constitutes: it is not about becoming an equal amount of each element. It is about having each element functioning to the degree it needs to for you to be who you deeply are. And there may be certain elements that you quite happily spend your life largely ignoring. That is not in itself imbalanced, if it works.

Sometimes a chart might be almost completely lacking in an element. Like I said, the person may happily live without it. Or it may become the focus of their lives. It is as if having a planet in a sign adapts it to human use, it can become part of our personality. If that element is lacking, then it retains an undifferentiated elemental power that can be enormously creative. Albert Einstein famously only had one Air planet, and that was Jupiter, which isn't as personal as the planets closer to the Sun. And yet he generated ideas that changed how humanity saw the universe. There was huge power in that element for him. Arnold Schwarzenegger only has one Earth planet, and his response was to become Mr Universe: someone with an outstanding physique.

So, it is worth looking at your own elemental balance in this way: even if you don't have a chart, you can make your own assessment in terms of the Wheel. Which element comes to you least naturally? You may happily overlook it, or it may be something of an issue for you, or it may be something you are enormously drawn to.

The Mandorla and the Centre of the Wheel

In his book *Owning your Own Shadow*, Robert Johnson draws a distinction between contradiction and paradox. Contradiction is the normal human condition: we view one half of our experience as good, as desirable, and we judge and shut out that which is not so.

In our work and busyness-obsessed culture, for example, you may feel guilty because you got up at 11am when there were all these things needing to be done. Or virtuous because you did indeed get up at 8am and got busy. The truth of it probably was that you had two conflicting wants: to lie around and dream, and to get things done. (And a guy with a big stick telling you one of them is right and the other wrong.) If you can hold both of these urges without judging either, without having to come down on one side or the other by feeling virtuous or guilty, than you are in paradox rather than in contradiction. And a new type of consciousness can emerge, that is outside of the usual boxes in which we and in which society finds its life.

Really, it is outside of space and time, and there is joy and a deep relief around it, since we are no longer 'doing' something to ourselves, not carving ourselves up. We are with the Divine, with Spirit.

Contradiction is fundamental to the way we generally work. It is easier than paradox, though it comes at the price of being a partial human being. Try it with politics: argue the case for the bunch you don't vote for, appreciate their humanity. Most people don't seem able to do this. In fact, it often seems to be part of their 'spirituality' to remain in contradiction about their politics, and to heavily judge the other side as uncaring or whatever, instead of moving into paradox.

William Blake puts it thus in *The Marriage of Heaven and Hell:*

"Without Contraries is no progression"

The Mandorla is a mystical medieval Christian symbol created by two overlapping circles, like a Venn diagram. The almond shape where they overlap is the Mandorla – the word itself is Italian for almond. The two circles are the state of contradiction – of good and bad – in which we normally live, and in which religion finds it place. Where the circles overlap is where good and bad are held together in paradox. It is where the mystic goes, the mystic who knows God, who is an open channel for Spirit.

Notice it is only an overlap. It is an overlap because it is not a place where we can live all the time. It is a special place, the place of vision, of visitation by poetry and by angels and other beings. Like it or not, we live in the world, experiencing opposites such as pain and pleasure, life and death, which come with having a body. It is important to incarnate, as well as to be aligned with the visionary dimension.

In the Medicine Wheel, the equivalent of the Mandorla overlap is at the Centre, the point of balance. The Centre of the Wheel is not a mild dilution and equalising of the four elements that we find in each direction, but a dynamic fusing of them that creates something new, a new level of consciousness that is more complete. We find this idea in the Middle Way in Buddhism, which can sound a bit watered down, neither one thing nor the other. But again, it points to the diamond that is formed when large opposing forces are allowed to synergise.

The four directions of the Medicine Wheel are four polarities within which ordinary human consciousness usually finds itself. As we have seen, each direction needs to be balanced with its opposite so that it does not fall into its shadow form. This balance does not generally mean equal, as we saw in the discussion on Jung's typology. Synergy is a good word to use here. If we are, say, one-sidedly North, good at thinking but unaware of the emotions fuelling that thinking, then developing emotional awareness brings in something new that is not just emotion plus thought, it is something more than that, along the lines of poise and self-mastery. It is in the nature of synergy that some new element or new consciousness is created. It is the same with the East and West. The point of balance or synergy here is incarnation, bringing spirit into matter. This can be an ongoing, gradual experience over the years. And it can also have its peak moments that are illustrative, such as when we create something, or in trance dance, where there can be the ecstasy of the spirit moving through the body.

And then there is the putting together of the North-South synergy with the East-West synergy, and that is the real, eventual purpose of the Medicine Wheel. I won't attempt to describe that in words. William Blake's Fourfold Vision comes to mind. And, of course, the Mandorla.

About the Author

Barry Goddard first came across the Shamanic Path in the mid-1990s, when the organised Buddhism that he had been around for 15 years was no longer working for him. The idea that the Earth herself is alive, and that a meaningful life does not involve ascending to a 'higher' realm, was deeply appealing to him. Within a few years, Shamanism changed his life completely, and did so again another 15 years later. For Barry, Shamanism is a path of alignment and engagement with the Spirit, and the often challenging transformational processes that come with that. For the last 20 years, Barry has been writing about and teaching both shamanism and astrology. He lives in Devon, and walks regularly on Dartmoor.

www.shamanicfreestate.blogspot.com www.astrotabletalk.blogspot.com

Bibliography

Audlin, James David, *The Circle of Life* CreateSpace 2012

Baring, Anne, *The Dream of the Cosmos* Archive Publishing 2019

Borrows, John, *Drawing Out Law* University of Toronto Press 2010

Boyd, Doug, *Rolling Thunder* Dell 1974

Bregman, Rutger, *Humankind* Bloomsbury Publishing 2020

Browning, Christopher, *Ordinary Men* Harper Perennial 2017

Campbell, Ffyona, *The Hunter Gatherer Way Wild* Publishing 2012

Clerc, Olivier, *The Gift of Forgiveness* Findhorn Press 2010

Davis, Wade, *The Wayfinders* House of Anansi 2009

Duran, Eduardo, *Healing the Soul Wound* Teachers College Press 2019

D'Escola, Philippe, *Spears of Twilight* Flamingo 1997

Duffell, Nick, *The Making of Them* Lone Arrow Press 2000

Ehrenreich, Barbara, *Dancing in the Streets: A History of Collective Joy* Granta 2007

Fox, Kate, *Watching the English* Hodder 2004

Greene, Liz, *The Astrology of Fate* Allen & Unwin 1984

Haidt, Jonathan, *The Righteous Mind* Penguin 2013

Harpur, Patrick, *Daimonic Reality* Penguin 1995; *The Philosopher's Secret Fire* Penguin 2002

Healy, Nan Savage, *Toni Wolff and CG Jung: A Collaboration* Tiberius Press 2017

Hollis, James, *The Middle Passage* Inner City Books 1993

Jenkinson, Stephen, *Die Wise* North Atlantic Books 2015

Johnson, Robert, *Owning Your Own Shadow* Bravo Ltd 1994

Kornfield, Jack, *After the Ecstasy, the Laundry* Rider 2000

McGilchrist, Iain, *The Master and His Emissary* Yale University Press 2019

Mehl-Madrona, Lewis, *Coyote Medicine* Fireside 1998; *Coyote Healing* Bear and Company 2003; *Coyote Wisdom* Bear and

Company 2005

Milton, Richard, *Shattering the Myths of Darwinism* CreateSpace 2017

Morris, Jan, *Conundrum* Faber 1974

Moore, Robert and Gillette, Douglas, *King, Warrior, Magician, Lover* Bravo Ltd 1992

The Native American novels of Leslie Marmon Silko, Louise Erdrich, Sherman Alexie and D'Arcy McNickle

Plomin, Robert, *Blueprint: How DNA Makes Us Who We Are* Penguin 2019

Rosenberg, Marshall, *Non-Violent Communication* Puddle Dancer Press 2015

Ruiz, Don Miguel, *The Four Agreements Amber-Allen 1997*

Rutherford, Leo, *The View Through the Medicine Wheel* O Books 2008

Sacks, Oliver, *The Man Who Mistook His Wife for a Hat Duckworth 1985*

Sanchez, Victor, *The Teachings of Don Carlos* Bear and Company 1995

Sarangerel, *Chosen by the Spirits* Destiny Books 2001

Schaverien, Joy, *Boarding School Syndrome* Routledge 2015

Silko, Leslie Marmon, *Ceremony* Penguin 2020

Tree, Jim, *The Way of the Sacred Pipe* Blue Sky Publishing 2004

Tupy, Marian, *Ten Global Trends That Every Smart Person Needs to Know* Cato 2020

Van Gelder, Dora, *The Real World of Fairies* Quest Books 1999

Van Ysslestyne, Jan, *Spirits from the Edge of the World* Pathfinder Communications 2018

Vitebsky, Piers, *Reindeer People* Harper 2005

Vuillard, Eric, *The Order of the Day* Picador 2019

Wolff, Toni, *Structural Forms of the Feminine Psyche* https://ufdc.ufl.edu/AA00001582/00001/3x

Znamenski, Andrei, *The Beauty of the Primitive* Oxford University Press 2007

Yalom, Irvin, *Momma and the Meaning of Life* Platkus Books 1999

Films And Documentaries

Surviving Death, Netflix 2021

Face To Face | Carl Gustav Jung, BBC (1959)

TED talk: *The Moral Roots of Liberals and Conservatives,* Jonathan Haidt 2008

YouTube: Jordan Peterson interviewed by Cathy Newman

Wild, Wild Country, Netflix 2018

American Beauty, Sam Mendes 1999

Kiss the Ground, Netflix 2020

YouTube: *The Science Delusion,* Rupert Sheldrake Ted Talk

Matter of Heart (Documentary on Jung), Dir Mark Whitney 1986

2 Spirit Documentary: *vimeo.com/ondemand/twospirits*

YouTube: *Nonduality and the Consciousness of 'Things' (Thich Nhat Hanh)*

Dreamkeeper, Dir Steve Barron 2003

Smoke Signals, Chris Eyre 1998

MOON
BOOKS

PAGANISM & SHAMANISM

What is Paganism? A religion, a spirituality, an alternative belief system, nature worship? You can find support for all these definitions (and many more) in dictionaries, encyclopaedias, and text books of religion, but subscribe to any one and the truth will evade you. Above all Paganism is a creative pursuit, an encounter with reality, an exploration of meaning and an expression of the soul. Druids, Heathens, Wiccans and others, all contribute their insights and literary riches to the Pagan tradition. Moon Books invites you to begin or to deepen your own encounter, right here, right now.

If you have enjoyed this book, why not tell other readers by posting a review on your preferred book site.

Medicine for the Soul

The Complete Book of Shamanic Healing

Ross Heaven

All you will ever need to know about shamanic healing and how to become your own shaman…

Paperback: 978-1-78099-419-2 ebook: 978-1-78099-420-8

Shaman Pathways – The Druid Shaman

Exploring the Celtic Otherworld

Danu Forest

A practical guide to Celtic shamanism with exercises and techniques as well as traditional lore for exploring the Celtic Otherworld.

Paperback: 978-1-78099-615-8 ebook: 978-1-78099-616-5

Traditional Witchcraft for the Woods and Forests

A Witch's Guide to the Woodland with Guided Meditations and Pathworking

Mélusine Draco

A Witch's guide to walking alone in the woods, with guided meditations and pathworking.

Paperback: 978-1-84694-803-9 ebook: 978-1-84694-804-6

Naming the Goddess

Trevor Greenfield

Naming the Goddess is written by over eighty adherents and scholars of Goddess and Goddess Spirituality.

Paperback: 978-1-78279-476-9 ebook: 978-1-78279-475-2

Shapeshifting into Higher Consciousness
Heal and Transform Yourself and Our World with Ancient Shamanic and Modern Methods
Llyn Roberts
Ancient and modern methods that you can use every day to transform yourself and make a positive difference in the world.
Paperback: 978-1-84694-843-5 ebook: 978-1-84694-844-2